DEMYSTIFYING DATABASES

A HANDS-ON GUIDE FOR DATABASE MANAGEMENT

DEMYSTIFYING DATABASES
A HANDS-ON GUIDE FOR DATABASE MANAGEMENT

Shiva Sukula
Ph.D., A.D.I.T

Ess Ess Publications

4837/24, Ansari Road, Darya Ganj,
New Delhi-110002
Tel. : 23260807, 41563444
Fax : 011-41563334
E-mail: info@essessreference.com
www.essessreference.com

Ess Ess Publications
4837/24, Ansari Road,
Darya Ganj,
New Delhi-110 002.

Tel.: 23260807, 41563444
Fax: 41563334
E-mail: info@essessreference.com
www.essessreference.com

© **Author**

Rs.725/-

First Published - 2008

ISBN: 81-7000-534-5   (10 Digit)
        978-81-7000-534-6 (13 Digit)

Published By Ess Ess Publications and printed at Salasar Imaging Systems

Cover Design by W&P Graphics Pvt. Ltd.

PRINTED IN INDIA

Preface

Information Technology (IT), which include technologies for data storage and retrieval, computing, and communication, and their direct and indirect applications—are transforming our lives. Although researchers in many fields have gathered data about people's IT use, the data are of highly variable quality; there has been little integrated analysis, and the overall impact of the phenomena is not clear. Important information about the shape and direction of IT use, and especially its impact in the home, remain uncharted. Databases evolved into a classic component of computing degrees. The subject became well supported by a wealth of research, exceptional industrial experience and numerous books covering a wide range of topics. However, books on databases run into voluminous proportions and tend to cover the whole spectrum of the subject thus constituting a monographic source of reference rather than being a learning aide. This book presents the concepts for design and implementation of modern databases. An analytical approach is followed so that the concepts learned can be applied not only to the wide variety of databases that exist today but can also be used build systems for the future.

This textbook differs from others in its field by its emphasis on design and the formalization databases. While anyone who has read about databases will have encountered the various conceptual models, as relational, hierarchical, networks, entity-relationships, etc., they are typically placed in opposition of each other rather than in a continuum of implementations of semantics. Similarly, the mathematical aspects of concepts such as functional dependencies are stressed without providing much interaction on their meaning. Once we have a formal understanding of how the structure of a database is related to the semantics of the stored information, then we can consider the transactions that are being performed as transformations of the represented knowledge. The users are an integral component of such systems. The results they obtain are combinations of the stored data and the transactions they specify. Transactions that update the database incorporate such knowledge in the system and make it available to others. Naturally, the book does not aspire to cover all aspects of databases nor does it pretend to present the relational theory in its entirety. The focus is on a coherent, systematic coverage of database design, applications and trends. The primary objective of this book is to present a reasonably comprehensive explanation of the process of the development of database application systems within the framework of the set processing paradigm. However, for applications that require processing of complex data structures the relational approach may not necessarily be advantageous. Application software built around the relational DBMS may require user-defined, complex data structures, appropriate to the domain of that application. Furthermore, certain types of applications do not naturally lend themselves to the relational paradigm. Thus we chose, and not without discussion and controversies, to include a separate chapter covering the object-oriented paradigm as applicable to databases.

When we look at individual libraries, the picture becomes even murkier. Information technology has changed the way libraries carry out many important activities, but it has not—at least yet—led to any alteration in the essential form or size of information services organizations. It has delivered great benefits to a handful of libraries, even propelling a few into positions of library leadership. Databases are presented in a setting of transaction processing. Transaction processing introduces modularity into database usage. We also present the implementation of database management in a modular fashion. Modularity is beneficial in presentation as well as in actual system design. The analytical approach permits that the performance of database transactions can be evaluated, both for centralized and distributed systems. Some background of File Organization for Database Design will be helpful to reduce the conceptual analysis shown here to practical design details. The emphasis throughout is on concepts and structure. No actual database management systems are described completely, nor are systems surveyed and compared. Specific and realistic examples are used throughout to illustrate points being made.

Simply put, it remains difficult, if not impossible; to draw any broad conclusions about databases' effect on the competitiveness and profitability of individual libraries. Databases have become the largest of all library expenditures—and an intrinsic element of nearly every modern information process—but libraries continue to make IT investments in the dark, without a clear conceptual understanding of the ultimate strategic or financial impact. The goal of this book is to help promote such an understanding, to provide library and information managers, as well as administrators and policy makers, with a new perspective on how technology, competition, and information services intersect.

Through an analysis of its unique characteristics, evolving role, and historical precedents, it is visible that databases' strategic importance is growing, as many have claimed or assumed, but diminishing. As databases have become more powerful, more standardized, and more affordable, it has been transformed from a proprietary technology that companies can use to gain an edge over

their rivals into an infrastructural technology that is
shared by all competitors. Databases have increasingly
become, in other words, a simple factor of production—a
commodity input that is necessary for competitiveness
but insufficient for information advantage. The emergence
of a ubiquitous, shared IT infrastructure has, as the book
will show, many important practical implications, both
for how libraries manage and invest in technology itself
and, more broadly, for how they think about creating
and defending competitive advantages. The way librarians
respond to IT's changing role will influence their libraries
fortunes for years to come.

Shiva Sukula

℡ Office {2760554 / 2760551}
Fax 2762838
Resi. 2600066
Fax 2760577

चौ० चरण सिंह विश्वविद्यालय, मेरठ
CH. CHARAN SINGH UNIVERSITY, MEERUT

प्रो० सन्त प्रसाद ओझा
एफ़० इन्स्टी० पी० (लन्दन)
कुलपति

Prof. S.P. Ojha
F. Inst. P. (London)
VICE-CHANCELLOR

Foreword

Databases are making significant contributions to the library and information services. There are increasing number of services looking towards libraries as innovative centers for new products, ideas, expertise and skills. This crossover between conventional to modern services is providing a balance which is helping libraries to consolidate its reputation for excellence in the perspectives of information technology. Computer databases have become essential part of many organizations. These databases must be dependable and must not become bottlenecks. In its fifth generation of computing products, databases have stressed robustness and performance in the libraries.

In designing libraries information products and services, IT application placed great emphasis on databases stability, particularly under conditions of information overload. These are not qualities that library customers will necessarily appreciate unless they have experienced their absence in an overloaded information environment. New applications and larger data storage mandate higher database throughput. High-speed local area networks create the expectation of high-performance database services from the libraries. Achieving this level of performance takes more than fast hardware, however. It requires careful attention to details of database implementation and interaction with the hardware, the processor and memory system, and the operating system.

This book by Dr. (Ms.) Shiva Shukla highlights the database application and the services in the modern library and information system. The book is divided into chapters: database: an overview, architecture of database, indigenous databases in libraries, types of databases, information retrieval from databases, growth and development of databases, linguistics in databases, marketing of information and databases, database and web applications and online database services worldwide. The key purpose of this work is to communicate information about databases from their basic hereabouts to application in the modern information services and transaction to the students and teachers and professionals as well. It has been able to keep pace with the scope and diversity of databases and the nature of databases research and technology activities. This book on current research in database and information technologies also reinforces the excellence which libraries strive for and achieve in information services and demonstrates the foundation which the libraries and information centers have built for future growth in the IT based information services.

I congratulate Dr. (Ms.) Shiva Shukla for bringing out such an excellent piece of work.

Prof. S.P. Ojha

Contents

1. **Database: An Overview**................................. 1

   Definitions of a Database 3

   How is a database organized? 7

   Categories of fields 9

   Types of Databases 10

   Features of Good Database Design 12

   Database Scheme 13

   Applications of databases 14

   Copyright of databases 17

   Significant Aspects of Database Production 18

   Importance and Use of Scientific
   and Technical Databases 20

   References 21

   Other References 23

2. **Architecture of Database** 25

   Flat Model 26

   Hierarchical Model 27

   Network Model 29

   Relational Model 30

   Dimensional Model 33

   Flat, Hierarchical, and Relational
   Files Compared 36

   References 37

3. **Indigenous Databases In Libraries** 39

   Genesis of Indigenous Databases 39

   Scientific and Technical Data and the
   Creation of New Knowledge 44

The Uniqueness of Many S&T Databases 45

Dissemination of Scientific and Technical
Data and the Issue of Access 47

Limitation of Online Databases 47

Indigenous Databases & Their Implicit Properties 50

Implicit Properties 50

Essentials of the Indigenous Databases 51

Design and Development of Indigenous Databases 53

Database' Correction 53

Objectives of Indigenous Database 54

Types of Indigenous Databases 54

Other Databases 54

Indigenous Databases: Effect on Library Services 56

Features of Networked Indigenous Databases 57

Searching Indigenous Databases 57

Database Searching Through E-Mail 58

Planning and Handling of Information 58

Policies Related With Indigenous Databases 59

Issues of Indigenous Databases 60

Barriers Related With Indigenous Databases 60

R&D Libraries and Their Role 61

Indigenous Databases Development in India 62

Initiation of Databases Development 62

Databases in Hard Copy Form 64

Databases on Magnetic Media 64

Indigenous Databases in Library &
Information Services 65

Indigenous Databases Market 67

Use of Scientific and Technical Databases 69

References 70

4.   Types of Databases 75

Bibliographic Databases 75

Database Creation Options 76

The Importance of Adherence to Marc 76

Appropriate Fields: Consistent Formats 77

Correcting A Defective Database 78

Guidelines For A Healthy Bibliographic File 78

Planning of Bibliographic Databases 80

Metadatabase 82

Full-text Databases 82

Future of Full-text Databases 84

Image databases 86

Maintenance of Databases 95

Mixed-Format Databases 97

Derivative Databases and New
Data-driven Research and Capabilities 97

References 100

5. Information Retrieval From Databases 104

Basic Searches 105

Database Indexing 108

Basics of the database Query 109

Data Types 110

Query Language 111

Overriding Precedence by
Nesting Search Terms 112

Using Nesting to Make the Not Operators Exclusive ... 113

Embedding Wildcard Characters in a Search Term 117

Using a Wildcard Character as a Literal 118

Subject Headings 135

Refining / Fine-tuning the Search 138

References 143

6. Growth and Development of Databases 144

Need of Information Planning 144

Need of Indigenous Information 146

Indigenous Databases: Importance for
National Information Accessibility 147

National Database 148

Databases 152

Growth and Development of Databases 155

Man Power and Development 157

Online Information, Databases and Gateways 159

Role of Govtenrment 162

Role and Importance of Databases............................. 162

References 167

7. Linguistics in Databases 172

Indexing in Databases 172

Validity and Improvement of Data 173

Updating Information in Databases 174

Searching of Databases 175

Linguistics and Full-text searching 176

References 185

8. Marketing of Information and Databases .. 188

Professional Attitude.. 195

Users Attitude and Behaviour Related to Databases .. 197

Suggestion for Databases 200

Feedback from Users 200

User Education: Searching 201

Future of User 204

Budgeting... 204

Funding 205

Man Power and Development...................................... 205

Training Strategies 206

References 207

9. Database and Web Application 211

Technologies... 214

Database Design and Development Process 219

Creating Web Based Database Services 219

Three-tier Architectures 221

Database Applications and the Hypertext
Transfer Protocol 221

Client and the Three-tier Model 224

Web Scripting With PHP 226

The Database Tier 228

Database Server 231

The Mysql Server 234

References 235

10. Online Database Services Worldwide 238

OCLC 238

OCLC Databases by Topic 246

Features of FirstSearch Database 247

Customizing the FirstSearch Databases 265

PUBMED 268

MEDLINE 269

Pubmed Services 272

BIOSIS 273

Databases 274

DIALOG 284

PRODUCTS 286

References 292

Index 294

Chapter 1
Database: An Overview

The term or expression database originated within the computer industry. Database is a collection of information in a structured way. One can say that it is a collection of a group of facts. The personal address book is a database of names a person likes to keep track of, such as personal friends and members of the family. A database is a collection of related data. It can be defined as a computerized collection of logically related data or data records about something that are stored, organized, or structured in a computer in such a flexible manner that it enables people to get information out of it very quickly[1]. A database can also be seen as a collection of interrelated largely similar data or data records in a set linked filed designed to facilitate the retrieval of information, which may be processed by one or more application programmes[2]. In other words a database is a machine- readable file or organized form of related records collected to satisfy the information requirements of a given user commodity[3]. Such organized collection can be about many things e.g. Database of books in a library of periodical articles, database of office orders etc. A large database is known as databanks. Each unit of information stored in a database consists of discrete characteristics of the entity being described[4] e.g. a bibliographic database will contain information relating to books, periodical, articles, reports, etc.

A database is essentially a file management system that comprises of records and fields where a record is a set of information of an individual or an item and distinct pieces of information are fields[5]. To begin with, a telephone directory or a railway timetable is an example of a database of special utility. Computers come into the picture when the question of handling volumes of records with a number of fields is considered along with a larger user group requiring the updated information immediately and then people speak of database management systems (DBMS). Generally speaking database is an organized set of records on a subject in whatever from, updated on a continual basis and available for national/regional consumption[6]. Databases are assembled and marketed by commercial firms and consortia, and may exist also in a conventional printed from[7]. Each database generally concerns one subject. The term 'database' has been used in two different connotations. In Library and Information Science, these are referred to as bibliographic or inventory in nature and consist of collection of related logical records. In Computer Science these are referred to as a database management system. In this sense a database has a logically consistent structure in which records are actually linked[8],[9].

Databases play an important role in the development of information market and its products. A large number of databases are available online from foreign vendors which are finding an increasing market in the country[10]. Over the past few years, India is gradually building up capability in the database field. Initiatives are taken by domestic vendors and institutions to commercialize databases and related services in a number of fields[11]. The vast expertise and capabilities in computer software, that are available in the country, provide excellent opportunities for the establishment and development of a strong commercial base for databases

in the country [12], [13]. The term 'database' generally refers
to an aggregate of information systematically arranged
and stored in a computer system or in any other form [14].
A database can be conceived as a system whose base,
whose key concept, is simply a particular way of handling
data. In other words, a database is nothing more than a
computer-based record keeping system. The overall
objective of a database is to record and maintain
information[15].

Definitions of a Database

The Macmillan Dictionary of Information Technology
defines a database as a collection of interrelated data
stored so that authorized users with simple user-friendly
dialogues may access it.

The Chambers Science and Technology Dictionary
provides a more simple definition of a database- a
collection of structured data independent of any particular
application.

Ellingen[16] defines a database as a collection of
information that can be searched as a single entity.

According to Oxborrow[17] a database can be
considered as an organized collection of related sets of
data, managed in such a way as to enable the user or
application program to view the complete collection, as a
single unit.

Harrod's Librarian's Glossary defines a database as
information stored in computer files and accessible via
remote terminal and telecommunication link.

According to Chingchick Chen and Schweizer[18], a
database is a collection of information in a machine-
readable form, accessible by a computer.

According to Williams[19], a database is an organized
set of machine-readable records containing bibliographic
or documents related data.

According to Rowley[20], a database is a collection of
records in accessible sequence, stored on an auxiliary

storage device such as magnetic tape of dispark.

According to Lomis[21], database is a collection of logically related data that supports shared access by many users and is protected and managed to retain in its value.

European Commission Directive on Databases Copyright states, "Database means a collection of works, data or other materials arranged in a systematic and methodological way and capable of being accessed by electronic or other means. It includes the materials necessary for the operation and consultation of a database, such as a thesaurus and indexing."

James Martin[22] says, "A much publicized but impracticable idea of a database says that a corporation keeps all its processable items of data in a large reservoir in which a diversity of data users can go fishing."

According to John Convey[23], "Databases are collections of records in machine readable form that are made available for searching from remote computer terminals."

In a library context, most electronic databases are based on an equivalent printed index but after greater flexibility and sophistication in the searching process. A database represents some aspect of the real world, sometimes called the miniworld or the Universe of Discourse. Changes to the miniworld are reflected in the database.

A database is a logically coherent collection of data with some inherent meaning [24]. A random assortment of data cannot be referred to as a database.

Simply put, a database is a computerized record keeping system. More completely, it is a system involving data, the hardware that physically stores that data, the software that utilizes the hardware's file system in order to 1) store the data and 2) provide a standardized method for retrieving or changing the data, and finally, the users who turn the data into information. Databases, another creature of the 60s, were created to solve the problems with file-oriented systems in that they were compact, fast, easy to use, current, accurate, allowed the easy sharing of data between multiple users, and were secure. Clement[46] suggests following points for developing an information environment. A consistent, yet open, computing and communication base adapted to users' needs in all phases of the research process;

1. Access to expert help, including means for supporting an rewarding peer and specialist expertise within the research professions;

2. Tools for developing database, along with feed back mechanisms to evaluate, modify and disseminate the database developed; and

3. Analogues to the library and information resources (not necessarily central physical locations) in which search information can be stored, organized and retrieved.

A database might be as complex and demanding as an account tracking system used by a bank to manage the constantly changing accounts of thousands of bank customers, or it could be as simple as a collection of electronic business cards on the laptop. The important thing is that a database allows storing data and getting it or modifying it when needed easily and efficiently regardless of the amount of data being manipulated. What the data is and how demanding library-routines will be when retrieving and modifying that data is simply a matter of scale. Traditionally, databases ran on large, powerful mainframes for business applications. Leung[47] discusses the architecture of an image database. He discusses the storage, management of image data; system organization and architecture; picture indexing and filing component. Maxon-Dadd[48] discusses the refurbishing an elegant Victorian database a view from DIALOG. She says that the creators and caretakers of a lovely old Victorian database have an irresistible impulse to give it a fix-up frequently. Sometimes structural repairs are needed. She points out some advantages and disadvantages of remodeling for database producers, search services etc. Stern and Tarkowski[49] discuss the need for a unified European environmental health database. They say that data on which to base the setting of priorities for implementing strategies to reduce public health risks must be sufficient quality to justify semiquantitative risk assessment. Ydreborg[50] discusses the questionnaire-based database on occupation and health status. Jarvis[51] discusses developing an expert system using a PC-based shell. He describes an expert system and briefly examines possible relationship between expert, system and database. Mukhopadhyay[52] states that more and more libraries in India are getting access to microcomputer facilities, yet little progress has been achieved so far towards library computerization. Culturally, the libraries are not yet ready to exploit computer power. These factors apart, non-availability of suitable application software may be considered one of the major impediments. There is hardly any software available for their use that is truly user-friendly, presupposing minimal computer skills to operate. While there is hardly any alternative for the average library there are many possibilities for those resourceful ones who may afford considerable investment on software development or procurement of commercial software. Some of the have-nots may hope to participate in one or another library networking programs in the near future and gains the privilege of using network software. The rest might continue to grapple with increasing information management problems even though a microcomputer is just there on the library desk but performing only general-purpose packages. Further he says that library use of general-purpose software has concentrated on routine applications. Relational databases like dBase have potential to solve problems of variable field, variable record structure and repeatable fields. One will probably have heard of such packages as Oracle 8 or Sybase SQL Server for example. However with the advent of small, powerful personal computers, databases have become more readily usable by the average computer user. Microsoft's Access is a popular PC-based engine.

How is a database organized?

Understanding records and fields

Understanding how databases are organized can help user retrieves information more efficiently. Information about each item in a database is called a record.

Elements of an individual record are called fields. Fields can be used as points of access when searching a database. A record in a periodical database would include information about a periodical article (author, source, date, title, etc.).

User might try visualizing a record in an electronic database as being part of a table. Each column in the table represents the fields and each row represents the individual record.

Structure of a Database

A database is comprised of records. Each record has a field structure. Each field is comprised of sentences and words. In what follows, note that the label (TX) refers to a field containing text that may be more than one paragraph long (in the English grammer sense of the word "paragraph."). Some database calls such a "field" a full-text field, and calls each individual "paragraph" within the full-text field a subparagraph. Such long fields are often called "memo fields" in the computer industry.

Fields

A field is the basic unit of a record. Most of the database record is divided into fields. Some of these fields resemble a grammatical paragraph. However, sometimes a database field will contain only one sentence or one word. Sometimes it will only contain a number (such as a publication date). Sometimes a database field will contain several grammatical paragraphs. Each database field was created to contain a particular piece of information. For instance, one field has been designed to contain only a date (publication date); another only a name (author). In fact, a database is defined to a large extent by the number of fields, the type of fields, and the search and display qualities of each field. All records in a database share the same field structure although it is possible for a field to be blank, for example, when the date of publication is unknown.

a. Standard and Fulltext Fields

A standard field can contain a word or number, a sentence, or a few sentences. A standard field could contain text that is comprised of one or more grammatical paragraphs. Most of the databases use standard fields for information that identifies the source of a description of software technology, such as the author, title, facts of publication, and the like. A fulltext field is usually created to contain consecutive, textually similar data. This information is similar enough to be in the same field, but extensive enough for users to want to search on and retrieve a unit of data smaller than the entire field itself.

A unit of data within a fulltext field is called a subparagraph. The advantage of a fulltext field is that it lets the user assign large blocks of text to a single field. However, because this large block of text is now in subparagraphs (instead of one large field) the field-wide search operator (same) will operate only on the text in each subparagraph.

b. Short Labels and Long Labels

Field labels are assigned by the database designer and used to describe individual fields. Each field has both a short label and a long label. Short labels and long labels also give a way to select the fields that users want to include in a search or display operation.

i. Short Label : A field's short label is the most common way to reference field, and is comprised of two to four characters. For some database operations, the short label are the only field name that can be used. If a field is a fulltext field, one or more subparagraphs may be viewed at one time. The label that identifies subparagraphs is called a subparagraph label. A subparagraph label is assigned to each subparagraph in a fulltext field. Such a label can appear either as the short label (of the fulltext field) or a number (the first subparagraph being one), or not be displayed at all.

ii. Long Label : A field's long label is comprised of up to 60 characters and should describe the text contained in the field. Since the text of the long label can (potentially) be quite long, it is usually not practical to use this label to select fields during database operations.

c. Search and Display Qualities of a Field

Most of the databases have attempted to assign the search and display characteristics for each field that are appropriate for the way users will search for and/or display text in that field. For example, fields may differ in the way users have to search for hyphenated words, the possessive form of words, abbreviations, initials, and numbers. In some databases, each field is discussed there in terms of its search and display qualities in their design aspect.

Categories of fields

In database there are five categories of fields
They are:
* Numeric
* Character
* Logic

* Memo
* Date

All the related fields for a particular event are called a Record. Thus, a record can be defined as a collection of logically related fields. Now database can be defined in a formal manner. It can be said that it is a collection of logically related records. In other words a database is a collection of database files, and each database file is a collection of records.

The task before any organization is creation of a database and its management. Data management involves creating, modifying, deleting and adding data in files, and using this data to generate reports or answer queries. The software that allows performing these functions easily is called a Data Base Management System (DBMS). Using a DBMS files can be retrieved easily and effectively.

There are many DBMS packages available in the market. Some of them are:
* DBASE III Plus
* FoxBASE Plus
* SoftBASE
* Clipper
* Paradox

There are some WINDOWS based database packages available in the market such as MS ACCESS (part of MS OFFICE).

Types of Databases

These days, when somebody talks about databases in general, he is primarily talking about two types: analytical databases and operational databases.

a. Analytic Databases

Analytic databases (OLAP- On Line Analytical Processing) are primarily static, read-only databases, which store archived, historical data used for analysis. For example, an organization might store sales records over the last ten years in an analytic database and use that database to analyze marketing strategies in relationship to demographics. On the web, it is often see analytic databases in the form of inventory catalogs such as the one shown previously from Amazon.com. An inventory catalog analytical database usually holds descriptive information about all available products in the inventory. Web pages are generated dynamically by querying the list of available products in the inventory against some search parameters. The dynamically-generated page will display the information about each item (such as title, author, ISBN) which is stored in the database.

b. Operational Databases

Operational databases (OLTP; On Line Transaction Processing), on the other hand, are used to manage more dynamic bits of data. These types of databases allow doing more than simply view-archived data. Operational databases allow modifying that data (add, change or delete data).

These types of databases are usually used to track real-time information. For example, a company might have an operational database used to track warehouse/stock quantities. As customers order products from an online web store, an operational database can be used to keep track of how many items have been sold and when the company will need to reorder stock.

c. Client/Server Databases

As it is said before, most databases will be relational databases. However, there are many types of relational databases and not all of them will be useful for web applications.

In particular, it will be the client/server databases rather than the stand-alone packages that library will use for the web.

A client/server database works like this: A database server is left running 24 hours a day, and 7 days a week. Thus, the server can handle database requests at any hour. Database requests come in from "clients" who access the database through its command line interface or by connecting to a database socket. Requests are handled as they come in and multiple requests can be handled at one time.

For web applications, which must be available for worldwide time zone usage, it is essential to build upon a client/server database, which can run all the time.

Features of Good Database Design

It is most likely that as a web developer, one will be working with one of the modern relational databases and that he will be able to work in conjunction with an existing database administrator. After all, database administration is its own entire job description.

However, libraries have been spending a lot of time going through general database theory because although users may not be designing databases themselves, in order to take the most advantage of them, it is important that user understand how they work. Likewise, it is important that users have a feel for good database design. After all, a database's usefulness is directly proportional to the sleekness and efficiency of its design. And their ability to take advantage of a database is directly proportional to their ability to decipher and internalize that design.

When thinking about good database design, it is important that library keep data retrieval, storage and modification efficiency in mind. It will pay off one thousand fold if library take a week or two to simply play with different arrangements of data. Library will find that certain table structures will provide easier and more intuitive access than others.

Tables should describe only one subject, have

distinct fields, contain no redundant data, and have a field with unique values so that the table can be related to others.

Library should also keep in mind future expansion of the database and make sure that the design is easily extensible.

Typically, library will go through a requirements phase in which it should simply sit with the problem, interview users, and achieve an intuition about the data and the project.

Next, library should spend time modeling the data, preferably using some standard methodology like ER Diagramming. However, even if library does not model in any traditional way, it can still play with different ideas and think about the pros and cons.

Finally, library should try out the ideas and hone them through limited trials.

Hopefully, library will also choose a database with full- functionality such as security and concurrency control (making sure that two users cannot simultaneously change a record). There are many excellent choices available in the market today from freeware to commercial products. In this case, library should work closely with the database administrator to define the database.

At the very least librarian should sit down over a brew one evening and discuss the database design thoroughly.

Database Scheme

1. Libraries distinguish between a database scheme (logical design) and a database instance (data in the database at a point in time).
2. A relation scheme is a list of attributes and their corresponding domains.
3. The text uses the following conventions:

* Italics for all names
* Lowercase names for relations and attributes
* Names beginning with an uppercase for relation schemes

These notes will do the same.

For example, the relation scheme for the deposit relation:

* Deposit-scheme = (bname, account#, cname, balance)

Applications of databases

In order to store all the new information, humanity invented the technology of writing. And though great scholars like Aristotle warned that the invention of the alphabet would lead to the subtle but total demise of the creativity and sensibility of humanity, data began to be stored in voluminous data repositories, called books.

As it is known, eventually books propagated with great speed and soon, whole communities of books migrated to the first real "databases", libraries.

Unlike previous versions of data warehouses (people and books), that might be considered the australopithecines of the database lineage, libraries crossed over into the modern-day species, though they were incredibly primitive of course. Specifically, libraries introduced "standards" by which data could be stored and retrieved. After all, without standards for accessing data, libraries would be like my closet, endless and engulfing swarms of chaos. Books, and the data within books, had to be quickly accessible by anyone if they were to be useful.

In fact, the usefulness of a library, or any base of data, is proportional to its data storage and retrieval efficiency. This one corollary would drive the evolution of databases over the next 2000 years to its current state. Thus, early librarians defined standardized filing and retrieval protocols. Perhaps, if one has ever made it off the web, he will have seen an old library with its cute little indexing system (card catalog) and pointers (Dewey decimal system). And for the next couple thousand years libraries grew, and grew, and grew along with associated storage/retrieval technologies such as the filing cabinet, colored tabs, and three ring binders.

Databases are used in many applications, spanning virtually the entire range of computer software. Databases are the preferred method of storage for large multiuser applications, where coordination between many users is needed. Even individual users find them convenient, though, and many electronic mail programs and personal organizers are based on standard database technology. Software database drivers are available for most database platforms so that application software can use a common application programming interface (API) to retrieve the information stored in a database.

Databases Information Services

Large bibliographic databases have a future, but publishers should not assume that there is a market for a database just because data exist the report [24] of Association of Information and Dissemination Centers 1984 Fall Meeting. Publishers should exploit existing databases, find new markets for them, ad place a heavy emphasis on new technology. Examples are customized subsets and non-primetime access (such as Knowledge Index). Front –end packages might draw a few new users, but this group felt they would have no large impact because of the time needed to learn and the voluminous documentation. Optical disks have possibilities, but frequent updating could present a problem. A hybrid system-disk and online–might be best. The future of full-text will depend on the type of information available. Large database producers find it difficult to know their markets when vendor information is scant; small database

producers can be more nimble and can make a database
more widely available. Because dynamic information is
needed rapidly, it may help to create subsets of large
databases. Auld[25] states that we've all seen the rapid
expansion of database development in the last few years.
We also know that very few are making any profits at all.
Many database publishers still are supporting the
electronic product with the revenue of the print product.
For those who wish to enter the game with an electronic
only offering, it's a tough road. So he needs to understand
his current market:

* Their likes and dislikes about the database
* To what uses these conditions the database will be
  used
* What type and how much support is necessary
* What factors can be implemented that will improve
  the database's ability to match the users' needs
  In addition to questioning the current offerings:
* What new opportunities exist in providing the
  current information that currently is not being
  pursued?
* What information is not currently being provided
  that he could economically provide
* What other markets could he get into, at what cost
* Alternative forms of delivery to his existing markets-
  the question of vertical integration, gateways, and
  optical disks: where is the technology taking us.

These are aspects concerned with the future of the
database information services industry. The future of the
industry, and, in particular, that of database producers
looks very good. Never before have there been
opportunities such as those before now. Technological,
legislative, economic, and sociological factors are all
playing vital roles in shaping the environment with in
which we operate. They all have impact on the single
most important factor to all of us-that of the speed, depth,

and degree to which society embraces electronic delivery of information to enhance, supplement, or replace traditional print forms.

Copyright of databases

Srividya[26] discussed Intellectual property rights issues in databases and said that database as a concept has undergone a change after Internet has narrowed the distances for transacting businesses. Databases were initially seen primarily as stored information, say, in the form of share prices, details of employees, products and such other information. This information was restricted in terms of the number of persons who could get access to it and the holder or the proprietor of the information had a control over the information by and large. Today the term database constitute data stored in the World Wide Web, CDs, multimedia products, network and so on. Mirchin[27] discusses the European Union Database Directive and its applications and implications as worldwide agenda. He discusses the protection of databases in the "Bad Old Days". Sui-generis as a new category of intellectual property right has been discussed. The impact of the directive is somewhat dependent on how stringent the penalties will be for violations. It states that electronic and prints are protected. Further he discusses about the databases makers and their enforcement of right. Further he discusses about the rights received by Database Makers and terms of protection. Rights of researchers, libraries and users and harmonized copyright protection under the Directive are also discussed. He recommends to the databases makers that records of time, money, or ideas contributed to the databases need to be maintained in order to assure the company can benefit from the Directive. Cuadra[28] discusses the proprietary rights and beyond in databases. He says that both databases publishers and online service vendors must define much more clearly the terms and conditions, if any, under which owners of microcomputers will be allowed to copy, retain, and re-use data downloaded by users from large, centralized computer service bureaus. He argues that most users will adhere to the terms and conditions set by the owners of data, if those terms and conditions are made clear and seem even halfway reasonable. Database owners should not remain silent about those terms and conditions but, instead, to give immediate attention to the nature of emerging user needs and to develop pricing policies-including "no-charge" policies-that serve those needs, while protecting their proprietary interests in the data.

Significant Aspects of Database Production

The rate of scientific progress depends not only on the collection of new data, but also on the quality of the data collected, their ease of use, and the dissemination of information about the database. Considerable attention must be given to all those activities necessary to organize raw or disparate data into databases for broader use. These functions and methods typically include digitally processing the data into successively more highly refined and usable products; organizing the data into a database with appropriate structure, format, presentation, and documentation; creating the necessary accompanying analytical support software; providing adequate quality assurance and quality control; announcing the availability of the database; and arranging for secure near-term storage and eventual deposit in an archive that preserves the database and enables continued access.[17] As databases become ever larger and more complex, effective database production methods become increasingly important and constitute a significant component of the overall cost of the database.

The production of S&T databases requires at least some involvement by those responsible for collecting the original data. Typically, those closest to the collection of the data have the greatest expertise and interest in organizing them into a database whose contents are both available to and readily usable by others. Furthermore, the highly technical and frequently esoteric nature of S&T databases is likely to require that the original data collectors (or project scientists) participate in at least the initial stages of organizing, documenting, and reviewing the quality of data in the database. Involvement by the original data collectors in managing that part of the database production process decreases the probability that unusable or inaccurate databases will result, reduces the need for subsequent attempts to rescue or complete such data sets, and saves time and expense overall.

The level of processing and related database production activities is a significant factor in defining the ultimate utility (and legal protection) of a digital data collection. It is the original unprocessed, or minimally processed, data that are usually the most difficult to understand or use by anyone other than the originator of those data, or an expert in that particular area. With every successive level of processing, organization, and documentation, the data tend to become more comprehensible and easier to use by the nonexpert. As a database is prepared for more widespread use with the addition of more creative elements, it also tends to become more copyrightable as well as more generally marketable. In the case of observational sciences, it is the raw, noncopyrightable data that are typically of greatest long-term value to basic research. Increased or new protection for noncopyrightable databases previously in the public domain could therefore have a disproportionate impact on the heretofore unrestricted access to and use of raw data sets for basic research and education.

Although the production of many S&T databases is performed by, or with the active participation of, the originating researchers, it also is common for third parties to be involved in an aspect of database production referred

to as "value adding." Because the comprehensive
production of very large or complex databases can be
quite expensive, organizations that collect data, especially
in government, are increasingly "outsourcing" database
production and subsequent distribution to third parties
in an effort to contain costs. In such instances, the raw,
or minimally processed, data are provided to a private-
sector vendor expressly contracted with by government
to add value to the data and produce a database in a
commercially marketable format to meet broad user
requirements. However, since most federal government
databases are openly available and in the public domain,
adding value to them may be undertaken as an initiative
by entrepreneurs that see a business opportunity in such
activities, without any formal contractual arrangement
with the government data source.

Importance and Use of Scientific and Technical Databases

Modern technology has propelled us into the
information age, making it possible to generate and record
vast quantities of new data. Advances in computing and
communications technologies and the development of
digital networks have revolutionized the manner in which
data are stored, communicated, and manipulated.
Databases, and uses to which they can be put, have
become increasingly valuable commodities.

The now-common practice of downloading material
from online databases has made it easy for researchers
and other users to acquire data, which frequently have
been produced with considerable investments of time,
money, and other resources. Government agencies and
most government contractors or grantees in the United
States (though not in many other countries) usually make
their data, produced at taxpayer expense, available at no
cost or for the cost of reproduction and dissemination.
For-profit and not-for-profit database producers (other

than most government contractors and grantees) typically charge for access to and use of their data through subscriptions, licensing agreements, and individual sales.

Currently many for-profit and not-for-profit database producers are concerned about the possibility that significant portions of their databases will be copied or used in substantial part by others to create "new" derivative databases. If an identical or substantially similar database is then either redisseminated broadly or sold and used in direct competition with the original rights holder's database, the rights holder's revenues will be undermined, or in extreme cases, the rights holder will be put out of business. Besides being unfair to the rights holder, this actual or potential loss of revenue may create a disincentive to produce and then maintain databases, thus reducing the number of databases available to others. However, preventing database uses by others, or making access and subsequent use more expensive or difficult, may discourage socially useful applications of databases. The question is how to protect rights in databases while ensuring that factual data remain accessible for public-interest and other uses.

References

1. Bjelland, Harley. Using Online Scientific and Engineering Databases. U.S.A.: Mc Graw Hill, 1992, p. 2-5.

2. Feldman, Tony. Turn of the Tide: A New Age in Multimedia Publishing. *Annals of Library Science and Documentation* , 39(3), 1992, p 86-88.

3. Lupovici, Christian. Towards a full electronic information system at INIST. *Information Services & Use*, 15, 1995, p 229-236.

4. Dugal, H. S. and Brown, C. L. The future of a small technical data base. *Information Services & Use*, 5, 1985, p 157-165.

5. Tell, Jorn B. Paperless Communication. *International Information, Communication and Education*, 9(2), Sept. 1990, p156-163.

6. Devarajan, Dr. G.(ed.) Progress in Information Technology. New Delhi: ESS ESS, 1996, p. 115-138.

7. Chopra, Dr. H.S.(ed.). Library Information Technology in Modern Era: Libraries and Librarians in New Mellenium. New Delhi: Efficient Offset Press, 1999, p. 36-42.

8. Ramaiah, L.S. Images and Perceptions in Library and Information Science. Electronic Media with Special Reference to Optical Media: Impact on Libraries. New Delhi: ESS ESS, 1998, p. 168-174.

9. Mahapatra, P.K. and Chakrabarti, B. Book Byte and Beyond: Library Without Walls. New Delhi: ESS ESS, 2000, p. 156-168.

10. Arenas, Judith Licea De. Online Databases and Their Impact on Bibliometric Analysis: The Mexican Health Science Research Case. *International Forum of Information and Documentation*, 18(1), Jan 1993, p 18 -19.

11. Parvathamma, N; Nijagunappa, R. and Murthy, P. Sadaswa. Creation of an Inhouse Database. *IASLIC Bulletin*, 31(1), 1986, p. 1-8.

12. Vijay Kumar, K.P. Databases in Information Retrieval. Library Computerization in India. New Delhi: ESS ESS, 1990, p. 66-80.

13. Vyasaomarthy, P. Database Industry in India: A Current Scenario. *DESIDOC Bulletin of Information Technology*, 15(4), 1995, p. 11-22.

14. Neelameghan, A. Online Glossary for Multilingual Database. *Information Studies*, 5(2), 1999, p 83-98.

15. McPherson, Malcolm G., Harrap, Chris and O'Reilly, Jan E. Enhancing search results by editing, analysis and packaging. *Information Services & Use*, 9, 1989, p 101-106.

16. Ellingen, O. Service bureau in multimedia diversification. *Information Services & Use*, 9, 1989, p 271-277.

17. Oxborrow, M. Online Databases. *Information Services and Use*, 7(2), 1987, p. 77-83.

18. Chingchick, Chen and Schweizer,V. Productivity and organizational implications of databases. *Information Services & Use*, 9, 1988, p 133-138.

19. Williams, A. Decentralized Intranet Access. *Bulletin of Medical Library Association*, 88(2), 2000, p 152-156.

20. Rowley, K. Online Databases. *Bulletin of Medical Library*

Association, 88(3), 2000, p 135-143.

21. Lomis, Y. Growth in Databases. International Information Communication and Education, 14 (3), 1985, p 118-193.

22. James Martin. Patent Information System. *Information Services & Use,* 6, 1986, p 113-119.

23. John Convey. Research Libraries and the Dissemination of Information in Genetic Engineering and Biotechnology. *Information Services & Use,* 6, 1986, p131-142.

24. Mahesh, G. and Das, K. Mohan. Quality Assurance in CD-ROM Based Information Products. *Annals of Library Science and Documentation,* 19(2), 2001, p 167-171.

25. Auld, Dennis. Information on Vu/text –an experiment. *Information Services & Use,* 5, 1985, p107-111.

26. Srividya, G.S. Intellectual Property Rights: Issues in Databases. *International Information Communication and Education,* 20(2), 2001, p 253-261.

27. Mirchin, David. The European Union Database Directive sets the world-wide agenda. *Information Services & Use,* 17, 1997, p 247-252.

28. Cuadra, Carlos A. Proprietary Rights And Beyond In Databases. *International Information, Communication and Education,* 3(1), 1984.

Other References

46. Clement, J. B. Increasing Research Productivity through Information Technology: A User-Centred Viewpoint. *International Forum of Information & Documentation,* 15(2), April 1990, p 25-31.

47. Leung, C.H.C. Architecture of an image database. *Information Services & Use,* 10, 1990, p 391-397.

48. Maxon-Dadd, Josephine. Refurbishing an elegant Victorian database- a view from DIALOG. *Information Services & Use,* 10, 1990, p 361-369.

49. Stern, Richard M. and Tarkowski, Stanislow. The need for a unified European environmental health database. *Information services & Use,* 10, 1990, p 5-14.

50. Ydreborg, Berit. Questionnaire based database on occupation and health status. *Information services & Use,* 10, 1990, p 47-51.

51. Jarvis, J. R. Developing an expert system using a PC-based shell. *Information Services & Use*, 9, 1989, p 67-77.

52. Mukhopadhyay, A. Database Management. *International Information, Communication and Education*, 17(2), 1998, p 196-213.

53. http://www.nos.org/htm/course.htm

Chapter 2
Architecture of Database

The central concept of a database is that of a collection of records, or pieces of knowledge. Typically, for a given database, there is a structural description of the type of facts held in that database: this description is known as a schema. The schema describes the objects that are represented in the database, and the relationships among them. There are a number of different ways of organizing a schema, that is, of modelling the database structure: these are known as database models or data models.

A possible definition is that a database is a structures collection of records or data which is stored in a computer so that a program can consult it to answer queries. The records retrieved in answer to queries become information that can be used to make decisions. Database architecture is the fundamental schema, or physical layout, of a database. Rooted in mathematical/ structural theory, the most common database architectures are: Hierarchical, Networked, Object-Oriented and Relational. Besides differentiating databases according to function, databases can also be differentiated according to how they model the data. Well, essentially a data model is a "description" of both a container for data and a methodology for storing and retrieving data from that container. Actually, there isn't really a data model "thing". Data models are abstractions, sometimes-mathematical algorithms and concepts. One cannot really touch a data model. But nevertheless, they are very useful. The analysis and design of data models has been the cornerstone of the evolution of databases. As models have advanced so has database efficiency. Before the 1980's, the two most commonly used Database Models were the hierarchical and network systems.

A database model is a theory or specification describing how a database is structured and used. Database models. A data model is not just a way of structuring data: it also defines a set of operations that can be performed on the data. Various techniques are used to model data structure. Most database systems are built around one particular data model, although it is increasingly common for products to offer support for more than one model. For any one logical model various physical implementations may be possible, and most products will offer the user some level of control in tuning the physical implementation, since the choices that are made have a significant effect on performance. An example of this is the relational model: all serious implementations of the relational model allow the creation of indexes which provide fast access to rows in a table if the values of certain columns are known.

1. Flat Model

Flat model may not strictly qualify as a data mode. The flat or table model consists of a single, two-dimensional array of data elements, where all members of a given column are assumed to be similar values, and all members of a row are assumed to be related to one another. A flat file is a simple method for storing data. All records in this database have the same number of "fields". Individual records have different data in each field with one field serving as a key to locate a particular record. For example, the social security number may be the key field in a record of a person's name, address, phone number, sex, ethnicity, place of birth, date of birth, and so on. For a person, or a tract of land there could be hundreds of fields associated with the record. When the number of fields becomes lengthy a flat file is cumbersome to search. Also the key field is usually determined by the programmer and searching by other determinants may be difficult for the user. Although this type of database is simple in its structure, expanding the number of fields usually entails reprogramming. Additionally, adding new records is time consuming, particularly when there are numerous fields[1][2][3]. For instance, columns for name and password that might be used as a part of a system security database. Each row would have the specific password associated with an individual user. Columns of the table often have a type associated with them, defining them as character data, date or time information, integers, or floating point numbers. This model is, incidentally, a basis of the spreadsheet.

2. Hierarchical Model

In a hierarchical model, data is organized into a tree-like structure, implying a single upward link in each record to describe the nesting, and a sort field to keep the records in a particular order in each same-level list. Relationships in such a system are thought of in terms of children and parents such that a child may only have one parent but a parent can have multiple children. Parents and children are tied together by links called "pointers" (perhaps physical addresses inside the file system). A parent will have a list of pointers to each of their children.

Hierarchical structures were widely used in the early mainframe database management systems, such as the Information Management System (IMS) by IBM, and now describe the structure of XML documents. This structure allows one 1:N relationship between two types of data. This structure is very efficient to describe many relationships in the real world; recipes, table of contents, ordering of paragraphs/verses, any nested and sorted information. However, the hierarchical structure is inefficient for certain database operations when a full path (as opposed to upward link and sort field) is not also included for each record.

Hierarchical files store data in more than one type of record. This method is usually described as a "parent-child, one-to-many" relationship. One field is key to all records, but data in one record does not have to be repeated in another. This system allows records with similar attributes to be associated together. A key field in a hierarchy of files links the records to each other. Each record, except for the master record, has a higher-level record file linked by a key field "pointer". In other words, one record may lead to another and so on in a relatively descending pattern. An advantage is that when the relationship is clearly defined, and queries follow a standard routine, a very efficient data structure results. The database is arranged according to its use and needs. Access to different records is readily available, or easy to deny to a user by not furnishing that particular file of the database. One of the disadvantages is one must access the master record, with the key field determinant, in order to link "downward" to other records. Hierarchical structures were widely used in the first mainfram database management systems. Hierarchical relationships between different types of data can make it very easy to answer some questions, but very difficult to answer others. If a one-to-many relationship is violated (e.g. a customer can have more than one retailer), then the hierarchy becomes a network[4, 5, 6, 7, 8].

The most common form of hierchical model used currently is the Lightweight Directory Access Protocol

(LDAP) model[9]. Other than that, the hierarchical model is rare in modern databases[10,11]. It is, however, common in many other means of storing information, ranging from file systems to the windows registry to XML documents[12,13]. However, as one can imagine, the hierarchical database model has some serious problems. For one, you cannot add a record to a child table until it has already been incorporated into the parent table. This might be troublesome if, for example, someone wanted to add a student who had not yet signed up for any courses. Worse, yet, the hierarchical database model still creates repetition of data within the database. One might imagine that in the database system discussed above, there may be a higher level that includes multiple courses. In this case, there could be redundancy because students would be enrolled in several courses and thus each "course tree" would have redundant student information.

3. Network Model

In many ways, the Network Database model was designed to solve some of the more serious problems with the Hierarchical Database Model. Specifically, the Network model solves the problem of data redundancy by representing relationships in terms of sets rather than hierarchy. The model had its origins in the Conference on Data Systems Languages (CODASYL), which had created the Data Base Task Group to explore and design a method to replace the hierarchical model. The Network model organizes data using two fundamental constructs, called *records* and *sets*. Records contain fields. Sets (not to be confused with mathematical sets) define one-to-many relationships between records: one owner, many members. A record may be an owner in any number of sets, and a member in any number of sets[14]. The operations of the network model are navigational in style: a program maintains a current position, and navigates from one record to another by following the relationships in which the record participates[15][16]. Records can also be located by supplying key values. Although it is not an essential feature of the model, network databases generally implement the set relationships by means of pointers that directly address the location of a record on disk[17]. This gives excellent retrieval performance, at the expense of operations such as database loading and reorganization. Visually, a Network Database looks like a hierarchical Database in that you can see it as a type of tree. However, in the case of a Network Database, the look is more like several trees which share branches. Thus, children can have multiple parents and parents can have multiple children. Most profoundly, the model was difficult to implement and maintain. Most implementations of the network model were used by computer programmers rather than real users. What was needed was a simple model which could be used by real end users to solve real problems.

4. Relational Model

The *Relational model* was introduced in an academic by in 1970 as a way to make database management systems more independent of any particular application[18]. It is a mathematical model defined in terms of predicate logic and set theory. Of course in the 80's the "Relational Database Model" became the rage.

Relational Files connect different files or tables (relations) without using internal pointers or keys. Instead a common link of data is used to join or associate records. The link is not hierchical. A "matrices of tables" is used to store the information. As long as the tables have a common link they may be combined by the user to form new inquires and data output. This is the most flexible system and is particularly suited to SQL (structured query language). Queries are not limited by a hierarchy of files, but instead are based on relationships from one type of record to another that the user establishes. It is important to note that how or where the tables of data are stored makes no difference. Each table can be identified by a unique name and that name can be used by the database to find the table behind the scenes[19]. As a user, all you need to know is the table name in order to use it. You do not need to worry about the complexities of how the data is stored on the hard drive.

The products that are generally referred to as relational database in fact implement a model that is only an approximation to the mathematical model defined by Codd. Three key terms are used extensively in relational database models: *relations*, *attributes*, and *domains*. A relation is a table with columns and rows. The named columns of the relation are called attributes, and the domain is the set of values the attributes are allowed to take.

A relational database stores all its data inside tables, and nothing more. All operations on data are done on the tables themselves or produce another tables as the result. You never see anything except for tables[20].

A table is a set of rows and columns. This is very important, because a set does not have any predefined sort order for its elements. Each row is a set of columns with only one value for each. All rows from the same table have the same set of columns, although some columns may have NULL values, i.e. the values for that rows was not initialized. Note that a NULL value for a string column is different from an empty string. You should think about a NULL value as an "unknown" value[21]

This is quite a bit different from the hierarchical and network models in which the user had to have an understanding of how the data was structured within the database in order to retrieve, insert, update, or delete records from the database.

The basic data structure of the relational model is the table, where information about a particular entity (say, an employee) is represented in columns and rows (also called tuples). Thus, the "relation" in "relational database" refers to the various tables in the database; a relation is a set of tuples. The columns enumerate the various attributes of the entity (the employee's name, address or phone number, for example), and a row is an actual instance of the entity (a specific employee) that is represented by the relation. As a result, each tuple of the employee table represents various attributes of a single employee.

All relations (and, thus, tables) in a relational database have to adhere to some basic rules to qualify as relations. First, the ordering of columns is immaterial in a table. Second, there can't be identical tuples or rows in a table. And third, each tuple will contain a single value for each of its attributes[22].

A relational database contains multiple tables, each similar to the one in the "flat" database midel. One of the strenghts of the relational model is that, in principle, any value occurring in two different records (belonging to the same table or to different tables), implies a relationship among those two records. Yet, in order to enforce explicit integrity constraints, relationships between records in tables can also be defined explicitly, by identifying or non-identifying parent-child relationships characterized by assigning cardinality (1:1, (0)1:M, M:M). Tables can also have a designated single attribute or a set of attributes that can act as a "key", which can be used to uniquely identify each tuple in the table. Well, in the relational model, operations that manipulate data do so on the basis of the data values themselves. Thus, if you wish to retrieve a row from a table for example, you 'do so by comparing the value stored within a particular column for that row to some search criteria.

A key that can be used to uniquely identify a row in a table is called a primary key. Keys are commonly used to join or combine data from two or more tables. For example, an *Employee* table may contain a column named

Location which contains a value that matches the key of a *Location* table. Keys are also critical in the creation of indexes, which facilitate fast retrieval of data from large tables. Any column can be a key, or multiple columns can be grouped together into a compound key. It is not necessary to define all the keys in advance; a column can be used as a key even if it was not originally intended to be one. The relational view (or model) of data described in Section 1 appears to be superior in several respects to the graph or network model [3,4] presently in vogue for non-inferential systems. It provides a means of describing data with its natural structure only — that is, without superimposing any additional structure for machine representation poses. Accordingly, it provides a basis for a high level data language which will yield maximal independence between programs on the one hand and machine representation and organization of data on the other [23].

The flexibility of relational databases allows programmers to write queries that were not anticipated by the database designers. As a result, relational databases can be used by multiple applications in ways the original designers did not foresee, which is especially important for databases that might be used for decades. This has made the idea and implementation of relational databases very popular with businesses.

6. Dimensional Model

The dimensional midel is a specialized adaptation of the relational model used to represent data in data warehouses in a way that data can be easily summarized using OLAP queries. In the dimensional model, a database consists of a single large table of facts that are described using dimensions and measures. A dimension provides the context of a fact (such as who participated, when and where it happened, and its type) and is used in queries to group related facts together. Dimensions tend to be discrete and are often hierarchical; for example, the location might include the building, state, and country. A measure is a quantity describing the fact, such as revenue. It's important that measures can be meaningfully aggregated - for example, the revenue from different locations can be added together.

In an OLAP query, dimensions are chosen and the facts are grouped and added together to create a summary.

The dimensional model is often implemented on top of the relational model using a star schema, consisting of one table containing the facts and surrounding tables containing the dimensions. Particularly complicated dimensions might be represented using multiple tables, resulting in a snowflake schema.

A data warehouse can contain multiple star schemas that share dimension tables, allowing them to be used together. Coming up with a standard set of dimensions is an important part of dimensional modeling.

Object Database Models

In recent years, the object - oriented paradigm has been applied to database technology, creating a new programming model known as object database. The methods of file organization discussed above depend upon the careful description of real-world phenomena in terms of their attributes, such as height, weight, or age. It is these attributes that are stored in the database and together they provide a sort of abstracted depiction of the real-world feature. Much recent attention has focused on how to organize this information in ways that more readily represent the way users gather and use information about the world around them. That is, humans recognize "objects" immediately in terms of their totality or "wholeness." Houses and skyscrapers are recognized immediately by form and function. The differences can be described in terms of the underlying attributes, but people recognize these from experience.

The idea of "object-oriented" database is to organize information (that is group attributes) into the sorts of "wholes" that people recognize. Instead of "decomposing" each feature a distinctive list of attributes, emphasis is placed on "grouping" the attributes of a given object into a unit or template that can be stored or retrieved by its natural name.

Consider the following situation involving two ways of organizing information about buildings zoned for different uses. These databases attempt to bring the database world and the application programming world closer together, in particular by ensuring that the database uses the same type system as the application program. This aims to avoid the overhead (sometimes referred to as the impedance mismatch) of converting information between its representation in the database (for example as rows in tables) and its representation in the application program (typically as objects). At the same time object databases attempt to introduce the key ideas of object programming, such as encapsulation and polymorphism, into the world of databases.

A variety of these ways have been tried for storing objects in a database. Some products have approached the problem from the application programming end, by making the objects manipulated by the program persistent. This also typically requires the addition of some kind of query language, since conventional programming languages do not have the ability to find objects based on their information content. Others have attacked the problem from the database end, by defining an object-oriented data model for the database, and defining a database programming language that allows full programming capabilities as well as traditional query facilities.

Object databases suffered because of a lack of standardization: although standards were defined by

ODMG, they were never implemented well enough to ensure interoperability between products. Nevertheless, object databases have been used successfully in many applications: usually specialized applications such as engineering databases or molecular biology databases rather than mainstream commercial data processing. However, object database ideas were picked up by the relational vendors and influenced extensions made to these products and indeed to the SQL language.

Flat, Hierarchical, and Relational Files Compared

Structure	Advantages	Disadvantages
Flat Files	* Fast data retrieval * Simple structure and easy to program	* Difficult to process multiple values of a data item * Adding new data categories requires reprogramming * Slow data retrieval without the key
Hierarchical Files	* Adding and deleting records is easy * Fast data retrieval through higher level records * Multiple associations with like records in different files	* Pointer path restricts access * Each association requires repetitive data in other records * Pointers require large amount of computer storage
Relational Files	* Easy access and minimal technical training for users * Flexibility for unforeseen inquiries * Easy modification and addition of new relationships, data, and records	* New relations can require considerable processing * Sequential access is slow * Method of storage an disks impacts processing time * Easy to make logical

Structure	Advantages	Disadvantages
*	Physical storage of data can change without affecting relationships between records	mistakes due to flexibility of relationships between records

References

1. websiteowner.info/articles/cgi/databasetypes.asp
2. doc.trolltech.com/qq/qq15-models.html
3. www.answers.com/topic/database
4. *www.cs.comell.edu/home/kleinber/bhs.pdf*
5. *www.cafeconleche.org/books/xmljava/chapters/ch04s05.html*
6. *www.nd.edu/.../Physics/Scalefree-Hierarchical_Sitges%20Proceedings-Complex%20Networks,%20.pdf*
7. *www.cl.cam.ac.uk/~av308/Project_Index/allHands05.pdf*
8. *www.cmm.bristol.ac.uk/team/mnhs.pdf*
9. *www.ietf.org/rfc/rfc1777.txt*
10. *www.gracion.com/server/whatldap.html*
11. www.kingsmountain.com/directory/doc/ldap/ldap.html
12. support.microsoft.com/kb/256986 ,
13. www.pctools.com/guides/article/id/1
14. www.pds-site.com/WhitePapers/wp_wdbfits.htm,
15. whitepaper.informationweek.com
16. www.theukwebdesigncompany.com/articles/article
17. www.ncbi.nlm.nih.gov/entrez/query
18. http://www.acm.org/classics/nov95/toc.html
19. *www.databasejournal.com/sqletc/article.php/1469521*
20. computer.howstuffworks.com/question599.htm
21. www.islandnet.com/~tmc/html/articles/orareln.htm
22. www.15seconds.com/issue/020522.htm
23. http://www.acm.org/classics/nov95/s1p1.html

Footnotes

1. websiteowner.info/articles/cgi/databasetypes.asp
2. doc.trolltech.com/qq/qq15-models.html
3. www.answers.com/topic/database
4. www.cs.cornell.edu/home/kleinber/bhs.pdf
5. *www.cafeconleche.org/books/xmljava/chapters/ ch04s05.html*
6. *www.nd.edu/.../Physics/Scalefree-Hierarchical_ Sitges%20Proceedings-Complex%20Networks,%20.pdf*
7. *www.cl.cam.ac.uk/~av308/Project_Index/allHands05.pdf*
8. *www.cmm.bristol.ac.uk/team/mnhs.pdf*
9. *www.ietf.org/rfc/rfc1777.txt*
10. *www.gracion.com/server/whatldap.html*
11. www.kingsmountain.com/directory/doc/ldap/ldap.html
12. support.microsoft.com/kb/256986 ,
13. www.pctools.com/guides/article/id/1
14. www.pds-site.com/WhitePapers/wp_wdbfits.htm,
15. whitepaper.informationweek.com
16. www.theukwebdesigncompany.com/articles/article
17. www.ncbi.nlm.nih.gov/entrez/query
18. http://www.acm.org/classics/nov95/toc.html
19. *www.databasejournal.com/sqletc/article.php/1469521*
20. computer.howstuffworks.com/question599.htm
21. www.islandnet.com/~tmc/html/articles/orareln.htm
22. www.15seconds.com/issue/020522.htm
23. http://www.acm.org/classics/nov95/s1p1.html

Chapter 3
Indigenous Databases In Libraries

The information explosion accompanied by the rapid developments in the field of IT has redefined the manner in which information products and services are rendered worldwide. One of the most profound impacts of the IT development on the information industry has been the paradigm shift from a paper-based media to the electronic media. The impact of IT has been all pervading. It has changed the way that information is stored and disseminated and threatened the traditional approaches to the library and its services. Faced with enormous increase in scientific and technological knowledge, growth in volume of information and endless requirements of information with various interpretations, the contemporary global situation is alarming and starting from the grass-root level of an individual to top State executives every one is well aware of the need of fast, easy, accurate and comprehensive access to the available resources.

Genesis of Indigenous Databases

Amidst ignorance and poverty in many developing countries, advanced scientific institutions also exist. Fortunately, today India has very good infrastructure for

research and development activities shared by central
government and state government all have done
considerable progress to achieve to link all through
interdisciplinary and, multi-disciplinary approaches into
functional network system so as to enable contacts with
isolated researchers, in order to avoid investments in
duplication of research efforts, to reach farmers and
industries as soon as the information is generated, and
to influence developmental agencies for acting
recommendations etc. According to Pant, K C. (1990)[1]
India was on the threshold of a revolutionary change in
its economic and social life largely occasioned by rapid
advances in Information technology, which could reduce
superstitions and prejudice in our country. He advised
the scientists and engineers to modify the technologies
to suit the Indian milieu. The information scientists and
database managers should use technology as a tool to
meet the needs of the end-users.

Moreover budgets for research are being restrained,
a better allocation of the existing resources is necessary,
by comparing research priority areas with scientific
expertise, the segments of research in which both
coverage and those in which gap exist can be identified
and the appropriate measures can be applied in order to
correct divergence and harness convergence. According
to Dashrathy (2002)[2], information technology (IT) has
revolutionized data management systems in molecular
biology. The advancement in IT is gradually
revolutionizing the traditional experiments methods and
interpretations made in classical biology research. One
of the main reasons for this is the availability of efficient
computational tools and relational database management
system.

The possibility that scientific and technical
information has become available in electronic form raised
a number of questions for librarians as well as
publishers[3]. Among the concerns that have been

expressed are those dealing with pricing and secondary distribution. Publishers have begun to talk about charging for information on an access rather than on a subscription basis; libraries are deciding how to find the cost of access when the total use of a particular file is unknown at the beginning of a budget period. With the increasing availability of microcomputers, librarians are interested in pursuing the matter of downloading of information for later scanning and retrieval. Some publishers have begun to provide mechanisms for downloading from large databases, but the cost of these arrangements is prohibitive for all libraries except perhaps those serving industrial research and development organizations. A longer-term issue involves data-storage for large files of numerical and bibliographical information. Despite the constantly decreasing cost of storage, the economic feasibility of maintaining large databases online that contain seldom-used information offers the potentiality of transferring such information to another medium such as microfiche or optical disc, relying upon research libraries to serve their traditional role as archival repositories. Software and databases can enhance ease and versatility. Further networking can be a strong way to provide information at right time to users. Required information can be made available and properly disseminated through the networks and the farmers will improve their production capacity. This will be accomplished through computers and telecommunication technology only.

The increase in the amount of electronic information sources available has been significant within Library and Information Services[4]. It is costly, results in a demand for information skills training for both staff and students and is causing a radical transformation within Library and Information Services, involving a shift from an original emphasis upon holding material towards the importance of being a gateway to networked information, providing access rather than holding[5].

At this point of time when progress is in an automated 21st century, the information specialist's role has been changed and enhanced because of the need of accessing and exploiting the information bank by a heterogeneous user group on various fields at different levels. Instead of gathering information to meet the required specification, one thinks of establishing an information core, which can be exploited and manipulated at any point of time and in any possible combination.

The influx of computers, backed by strong databases, into the information management activities has changed the entire scene and the information specialist is in a position to be designated as an information originator with this specialized knowledge in database handling. Library and Information Science personnel are increasing becoming aware of the fruits of IT as exemplified by the day to day use of such terms as electronic library, electronic journal, teleconferencing, videotext, optical disc, telesmile etc[6]. Another word, which is very much in use, is database. In simple terms, any centrally controlled, integrated, collection logically organized data can be called the database[7].

Now, when we speak of databases, it is pre-assumed that the data are stored and collected in computers because of their inextricable association with databases. In the present context a database is an organized integrated and often inter-related collection of computer-based data, records, files or information is general with advent of IT, data, or information stored on computer files could be made accessible via remote terminals and telecommunication links that resulted in the emergence of on-line databases[8].

While a great deal of public attention has been paid to the 'information explosion' and the 'computer revolution', dramatic changes have been taking place in the way that research libraries collect, organize and service the vast quantities of information within their purview[9]. The application of computer and optical disc technology in research libraries has the potentiality of creating as significant change as did two other major 'revolutions'-the invention of micro-technology. Over the past decades, significant technological enhancements are witnessed, which have provided us the ability to store, manipulate and retrieve information in large quantities. However, one can barely keep pace with the burgeoning of information-particularly, in science and technology. It is ironic that one of the precipitating factors creating a crisis for today's information age, that is information overload, not information scarcity. The challenge is problem of access to the right information at the right time, both in terms of comprehensiveness and specificity rather than lack of information[10].

The population Division of the United Nations Department of International Economic and Social Affairs announced the publication of a database of a new database "Global Review and Inventory of Population Policy (GRIPP)" on population policies in countries throughout the word[11]. This database contained data files and corresponding dictionaries on the diskette in four commonly used formats in order to increase the database's flexibility and user-friendliness. ACROME[12], a database produced by IDATE (Institut de l'Audiovisual et des Telecommunications in Europe-France), facilitated information flow and collaboration among European researchers active in the communication field as it is available online on the ECHO (European Commission Host Organization). While a seminar on online searching was organized, online searching of DIAOLOG databases telex and PSTN modes were demonstrated to the participants[13].

There are some advantages in the use of databases that may be particularly pertinent to developing countries[14]. Most important aspect is speed of access, which is particularly crucial for such ephemeral data as currency quotations and commodity prices[15]. With some full-text databases, users can instantly obtain a complete copy of a patent that was registered in a developed country. With the bibliographic databases that contain abstracts, users obtain essence of articles, reports and other publications without delay[16].

Scientific and Technical Data and the Creation of New Knowledge

Factual data are both an essential resource for and a valuable output from scientific research. It is through the formation, communication, and use of facts and ideas that scientists conduct research. Throughout the history of science, new findings and ideas have been recorded and used as the basis for further scientific advances and for educating students.

Now, as a result of the near-complete digitization of data collection, manipulation, and dissemination over the past 30 years, almost every aspect of the natural world, human activity, and indeed every life form can be observed and captured in an electronic database. There is barely a sector of the economy that is not significantly engaged in the creation and exploitation of digital databases, and there are many—such as insurance, banking, or direct marketing—that are completely database dependent.

Certainly scientific and engineering research is no exception in its growing reliance on the creation and exploitation of electronic databases. The genetic sequence of each living organism is a natural database, transforming biological research and applications over the past decade into a data-dependent enterprise and giving rise to the rapidly growing field of bioinformatics. Myriad data collection platforms, recording and storing information about our physical universe at an ever-increasing rate, are now integral to the study and understanding of the natural environment, from small ecological subsystems to planet-scale geophysical processes and beyond. Similarly, the engineering disciplines continually create databases about our constructed environment and new technical processes, which are endlessly updated and refined to fuel our technological progress and innovation system.

Basic scientific research drives most of the world's progress in the natural and social sciences. Basic, or fundamental, research may be defined as research that leads to new understanding of how nature works and how its many facets are interconnected. Society uses the fruits of such research to expand the world's base of knowledge and applies that knowledge in myriad ways to create wealth and to enhance the public welfare.

New scientific understanding and its applications are yielding benefits such as the following:

* Improved diagnosis, pharmaceuticals, and treatments in medicine;

* Better and higher-yield food production in agriculture;

* New and improved materials for fabrication of manufactured objects, building materials, packaging, and special applications such as microelectronics;

* Faster, cheaper, and safer transportation and communication;

* Better means for energy production;

* Improved ability to forecast environmental conditions and to manage natural resources; and

More powerful ways to explore all aspects of our universe, ranging from the finest subnuclear scale to the boundaries of the universe, and encompassing living organisms in all their variety.

The Uniqueness of Many S&T Databases

A key characteristic of original S&T databases is

that many of them are the only one of their particular kind, available only from a single source, which has significant economic and legal implications, as discussed in subsequent chapters of this report. For example, many S&T databases describe physical phenomena or transitory events that have been rendered unique by the passage of time. Measurements of a snowstorm obtained with a single radar observation, or a statistical compilation of some key socioeconomic characteristics such as income levels collected by a state agency, cannot be recaptured after the original event. The vast majority of observational data sets of the natural world, as well as all unique historical records, can never again be recreated independently and are thus available only as originally obtained, frequently from a single source. Other S&T databases are de facto unique because the cost of obtaining the data was extremely high. This is the case with very large facilities for physical experiments or space-based observatories.

Even when data similar but not identical to original research results or observations are available for use in non-technical applications, scientists and engineers will likely not find an inexact replica of a database a suitable substitute if it does not meet certain specifications for a particular experiment or analysis. For example, two infrared sensors with similar spatial and spectral characteristics on different satellites collecting observations of Earth may provide relatively interchangeable data products for the non-expert consumer, but for a researcher, the absence of one spectral band can make all the difference in whether a certain type of research can be performed. Thus a database generally deemed adequate as a substitute in the mass consumer market very likely will not be usable for many research or education purposes.

Dissemination of Scientific and Technical Data and the Issue of Access

S&T data traditionally were disseminated in paper form in journal articles, textbooks, reference books, and abstracting and indexing publications. As data have become available in electronic form, they have been distributed via magnetic tape and, more recently, optical media such as CD-ROM or DVD. The growing use of the Internet has revolutionized dissemination by allowing most databases to be made available globally in electronic form. Digitization and the potential for instant, low-cost global communication have opened tremendous new opportunities for the dissemination and utilization of S&T databases and other forms of information, but also have led to a blurring of the traditional roles and relationships of database producers, vendors, and users of those databases in the government, not-for-profit, and commercial sectors. In fact, virtually anyone who obtains access to a digital database can instantly become a worldwide disseminator, whether legally or illegally.[20]

Two of the most important mechanisms for the dissemination of public and publicly funded databases have been government data centers and public libraries. Government, or government-funded, data centers have been created in recent decades for dissemination of data obtained in certain programs or research disciplines

Limitation of Online Databases

Online database access is directed towards multiplicity of sources. On-line databases certainly cannot satisfy all the information needs of developing countries[17], in many cases they can nevertheless provide some useful information. As a group, the source databases-the numeric, textual-numeric and full-text databases-probably hold the greatest attraction for users in developing countries because they contain actual source

data. However, for a thorough search, reference databases
may have to be consulted as well. Referral databases can
provide useful data, such as the names, addresses and
telephone numbers of exporters or firms with technologies
to license-information that is not easily obtained in
developing countries. Bibliographic databases[18] contain
informative abstracts that may provide users with enough
information to satisfy their information needs, without
seeking the complete text of an item. Even databases that
provide only brief citations to articles or documents can
be of help, if only to tell users whether something relevant
to the inquiry has been published.

Over all it must be kept in mind that the vast
majority of databases and databases records are produced
in developed countries, in response to the demand of
users who are primarily from the same countries. The
contents of databases consist, therefore, of data that are
geared to the demand of users in developed countries,
which is not necessarily always the same as that of users
in developing countries. Yet it should be noted that the
relevance of many data in independent of the level of
development.

Using online foreign databases produced by
developed countries may not be cost-effective[19]. Some
countries may have to consider such problems as foreign
exchange for the payment of imported equipment or
telecommunication facilities. Sometimes ago, government
exercised stringent control over the import of some high-
tech equipment such as CD-ROM drives. It is felt that
indigenous databases available in developing countries
provide a valuable source of information. Here are various
aspects to be considered:

* What is the bibliographic information in the region
  and to what extent do available sources satisfy
  user's needs?

* Is an indigenous database the desirable solution
  and what would be the technical characteristics,

manpower requirements and financial burden of such a service?

* What form of co-operation is required to implement it?

Sociologists, economists, scientists, technologists, and other groups of potential users of information throughout the world have recognized information as an essential resource for development as a catalyst for scientific and technical development and advancement[19]. There is a close connection between a country's social needs, the satisfaction of those needs by production and services, and the application of science to determine the needs and choose the ways and means for economic and technical development. All these processes are interwoven with science. The intensive development of science and immediate penetration into production are characteristic features of our age. A country's economic growth is increasingly dependent on the tempo of scientific research and on the ability to apply the results of that research rapidly and completely to production. It can emphatically be said that science and research continue to produce new knowledge in developing countries and that ways and means are sought, nationally as well as internationally, to utilize that knowledge in thee national economies.

One of the inherent problems with bibliographic databases is that the coverage will be in most of the cases be judged inadequate by at least some users- whether form the point of view of time span, or from that of subject scope, or from the geographical coverage, or perhaps for that of document types indexed[20]. Another possibility is that the literature in some; languages is poorly represented – not only on certain files but across the whole spectrum of available online information resources for S&T.

Indigenous Databases & Their Implicit Properties

Indigenous databases are the need of every research area to obtain the local information, which is not available in international databases. Indigenous databases provide that store of knowledge, which is not only regarding the national output of information but also related with the particular field of knowledge produced with in the country.

Implicit Properties

* An indigenous database is designed, built, and populated with data for a specific purpose[21]. It has an intended group of users and some preconceived applications in which these users are interested.

* In an indigenous database the data are shared among different users and all the requirements or information needs of users are fulfilled.

* A common and controlled approach is used for adding or inserting new data as well as deleting, collecting, modifying and retrieving existing data records or portion thereof within an indigenous database[22].

* Users and application programmes which asses data do not need to be aware of the detailed storage structure of the data on a computer storage device; in other words, the data are stored in a way so that they are independent of one of more application programmes that use the data.

* It is integrated with provisions for different applications.

* It eliminates or reduces data duplication.

* It enhances data independence by permitting application programs to be insensitive to changes in an indigenous database.

* It permits shared access.

* It permits finer granularity[23].

* It provides facilities for centralized control of accessing and security control functions.

Thus it can be said that an indigenous database has some source from which data are derived, some degree of interaction with events in the real world, and an audience that is actively interested in the contents of a database.

An indigenous database can be of any size and of varying complexity. It may be generated and maintained manually or it may be computerized. A computerized database is to be created and maintained either by a group of application programmes written specifically for that task or by a database management system. An indigenous database can be conceived as a system whose base, whose key concept, is simply a particular way of handling data. In other words, an indigenous database is nothing more than a computer-based record keeping system. The overall objective of an indigenous database is to record and maintain locally available and produced information.

Essentials of the Indigenous Databases

An indigenous database should have following essential qualities:

* An indigenous database must be very good application generator to help the information specialist in achieving his goal of designing and developing in house databases without programmer assistance.

* A strong report generation and retrieval increases the adaptability of indigenous databases.

* The flexibility of indigenous databases is an equally important feature. Since files and records are generally maintained for long period, the translation facility of the database boosts its usability over others.

* Translation of files or records created through various and leading operating systems into the database file is another item to be highlighted for an indigenous database.

* Data entry is another area of importance for an indigenous database. A database must have an operator friendly approach, like the operator should not key in the serial number of the records as he goes on typing records after records.

* The indigenous database must be able to distinguish the mismatch to a field content.

* Efficient online help and screen tutorial facilities are among the most important features of a popular indigenous database.

* The design and layout of the indigenous database screen is of equal importance.

* A good indigenous database must have the features of suppressing of reviving certain information and messages during operation at a single-stroke of a function key and it should be at any stage of programme proceedings.

* The indigenous database must give ample scope to the user to reserve and write each record to the disk file as he finishes a record so as to tackle which sudden interruption and power failure.

* An indigenous database with rapid loading, accessing time and requiring less memory space and leaving more bytes free to define memory variables is suitable for handling long.

* Software support service and license should be considered well in advance.

* Redundancy can be reduced.

* In consistency can be avoided to some extent.

* The data can be shared.

* Security restrictions can be applied.

* Integrity can be maintained.

* Conflicting requirements can be balanced.

* Ready recover for the management.

* To make the data available to wide variety of users.
* Centralized control of database.

Design and Development of Indigenous Databases

The design and development of indigenous databases involves following steps:

1. Analysis of the data requirements: At the outset, analysis of data requirement should be done. It will facilitate the recording and storing of right kind of data that will be required by user community.

2. Logical database definition: Database must be defined logically. It means the internal definition of the database.

3. Physical database definition: Database is to be defined physically also.

4. Implementation: Implementation denotes the data entry, formatting, presentation etc.

5. Evaluation: Evaluation means the final assessment of recorded information on the user's point of view.

Database' Correction

Database should provide right kind of information to users. When it is required, the information must be corrected. Database correction involves a total checking up of recorded information and deleting the odd or incorrect records form the database. For example, for small number of errors which escape INSPEC's[24] extensive quality control and validation procedures, INSPEC is now able to provide replacement corrected records. Future tapes will be issued on an occasional basis, whenever a significant number of records in need of correction have been accumulated INSPEC database correction loaded on Data-Star.

Objectives of Indigenous Database

Objectives of indigenous databases are very specific in nature. They are as following:

1. To provide the locally and nationally produced information, which is not available in international databases.
2. To store the information which is of local relevance.
3. To function as the mediator of indigenous knowledge.

Types of Indigenous Databases

Indigenous databases are found as following types:

1. Factual-type databases
    A. Statistical databases
        - Crude data
        - Aggregated data
        - Time series data
    B. Quasi-statistical databases
    C. "Textual Facts" databases
    D. "Formalism and Physical Model" databases
2. Text databases
    *   Full text databases
    *   Bibliographic databases
3. Integrated databases

Other Databases

Object Oriented Database : Object oriented database[25] system represent the confluence of ideas from Object Oriented programming languages and database management. Database system provides long term reliable data storage, multi user access, concurrency control, query, and recovery and security capabilities. OODB's combine the advantages of object oriented programming languages with those of database system.

Portable Databases : Portable databases entered

the market in 1985 and reached the 1000 figure by the middle of 1990[26]. On line and portable database overlap somewhat in there subject matter and indeed some databases are available both on line and in portable form. However, whereas, online database are inherently limited by the technology and cost of telecommunications, portable databases can cover type of materiel, such as, sound and graphics that would be difficult or prohibitively expensive to offer online.

Word Oriented Databases : It consists primarily of characters and thus they require software designed specifically for handling such strings.

Number Oriented Databases : It consists of numbers and symbols are the principle data that are stored and processed, instead of string of characters.

Pictoral Databases : These are specialized database. Their data consist chiefly of specifications for shapes, distances, geometrical relationship, colors and the like.

National Database : A network supports nation wide, called National networks, such as INFLIBNET, NICNET, etc. It hosts union databases of all academic, R & D institutes, national institutes' libraries etc[27].

DVD-ROM Databases : The CD-ROM can deliver decent multimedia right now and the DVD, with its maximum capacity of 17GB, is currently the only credible true multi media format. The advent of DVD and its gigabyte storage capacity has provided new potentials to expand the capacity of CD-ROM databases, especially for multimedia applications. DVD-Digital Video Disc, or Digital Versatile Disc for the computer industry, is the next generation to Compact Disc in optical disc storage technology[28]. DVD players can also read CDs. The DVD technology provides a storage capacity that is at least 6 to 7 times greater than a CD, in the same arial space. The main feature of DVD is the compression technology and storing data on multi-layer sides. There are various kinds of DVD's like DVD-ROM, DVD-Audio, DVD-recordable, DVD-Erasable etc.

Distributed Databases : A distributed database is one in which the data is contained within a number of separate subsystems, usually, in different physical locations[29]. If the constituent sub-systems are essentially similar, the system is said to be homogenous, otherwise, it is said to be heterogeneous. Distributed database systems may vary considerably. At one extreme is the type where the computer system was conceived, designed, and set up as a single entity; such systems exist within large commercial organizations, and, are usually homogeneous. Distributed databases are currently an active topic in database research and development, largely, because of the availability of national and international communication facilities.

Indigenous Databases:
Effect on Library Services

Indigenous databases have very important place among the tools of information services[30]. They are affecting the library services in various ways such as:

* Online catalogue of indigenous databases has major value to effect the document delivery.

* Another value of online catalogues to libraries of the future will be their availability as platforms for other online services.

Other Uses

* Resource Sharing.
* Bibliographic control.
* Reference services such as CAS/SDI etc., Abstracting and Indexing services.
* Easy retrieval.
* Quick service.
* Remote accessible (Online and Offline both).

* Onetime cost / No need to go for another.
* Multi accessing.

Features of Networked Indigenous Databases

Library and information centers can improve the services provided by indigenous databases by using the network facility. The networked services will facilitate various activities such as[31]:

* Globalized reach.
* Users can use the same e-resources at same time at any place.
* Easily copied, stored, and disseminated.
* Easy to revise, manipulate, and merge.
* Less bulky than paper.
* Speedy delivery.
* Add value to services.
* The databases save users time.
* Generate satisfaction among users.
* Bring and selling of databases is available on WWW.
* Interaction with remote users.
* Users tracking online.
* Databases enhance the R & D effectively and efficiently.

Searching Indigenous Databases

The following are the advantages of searching the indigenous databases: -

* In-depth searches of computer held files could be carried out at a speed, which on human can hole to match.
* The user is an active participant and can instantly adapt his request to the reality of what is actually in the reference- perhaps, very different from what he expects and also readily recover from errors of query formulation[32].

* Databases can easily be researched, using new clues, whereas in manual searching the time available does not often permit full searching[33].

* The user has easy access to an extremely wide range of indexes/ databases, many of which may not be available locally.

* Databases searchable online often offer a far great number of access points than the corresponding printed index[34].

* There is almost no need for irksome note taking so typical of many conventional searches.

* Online searches save time.

* Many publications can be searched at one time.

* Some databases are available only online and do not have printed counter parts.

* Most databases can be available around the clock.

* Searches can be saved and updated or modified periodically[35].

Database Searching Through E-Mail

Database searching through e-mail can be a very effective and impressive mode of accessing information. With the use of online and offline services, users can access information by e-mail. DELNET has taken pleasure in the launching of DELSEARCH the software developed in-house by DELNET for searching DELNET databases through e-mail[36]. This service should be included for exploring the indigenous databases.

Planning and Handling of Information

Planning and handling information is very important while developing and maintaining indigenous databases[37]. Providing information services on the basis of indigenous databases, it involves complex planning and handling of information in indigenous databases.

Various aspects are as following:

1. Planning and Handling scientific documentation and information by specialists with a scientific background using specific methods and techniques.
2. The development programmes are not carried out at random but on the contrary should be based on the philosophical and knowledgeable principles, which are shared by other library and information centers also[38].
3. Indigenous information is strategic since it constitutes an important component of the wealth of the nation. Most library and information centers suffer from an acute imbalance in the distribution of information among the various groups of information society[39].
4. Indigenous databases should be developed to promote the collection and preservation of indigenous information.
5. Library and information centers should stimulate in undertaking indigenous databases for disseminating indigenous information[40].

Policies Related With Indigenous Databases

Policies related with indigenous databases are as following:

1. Policies must be framed to develop indigenous databases.
2. Policies regarding indigenous database maintenance should be framed.
3. Policies regarding number and format of indigenous databases must be framed.
4. Policies regarding marketing of indigenous databases must be framed.
5. Policy guidelines on database access and for the preparation of an inter-agency product should be framed.
6. Policies regarding the co-operation of other library and information centers must be framed.

Issues of Indigenous Databases

Issues related with indigenous databases are as following:

1. User-access[41]
2. Non-standard public interfaces
3. Growing demand for full-text, numeric and graphic information
4. Standardization
5. Criteria for selection of quality information
6. Timeliness[42]

Advancements in the computing and communication technologies have made inroads into modern libraries and information centres. Information centres should now concentrate on the effective use of these technologies to communicate with the users on what they need and for providing exhaustive information through resource sharing.

Barriers Related With Indigenous Databases

Barriers related with indigenous databases are as following:

1. Socio-Institutional Barriers: establishing standards in national settings. This is the most difficult process.

2. Technical Adaptation Barriers: fine-tuning the technology to the end-users' needs[43].

3. Socio-technical Barriers: e.g. different language formats for the same software package.

4. Procedural integration Barriers: ensuring that the technology does not conflict with other established procedures.

5. Managerial[44]: Question of responsibility for technical and non-technical aspects; user interaction; cost recovery; non-standard working;

6. Hardware Interconnection: Non-standard working; lack of advice on which hardware to use, or control of what is obtained;

7. Software Related : The same questions as for hardware;

8. Data Communication[45]**:** Inadequate national telecommunications; high tariffs; physical movement of CD-ROMs and floppy disks;

9. Micro-Computer Related : The variety leads to incompatibilities, and there are insufficient skilled staff available;

10. Marketing Management: All the services are under-used, hence the need for more effort in promotion; promote as a total service, i.e. including document delivery[46].

Increasingly in recent times, R&D efforts have been mainly focused on problems, which require access to information that cuts across many disciplines. As an immediate response, new services and products were designed and developed. However, the user felt that they were not being served adequately and appropriately. This led to an in-depth analysis which revealed, surprisingly, that these services were not user oriented largely because of the non-involvement of users (in their design) and also that the extent of use made of the indigenous databases services was unknown to generators.

R&D Libraries and Their Role

Due to multidisciplinary nature of research, the role of a library in R&D organization is all the more important. Diverse subjects are studied and researched in one context or the other. Such a phenomenon has a direct impact on the R&D library, its users and managers. It is almost impossible to quantify the information output in any field of research and its related areas. Hence, the role of the libraries of the R&D organizations in acquiring, organizing and disseminating the required information to its patrons cannot be overestimated. Libraries are the only instruments, which bridge the gap of information downpour on the one hand and the information needs of the users on the other. The libraries attached to CSIR, being one of the premier R&D organizations of India, with their ever-dwindling financial resources and facilities, are trying their best to satisfy the information needs of their respective clientele. In addition to the routine library services, they offer current awareness services (CAS), selective dissemination of information (SDI), etc. to their clientele. But all such efforts, as of how, are individual and isolated and hence these remain largely underutilized, or even in cases, wholly unutilized due to lack of marketing approach.

Indigenous Databases Development in India

Indian efforts made, in the past or those planned for immediate future, had one or more of the following objectives:

1. To organize nationally produced information.
2. To create databases in restricted subject areas relevant to national socio-economic situation.
3. To develop endogenous capabilities for database creation and utilization.

In organizing national information system the aims had been that (a) that databases would complement and supplement international databases, and (b) the databases would serve the archival recording functions of informational generated indigenously.

Though these aims are generally the prime-overs and starters of database development in all countries. Unfortunately such efforts in India quickly lose the lustre. The Indian situation has also been fraught with slackening of Internets and piling of backlogs.

Initiation of Databases Development

Generations of an abstracting service on the papers published in Indian Science and Technology journals were taken up by the NISCAIR, (formerly INSDOC), New Delhi way back in 1965. The number of items getting into Indian Science Abstracts has been fluctuating mainly because of extra efforts made in particular years to clear the backlog.

The National Union Catalogue of Scientific Serials in India produced by the INSDOC contains holdings data relating to 35,000 titles of which 18,000 are current (and 2,300 are of Indian origin). Experiments are underway to install the NUCSSI database on networks for online search as a part of the larger concept of as Science and Technology Referral System. The Science citation Index (SCI) is now widely used for bibliographic studies for evaluating research outputs. In order to supplement the SCI database, the preparation of a National Citation Index (a project of NISSAT at INSDOC) has been conceived at the National Centre on Bibliometrics[47]. The National Social Science Documentation Research Centre (ICSSR) has prepared a union catalogue of Delhi.

Under the NISSAT programme, a major thrust was given to development of indigenous databases by the Sectoral information centers[48]. In the first phase (1977-1984) the following four sectoral centers were set up:

(a) National Information Centre for Leather and Applied Industries (NICLAI)

(b) National Information Centre for Food Science and Technology (NICFOS)

(c) National Information Centre for Machine Tools and Production Engineering (NICMAP)

(d) National Information Centre for Drug and Pharmaceuticals (NICDAP)

Later another information centres were opened. Apart from the databases efforts promoted by NISSAT, several institutions have made independent efforts to organize databases in their respective areas of interest. It provides support for establishment of information centres in different subject areas and helps in networking and building bridges between information resource

developers and users in Indian and other countries. Some
of the databases established by NISSAT are described
below[49]:

* Database activity PI Institution
* Database of Indian Chemical & Pharmaceutical
  Industries NICCHEM, NCL
* Directory of manufacture of various kinds of Ferrous
* and Non-Ferrous and Special Castings IIF, New
  Delhi
* Food Technology Abstracts (FTA) NICFOS, CFTRI
* INDAB : Database of Indian Databases, Abstracting
  and Indexing Services, and Directories ISAC-NISSAT
* Leather Science Abstracts (LESA) NICLAI, CLRI
* Metal Working Abstracts NICMAP, CMTI
* Index of Management Journals (JIND) NICMAN,
  IIMA.
* Oceanline NICMAS, NIO
* Indian Sugar Industry VDIS, Pune
* Texincon: Textile Information Condensed NICTAS,
  ATIRA
* Virus and Virology

NISTADS[50] has developed a significant database
named CLOSS (Current Literature on Science of Science).
At SNDT Women's University, *Suchak* is a computerized
database covering over 400 Indian and foreign journals
in English, Hindi, Marathi and Gujrati. India has achieved
a lot in preparing directory or registry type databases. In
most cases, individual institutions took initiatives.

Databases in Hard Copy Form

India has developed various Science and Technology
databases in hard copy form.

Databases on Magnetic Media

India started handling databases on magnetic media
since beginning.

Indigenous Databases in Library & Information Services

Within the field of library and information science a database is defined (rather understood) as "an organized and generally unlinked set of machine-readable bibliographic or information source records." Taken collectively, these records constitute a growing file of information that can be used to obtain a variety of products for a range of purposes. The variety of databases and types has grown over the last two decades and now include a range of specialist and smaller scale databases usually limited in scope to particular subject areas.

Impact

Databases can change the nature of customer interaction by speeding up routine process, by widening the choice of available information sources and making library services more accessible.

Current Awareness Service

Traditionally, current awareness services are mundane, less attractive, bulky and often absolute and only add to 'information overload' of users.

Bibliographic databases on CD-ROM with versatile software are the logical and efficient replacements of bulky and under used secondary journals. An innovative application of CD-ROM databases in providing regularly (as and when updates are received the contents {with abstracts} of costly and / or less relevant journals as well as those cancelled for various reasons including budgetary constraints after searching by journal name.

Retrospective Search

Customer accounting and security, search aids like thesaurus, several indexes, automatic spelling, variations, singular-plural versions, change disc options in single disc workstation, instantaneous display of library holdings information and any other features found in a typical online search facility are available on CD-ROM databases. Electronic database are able to fulfill all the three approaches namely; everyday, current and exhaustive approaches.

Developing Local Databases

CD-ROM databases with provision to download selected records and process and upload to other databases give ample scope for small libraries to develop their own local databases. As most of the databases follow standard formats and there are software, which can easily process and import data from CD-ROM databases, the task of developing databases is made simple, cheap and easy.

Networking, Cooperation and Resource Sharing

The potential of CD-ROM databases for exchange of bibliographic data is enormous and such standardized exchange of bibliographic data goes long way in helping libraries. Creation and production of authoritative bibliographic records for exchange, cooperative systems, individual libraries, abstracting and indexing services can augment library and information services.

CD-ROM as cheap storage alternative, today provides many national bibliographies and catalogues on it to economically download the required data for library automation and also to carry out quick and authentic cataloguing.

The use of database service in India involves various policies and conceptual issues. While developing database concept the following facts should be taken into consideration so far as its production, marketing and use of its services are concerned:

1. Using standard formats, library should make production and maintenance of database.
2. Installation of databases on national and

international networks.

3. Provision of alternative database service may be created such as direct database producer, installation of database on one or multiple hosts, provision of access through gateways, and also with the help of technology transfer agencies, information brokers.

4. Marketing practices of existing database producers, data hosts, gateways etc.

5. Education and training requirements for database service.

Indigenous Databases Market

Marketing is as such a pervasive activity that all organizations advertently or inadvertently practice it but under different terms. Librarians have carried myriad user studies and segmented their users basing on different criteria. Database production and distribution is a multibillion-dollar industry. Databases are produced by different kinds of organizations. The producers of bibliographic database in S & T are often non-profit making organizations. Many of the databases are produced by collecting information from various sources inputting it in an appropriate format for internal distribution. Databases are dispatched to host services on magnetic tapes, magnetic diskettes and CD-ROM. The usage of databases in online systems has grown steadily, but only a few services are reported as being profitable. Many of the systems have current marketing directed to end-users. Pricing principles various by charging only on the basis of actual usage. There are also differences in pricing of CD-ROM products.

'India is on the threshold of a revolutionary change in its economic and social life largely occasioned by rapid advances in Information technology, which could reduce superstitions and prejudice in the country. The scientists and engineers are modifying the technologies to suit the

Indian milieu. The information scientists and database managers should use technology as a tool to meet the needs of the end-users.

The impact of IT has been all pervading. It has changed the way that information is stored and disseminated and threatened the traditional approaches to the library and its services. Faced with enormous increase in scientific and technological knowledge, growth in volume of information and endless requirements of information with various interpretations, the contemporary global situation is alarming and starting from the grass-root level of an individual to top State executives; every one is well aware of the need of fast, easy, accurate and comprehensive access to the available resources.

India has very good infrastructure for research and development activities shared by central and state government, all have done considerable progress to achieve to link all through interdisciplinary and, multi-disciplinary approaches into functional network system so as to enable contacts with isolated researchers, in order to avoid investments in duplication of research efforts, to reach farmers and industries as soon as the information is generated, and to influence developmental agencies for acting recommendations etc.

In information management and services, International and Online database access is directed towards multiplicity of sources. These databases certainly cannot satisfy all the information needs of developing countries, in many cases they can nevertheless provide some useful information. It must be kept in mind that the vast majority of databases and databases records are produced in developed countries, in response to the demand of users who are primarily from the same countries. The contents of databases consist, therefore, of data that are geared to the demand of users in developed countries, which is not necessarily always the same as that of users in developing countries. Yet it should be noted that the relevance of many data in independent of the level of development.

In addition to the disadvantage of high cost, International online databases also suffer from a major drawback: the Indian user from seldom gets indigenous information from international databases. Coverage of global databases is often biased towards publication of western origin.

While the indigenous information industry has to grow and become globally relevant, there is a need to nurture, help develop some of the potential databases and facilitate their increased access.

Use of Scientific and Technical Databases

Prior to its public dissemination, the use of a database is limited to those involved in the collection of data or production, and therefore does not provide the opportunity to contribute broadly to the advancement of scientific knowledge, technical progress, economic growth, or other applications beyond those of the immediate group. It is only upon the distribution of a database that its far-reaching research, educational, and other socioeconomic values are realized. One or more researchers applying varying hypotheses, manipulating the data in different ways, or combining elements from disparate databases may produce a diversity of data and information products. The contribution of any of these products to scientific and technical knowledge might well assume a value far greater than the costs of database production and dissemination. The results of a thorough database analysis may reveal a value of the data not apparent in even a detailed examination of the individual elements of the database itself. With the widespread availability of information on the Internet have come abundant opportunities to search for scientific and technical gold in this ore of factual elements. The possibilities for discovery of new insights about the natural world—with both commercial and public-interest value—are extraordinary.

In considering how databases are used, it is important to distinguish between end use and derivative use. End use—accessing a database to verify some fact or perform some job-related or personal task, such as obtaining an example for a work memo—is most typical of public consumer uses. End use does not involve the physical integration of one or more portions of the database into another database in order to create a new information product. A derivative (value-adding or transformative) use builds on a preexisting database and includes at least one, and frequently many more, extractions from one or more databases to create a new database, which can be used for the same, a similar, or an entirely different purpose than the original component database(s).

References

1. Murthy, S S. International Conference on Bibliographic Databases and Networks. International Information, Communication and Education, 9(1), March 1990, p104-106.

2. Dasharathy, Radhika. Biological Databases: 'IT' Revolutionizing Data Management Systems in Molecular Biology. *SRELS Journal of Information Management,* 39(2), 2002, p. 169-176.

3. Association of Information and Dissemination Centers 1984 Fall Meeting. *Information Services & Use,* 5, 1985, p 49-56.

4. Rathore, R.S. and Kothari, D.V. Compact Disc: A Powerful Information Medium. *International Information Communication and Education ,* 19(2), 2000, p 229-235.

5. Kavi, Pradeep P. and Jayakant, Francis. Tools For Identification of Duplicate Records Downloaded for Multiple CD-ROM: A Case Study with SPIRS Based Database. *SRELS Journal of Information Management,* 38(4), 2001, p 279-286.

6. Chakrabarty, Bipul Kumar. Information Manpower- Strategic Issues for Development. *IASLIC Bulletin,* 38(2), 1993, p 67-72.

7. Tiamiyu, Mutawakilu Adisa. Pragmatics of Developing Information Resource Management Systems in Government Organizations in Developing Countries. *International Information, Communication and Education,* 12(2), Sept 1993, p 201-212.

8. Panda, Krishna C. Online Database: Some Basic Issues. *National Policies and Programmes. IASLIC,* p. 57-70.

9. Chowdhary, G.G. Information Retrieval System. New Delhi: ESS ESS, 1989, p 83-102.

10. Siddiqui, Moid A. Can CD-ROM Replace Online? *International Information, Communication and Education,* 10(1), 1991, p 40-45

11. Digests and Notes, *International Information, Communication and Education,* 9(1), March 1990, p 131.

12. ECHO Offers Greek Database. Digest and Notes. *International Information, Communication and Education,* 14(2), Sept. 1995, p 292-3.

13. Digests and Notes, *International Information, Communication and Education,* 9(1), March 1990, p 124.

14. Courrier, Yves. Information Technology Training Needs, Strategies and Objectives for the Developing Countries. *International Forum of Information & Documentation,* 12(3), July 1987, p 32-37.

15. Mahapatra, Piyush Kanti and Chakrabarti, Bhubaneswar. Knowledge Management in Libraries. New Delhi: ESS ESS, 2002, p 228-254.

16. Sur, S. N. And Chowdhury, G. G. A Prototype Design of a Bibliographic Database Based on CCF Using Micro-CDS/ISIS. *IASLIC Bulletin,* 38(1), 1993, p17-37.

17. Ramesh, D.B.; Seth, M.K. and Sahu, J.R. Use of Digital Information: A Study on CD-ROM and Online Databases. *Lucknow Librarian,* 28(1-4), 1996, p 1-3.

18. Smith, I. W. Evaluation of CD-ROM products. *Information Services & Use,* 9, 1989, p 85-90.

19. Singh, Surendra and Singh, Sonal (ed.). Library, Information Science and Society. New Delhi, 2002, p 259-308.

20. Graham, M. H. Information services as a corporate resource in Exxon. *Information Services & Use,* 5, 1985, p 207-212.

21. Samal, P.K. and Gupta, Sangeeta. Use of CD-ROM POPLINE Database in NIHFW: A Case Study. *IASLIC Bulletin,* 39(3), 1994, p125-128.

22. Granick, Lois. Assuring the quality of information dissemination: responsibilities of database producers. *Information Services & Use*, 11, 1991, p 117-136.

23. Singh, Shivpal ;Jambhekar, Ashok and Gautam, J.N. Authority control: Its requirement for maintaining quality in Indian Bibliographic databases. *SRELS Journal of Information Management*, 39(4), 2002, p 395-408.

24. *Vijayakumar, J.K. and Das, Manju. CD-ROM to DVD-ROM: A New Era in Electronic Publishing of Databases and Multimedia Reference Sources. IASLIC Bulletin, Vol. 45(2); 2000; p 49-54.*

25. Digests and Notes, *International Information, Communication and Education,* 9(1), March 1990, p 133.

26. Vishwanathan, T. Object Oriented Database Management System: A New Tool for Information Centres. *Annals of Library Science and Documentation,* 39(3), 1992, p 74-80.

27. Digests and Notes. *International Information, Communication and Education,* 12(1), 1993, p 138.

28. Kumar, S. and Goria, Sunil. Bibliographic Database Management in India: Problems and Prospects. *International Information Communication and Education,* 17(2), Sep. 1998, p. 196-213.

29. Dou, Henry, Hassanaly, Parina, Tela, La Albert and Quoniam, Luc. Advanced interface to analyze the automatically online databases set of answers. *Information Services & Use,* 10, 1990, p 135-145.

30. Nagarajan, S.; Sangameswaran, S.V. and Jain, H.C.(ed.). Distributed Databases: Plan for Interraction and Online Search. New Delhi: Informatics Publications, 1989, p. 103-111.

31. Mahesh, G. and Ghosh, S.B. Availability and Use of Indegenous Databases: A Case Study. *IASLIC Bulletin,* 43(2), 1998, p. 67-76.

32. Thiruvarasu, S. Online Databases. Satyanarayana, B. et.al. (ed.). Information Technology: Issues and Trends. Vol.I. New Delhi: Cosmo Publications, 1998, p. 58-68.

33. Hussain, K.H; Nair, R. Raman and Asari, K. Raveendra. Importance of Search And Retrieval in CD-ROM Full Text Publishing: Experiments Using PDF Documents And NITYA Archival System. *Information Studies,* 8(3), 2002, p 173-180.

34. Murthy, S S. International Conference on Bibliographic

Databases and Networks. *International Forum of Information and Documentation,* 9(1), March 1990, p104-106.

35. Rao, D.N. Online Bibliographic Services in Academic Libraries. *Lucknow Librarian,* 21(1), 1989, p 11-14.

36. Chowdhary, G.G. Introduction to Modern Information Retrieval. London: Library Association Publishing, 1999, p.12-19.

37. Databases Searching through E-mail. Digests and Notes. *International Information, Communication and Education,* 11(1), 1993, p 136

38. Rao, H.R. Achyutha; Ramesh, C.P. and Venkatesh, Y. An Analytical Study on the Use of CD-ROM Databases and other Digital Facilities in Mysore University Library: A case study. Library and Information Networking. *NACLIN 2001.* H.K. Kaul and E. Rama Reddy (ed.).

39. Kumar, Ram and Kumar, Ashok. Sharing of Inhouse Databases in India. *ILA Bulletin,* 28(3-4), 1983, p. 125-127.

40. Kashyap, M.M. Database System: Design and Development. New Delhi: Sterling, 1993, p. 129.

41. Ghosh, S.B. Need for National Database of Indian Medical Literature as a Feeder Service of Institutional Databases. New Delhi: ESS ESS, 1990, p. 171-175.

42. Chakravarti, A.K. et.al. Technology Watch: CD-ROM. *Annals of Library Science and Documentation, 42(1), 1995,* p 27-34.

43. Jarvelin, Kalervo and Niemi, Timo. Simplifying Fact Retrieval through Intermediary Systems: Problems and Requirements. *International Forum of Information & Documentation,* 15, (2) April 1990, p 8-15.

44. King Research Institute. Development in Communication and Education. *International Information, Communication and Education,* 14(2), 1985, p 173-176.

45. Liddle, L. Patent Information System. *Information Services & Use,* 5, 1985, p 113-119.

46. Sathyanarayan, N.V. Online Access: A Beginner's First Lesson. *Library Science with a Slant to Documentation,* 24(Paper H.), 1987, p. 89-97.

47. Keenan, Stella. Re-use and repackaging of Information: the Information Worker's View. *Information Services & Use,* 3, 1983, p1-6.

48. www.nissat.org

49. www.nissat.org

50. www.nistads.res.in

51. Slamet, Margono. An Analysis of Faculty Attitude towards the Cooperative Extensive Service at Lousiana State University. Lousiana, Lousiana University, 1973.

52. Krech, David, Crutchfield, Richard and Balllachey, Egerton. Individual in Society. New York: McGraw Hill, 1962, p 177.

53. Sellitz, Claire. Research methods in social relations. New York: Holt, Rinehard and Winston, 1976.

Chapter 4
Types of Databases

Clement[1] suggests following points for developing an information environment. A consistent, yet open, computing and communication base adapted to users' needs in all phases of the research process;

1. Access to expert help, including means for supporting an rewarding peer and specialist expertise within the research professions;

2. Tools for developing database, along with feed back mechanisms to evaluate , modify and disseminate the database developed; and

3. Analogues to the library and information resources (not necessarily central physical locations) in which search information can be stored, organized and retrieved.

Bibliographic Databases

Bibliographic databases generally include information about printed material such as books, articles, and maps. They consist of records with basic descriptive information about the items such as author, title, publisher, date, publication title, etc. Bibliographic databases may not contain the items themselves, but will give the information user needs to find the item. They provide citations (a listing of information about the item), and sometimes include abstracts (summaries) or descriptions of the items.

Database Creation Options

There are a number of ways of creating the bibliographic database to be mounted on a local automated library system. Most approaches rely on a resource file of machine-readable records to provide cataloging copy, in preference to creating and keying all records from scratch.

Cataloging resource files come in a variety of forms: a library database mounted on a local automated system, a CD-ROM stand-alone cataloging support system, or a remote file accessed via telecommunication linkages (such as OCLC). The resource file is searched for a record that describes the item being cataloged. If an exact match is not found but the file contains a record for a similar item, a derived catalog record is created by selecting and editing the near-matching record to represent the item in hand.

If no copy record can be identified, an original record is prepared. All copy cataloging requires some editing to add local library-specific data such as call number or local subject headings. Record creation and record editing can be performed either on the system that supports the resource file or on the local automated library system.

The Importance of Adherence to Marc

Some libraries unknowingly impose limits on future applications of their system (or make the implementation of such applications more expensive) by following the overall structure and conventions of MARC formatting, but failing to maintain data elements that seem obscure or redundant or otherwise appear to have little or no importance for the current automated system. This is particularly common when records are created by original cataloging or by editing a near-matching record to conform to the slightly different item in hand.

The data elements most frequently overlooked are those recorded as coded data in the record leader and the 008 fixed length field. For example, a record assigned the local library classification of PER and a local subject heading "Periodical" is clearly a record for a serial; why go to the added effort and expense of ensuring that the value "s" for serial is recorded in the bibliographic code element of the leader? Why not use a bibliographic level default of "m" (for monograph) or blank (in assigned meaning) in all records?

What may appear to be a reasonable time and labor saving variation from standard MARC practice can become a major limitation or expense. A library wishing to use its automated library system to inspect its bibliographic file, select all records for serials, and output these records in machine-readable form for submission to a union list of serials or as a printed list of holdings, will be unable to do so if the system bases the identification of serial records on the expectation that all serial records, and only serial records, contain "s" in the bibliographic level element of the record leader.

Other important data elements are standard numbers such as the Library of Congress Card Number (LCCN) and the International Standard Book Number (ISBN). Although often regarded as of little importance in local system databases, these numbers assume significance in external applications, such as when a library is seeking to produce a microfiche or CD-ROM catalog; to migrate the database from one automated library system to another; to merge its records with those from other libraries on a shared automated system; or to report holdings to a union catalog.

Appropriate Fields: Consistent Formats

It is not enough to record data in the appropriate field. It must also be recorded in a consistent format. Some automated library systems and cataloging support systems enforce formatting consistency by providing input validation routines that either alert the operator to an incorrectly formatted number and prevent it from being added to the database, or automatically reformat the data once it has been keyed. However, most multifunction integrated automated library systems neither check nor manipulate input data; they accept whatever is keyed and output it unchanged.

Appropriate and consistent formatting conventions must be followed if standard numbers are to be readily available for machine manipulation. Local automated system vendors' data recording guidelines tend to focus on formatting data for internal, local applications—use within the automated library system. Capabilities to support the output of MARC records from local automated systems are relatively new. Their introduction emphasizes the need for libraries to expand their data entry horizons beyond the confines of current local system usage.

Correcting A Defective Database

It is expensive to develop and maintain a bibliographic database, and the cost can escalate dramatically if ill-considered shortcuts result in records that cannot support the full range of automated library system applications, necessitating major revision or upgrade of the file.

A library can correct defective records by calling them up and changing them one at a time or, if the problems are widespread and consistent, it can contract with a bibliographic tape processing service to prepare custom software to correct the records automatically. Some automated library system vendors also provide these services. The more customization a vendor is required to perform to prepare a file for loading or transfer, however, the more the library can expect to pay for the service.

Guidelines For A Healthy Bibliographic File

1. Follow the established national standard for the recording and formatting of bibliographic data: the

US MARC Format for Bibliographic Data.

2. Include and maintain all relevant data elements in the records, especially the coded data in the record leader and the 008 fixed length data elements field.

3. Look beyond current system requirements to the time when additional system capabilities will be implemented, the file will be transferred to a new system, or standard output will be required for other applications. Specifically, include and maintain standard control numbers such as LCCN and ISBN.

4. Pay special attention to coded data elements and standard numbers in original record creation and in the editing of near-match records drawn from a resource file.

5. Select an automated library system that has the ability to output bibliographic records in the MARC format. (All current systems have the ability to accept the input of MARC formatted bibliographic records.)

6. Document changes in database creation practices, procedures, and policies. Many problems and inconsistencies in bibliographic databases can be overcome by external tape processing. It is easier, faster, and less expensive to fix known problems. Memory is not a reliable guide.

Endres-Niggemeyer[2] explains how documents are represented for bibliographic databases. A first individual model of an abstractor work is presented. She explains beginning of a procedural model of content analysis, based on the performance of competent colleagues. The individual model results form the model-driven interpretation of 11 abstracting processes, the initial model being a specialization of a model of expository writing with an integrated strategic model of text understanding and summarizing. The resulting abstractor's performance model is pragmatic in its respect for the comprehensive goals if the embedding information transfer environment; it is strategy oriented, goal-driven and constructive. She disposes of efficient intellectual tools that rely firmly on document structure. Kar, and Siddiqui[3] discuss the bibliographic database RIZA, its design, development using mini/micro CDS/ISIS Version 2.3. They discuss the advantages of version 2.3. They highlight the features of this software also. McDonald[4] identifies three major groups of non-bibliographic data:

1.   Full-text,
2.   Numeric, and
3.   Graphic
     He predicts following developments:
1.   Hybrid systems comprising both network and local options will become available for access to non-bibliographic data;
2.   Local work-station software will become more powerful in its ability to link with specific network applications, resulting in a demand for increased standardization; and
3.   The blurring of local versus network access may prove to be a marketing challenge given the costs inherent in providing, both local and network access.

Planning of Bibliographic Databases

Sur and Chowdhury[39] state that design aspect of bibliographic databases are of utmost importance for effective resource sharing and for providing better information retrieval services in libraries. Standard formats like CCF may be adopted for design of databases. However experiences show that some modifications to the CCF format may be more useful for manipulation of data for various library operations. Design of bibliographic databases based on CCF for use in Micro-CDS/ISIS has been proposed. Almost all the mandatory CCF fields have been adopted and a few new fields have been added for achieving better results. Formats for display of records conform to AACR-2. Further he says that a text retrieval system is designed to store a variety of textual and/or bibliographic information that can be accessed by one or more terms or keywords and the retrieved data can be displayed in a user-defined format. Two major characteristic features of text/bibliographic information systems are-they are designed to handle a number of fields most of which are unstructured, and they provide a wide range of retrieval facilities. Further he says that a text or bibliographic database is a key to both the information retrieval services and housekeeping operations in libraries. Jarvelin and Niemi[40] discuss that inconsistency in the naming of data items means that closely related data appears in different databases under totally different names and follow totally different naming principle. It is, therefore, difficult to determine reliability with data items have equaled meaning. Often databases provide data that are inconsistent. The inconsistency may follow from:

1. The technical representation of data
2. The dimensions of measurement
3. Naming of data item values
4. Composition of data items
5. Method and precision of measurement

They suggest that often it is possible to devise some method for overcoming such apparent incompatibilities due to data inconsistency.

Tell[41] states that industry because it works to tight time and financial scheduled requires confidence that the information or data to be used is reliable. It has been suggested that future database for industry should give:

* Service experience
* Techno-commerical data
* Advanced materials
* Computerized form of handbooks.

Further he discusses the features associated with the future information system:

* Validation of data (different levels)
* A data evaluation programmes
* Different security programmes
* Multilingual accessibility
* Bibliographic/factual data linkage
* Modeling algorithms and procedures
* Computer Aided Engineering interface
* Uploading and downloading options
* Expert systems

Metadatabase

Behling and Matthies[5] discuss the development of a metadatabase on environmental monitoring programs. They discuss the concept for a metadatabase on environmental monitoring programme. They tried to give an idea of the targets, the problems and even the possibilities for the development of an environmental monitoring programme metadatabase. Choros and Sieminski[6] state that the main aim of data compression is to reduce the conventional length of data representation. Numerous experiments have shown that data representation in bibliographic bases is very redundant; so compression is both feasible and desirable in this case, since it can reduce the costs of running information systems. Data compression algorithms are classified in their study into two groups: semantic and statistical. In their study they also find out that bibliographic databases are not well suited for semantic compression. The consecutive application of semantic and then statistical compression is possible in theory, but in practice it is effective only if the semantic algorithm does not change significantly the statistical properties of the field.

Full-text Databases

Full-text databases contain the full text of a work right on the screen. Full-text databases are usually bibliographic databases that contain the complete article. For example, Britannica Online contains entire encyclopedia articles, and Lexis-Nexis provides the full-text of articles from newspapers, magazines, and other publications. Hawkins[7] discusses the importance of full-text databases. He states that full-text databases are excellent in fulfilling today's interdisciplinary information needs. Frequently, the necessary data are mentioned only in passing in as article and will not be indexed in a controlled vocabulary database. Full-text databases are beginning to bring us close to true electronic publications and to solve the problems of document delivery and accessibility that have plagued the online bibliographic database user. Thorpe discusses[8] the tailored use of databases according to the requirements of users. This is another way in, which the database may be broken up into smaller sections more relevant to a specialized center's needs. Naturally SDIs may be extremely specific, and tailored to the needs of an individual user, but they may also be of a more general nature corresponding to the major activities of a specialized centre. Bibliographies and reading lists, compiled either on specific request or as a series of publications from the major suppliers, can also be extremely useful products for specialized centres.

Text Databases and Online Publication

This type of database is used extensively by the research community, consists primarily of text with data summarized or added as examples. These databases may consist of primary literature (as in the case of full-text databases of journal articles) or secondary literature (as in the case of bibliographic reference databases). Traditionally, this text has been available in print form, with publishers providing peer review, professional editing, indexing and formatting, and other services, including marketing and distribution. Increasingly this information is being provided as text databases with the publishers also providing the systems that allow access to these databases. These value-adding or information repackaging functions are performed by both not-for-profit and for-profit organizations. For example, the not-for-profit American Association for the Advancement of Science, a scientific society, produces a database containing the full text of articles from *Science* magazine, including enhancements to the content that do not appear in the print version. Similarly, the for-profit publisher Elsevier Science produces ScienceDirect, a database containing the full text of its journal articles. Bibliographic reference databases are also produced by government, not-for-profit, and for-profit organizations, such as the National Library of Medicine, Chemical Abstracts Service, and the Institute for Scientific Information, respectively. Where full-text databases include associated data collections, physical and legal possession of the data collections may be retained by the originator or may pass to the publisher.

As S&T data and results are increasingly digitized and made available online, publishers are seeking access to and inclusion of the underlying data collections on which published articles are based. The intent is not only to provide greater validity and support for published research articles, but also to make their online publications more interesting and useful to the S&T customer base. The ability to link to the underlying databases instantaneously and at different levels of detail adds an entirely new and exciting dimension to scientific publishing and to the potential for new research, but also raises the question of who will have the rights to exploiting those data.

Future of Full-text Databases

According to the report[42] of Association of Information and Dissemination Centers Fall Meeting, full-text databases have a future depending on their content, the availability of the original, and the appropriateness of the online system. Technology also has an influence. Problems with full-text files include synonyms and the large amount of labor in loading and copyright. Value pricing is not illogical if more value is being delivered for the higher price. Training emphases will shift from 'how to work the machine' to presenting the value of information. A standard common language is slow in coming; there needs to be more cooperation between database producers and vendors. Liddle[43] states that access to the various database components will be through index. There will be two principal types of indexes. One use is to locate text and image data based on the words that are contained in the character part of the database-i.e., full-text search. This is similar to what is done in commercial database systems such as Lexis and DAILOG. The other type of index provides identification of documents on the bases of other information, such as the Patent Classification System or the International Patent Classification system. With such indexes, the documents are so indexed can be identified and retrieved. The system will maintain the identity of external databases and systems that will be available, and will establish a communication path for accessing them as if they were to be a part of the internal databases. Bhattacharya[44] worked on the 'Computer readable databases and the future of information services' and discussed the varieties, genesis, and growth of Computer Readable Databases. He also explains some technical aspects of CRDB's, and also the CRDB-Services. He also indicates the future trend of CRDB. According to him a CRDB is an organized collection of Information computer-readable form. He also describes evident from the earlier presentation that CRDB's services and their associated technologies have set up new trends towards many new possibilities of great consequences.

Image databases

Image databases are becoming increasingly available, especially through the Web. These databases could include art prints, photos, animations, etc. Leung[9] discusses the architecture of an image database. He discusses the storage, management of image data; system organization and architecture; picture indexing and filing component. Maxon-Dadd[10] discusses the refurbishing an elegant Victorian database- a view from DIALOG. She says that the creators and caretakers of a lovely old Victorian database have an irresistible impulse to give it a fix-up frequently. Sometimes structural repairs are needed. She points out some advantages and disadvantages of remodeling for database producers, search services etc. Stern and Tarkowski[11] discuss the need for a unified European environmental health database. They say that data on which to base the setting of priorities for implementing strategies to reduce public health risks must be sufficient quality to justify semiquantitative risk assessment. Ydreborg[12] discusses the questionnaire-based database on occupation and health status. Jarvis[13] discusses developing an expert system using a PC-based shell. He describes an expert system and briefly examines possible relationship between expert, system and database. Mukhopadhyay[14] states that more and more libraries in India are getting access to microcomputer facilities, yet little progress has been achieved so far towards library computerization. Culturally, the libraries are not yet ready to exploit computer power. These factors apart, non-availability of suitable application software may be considered one of the major impediments. There is hardly any software available for their use that is truly user-friendly, presupposing minimal computer skills to operate. While there is hardly any alternative for the average library there are many possibilities for those resourceful ones who may afford considerable investment on software development or procurement of commercial software. Some of the have-nots may hope to participate in one or another library networking programs in the near future and gains the privilege of using network software. The rest might continue to grapple with increasing information management problems even though a microcomputer is just there on the library desk but performing only general-purpose packages. Further he says that library use of general-purpose software has concentrated on routine applications. Relational databases like dBase have potential to solve problems of variable field, variable record structure and repeatable fields.

Cawkell[15] discusses about the picture databases, image processing, Business Document Image Processing (DIP), Multimedia, and Picture Management. Willem[16] discusses the database DIANE-GUIDE that gave a detail account of offering information on European databases, database producers and host organizations. He describes the background to the new I'M-GUIDE database, its content, how the information is collected, the functions of the directory, and future developments. Philip, Crookes, and Juhasz[17] discuss an image database on a parallel processing network. They say that unlike textual databases, image databases are fairly new. They describe how they successfully harnessed the parallelism offered by a transputer network, which is a product of vlsi technology, in providing the necessary processing power for creating image databases.

Wanting[18] discusses about the Children's Culture Database (CCD). He says about coming of ides when it became clear that the pedagogical and the psychological views were so strongly represented in highly respected databases such as Eric and Psychological Abstracts that the cultural, aesthetic and humanistic views had vanished. He states that research in children and culture as a field is interdisciplinary, which in fact does not always stimulate the terminology between researchers. He discusses the database, its language, keywords, abstracts, coverage and feasibility of CDS/ISIS software for this database. The International Database on Disability was available on PC-Compatible diskette.

Audio and Video Databases

Audio and video databases are also becoming increasingly available, via the Web. These databases could include audio clips of sound effects and music samples or video excerpts from speeches, television shows, or other broadcast media.

Numeric Databases

Numeric databases provide mostly numeric data such as statistics, financial data, census information, economic indicators, etc. An example of a numeric database is Stat-USA, which contains statistics on United States imports and exports.

Scientific numeric databases (SND) are powerful, relatively new research tools for the scientific and technical community. They have certain attributes and capabilities. SND permit the direct location, retrieval and the subsequent analysis/manipulation of evaluated numeric data. Advances in telecommunications and increases in the number and types of SND produced greatly enhance the likelihood of relevant data being readily available. Although few percentage of all databases is accessible online in the world are SND, they are growing in importance and acceptance as more databases are developed and scientists and engineers become aware of their potential. Many organizations are active not only in the production of SND, involving some international collaboration, but also in their dissemination by means of a nation-wide online packet-switched network.

CD-ROM Databases

Hasan, Singh and Sharma[19] talk about CD-ROM: A Powerful Media for information packing, retrieval, and dissemination and described CD-ROM as one of the best storage tool, which has got tremendous capacity to store voluminous non- modifiable data/information. Architecture and the main features of CD-ROM and its uses with special reference to libraries have also been described. Advantages and disadvantages are also enumerated. The development of IT in regard to CD-ROM, DVD-ROM, CD Server and future prospects of CD-ROM has also been described. Hussain, Nair and Asari[20] study the Importance of search and retrieval in CD-ROM Full text publishing: Experiments using PDF, Documents and Nitya Archival system CD-ROM has indispensable role to play in the dissemination of electronic information. Full text archiving and publishing in CD-ROM have already found a special place in the rapidly growing digital libraries. Many of full text CD-ROM titles are coming with thousands of document files, but without efficient retrieval facilities. CD-ROM has growing importance on publishing and the necessity of providing search facilities in full text CDs.

Mahesh and Das[21] discuss about quality assurance in CD-ROM based information products and said that CD-ROM's have evolved as an effective information storage and dissemination centres. However, publishers, and database vendors are increasingly producing CD-ROM based information products and services without giving much attention to quality. Quality assurance in CD-ROM based information products is important in the present scenario and it looks at the various parameters that determine quality of CD-ROM based products. Kavi and Jayakant[22] talked about tools for identification of duplicate records downloaded from multiple CD-ROMs. They discuss that esearch becomes more and more interdisciplinary, literature search from CD-ROM databases is often carried out on more than one CD-ROM database. This results in retrieving duplicate records due to same literature being covered in more than one database. Scientific literature has grown exponentially over the years in the last century. With such a staggering growth, technological, tools to store, retrieve and disseminate the knowledge accumulated have also grown by leaps and bounds. Rapid developments in the field of Information Technology paved the way for development of electronic databases in all fields. Today hundreds of databases are available in electronic form on CD-ROMs and online hosts both. Rao, Ramesh, and Venkatesh[23] analysed the use of CD-ROM databases and other digital facilities in Mysore University Library. They discuss the use pattern of some of the CD-ROM databases available in the Mysore University Library, Mysore. The categories of users are segregated as faculty, researchers, and their graduate students and their access to databases is quantified to arrive at the conclusion. The users are also considered discipline-wise to know the extent of use and the constraints in the collection of databases. Data is also collected to examine the use of CD-ROM facilities by the consortium institutions particularly under the resource-sharing programme of Mysore City Libraries. They conclude with the important statement that subscription of CD-ROM databases is a necessity to meet the various academic and research needs of users. It is more an economical means of getting access to vast information available retrospectively chronologically than printed secondary journals. Infact, subscription to CD-ROM will supplement and complement the other information sources and services of the library for academic endeavor.

Rothore and Kothari[24] discuss about Compact Disc. This is powerful information medium and this electronic media is dominating our day to day routine activities. With the advancement of electronic media in the field of communication there have been tremendous changes in the every walk of life. CD databases keep up to date with latest developments and application in the entire premiere subject fields available all over the world. Under this paper types of CD-ROM products, science and technology databases, use of CD in document delivery and future of the CD-ROM is discussed. Vijayakumar and Das(2000)[25] discuss about CD-ROM to DVD-ROM. It is a new era in electronic publishing of databases and multimedia reference sources in the aspects of application of DVD technology in electronic publishing of reference sources and databases. There is a trend towards publishing reference sources and bibliographic databases in DVD format instead of CD-ROM due to its high storage capacity of 17 GB, high quality in data, diminishing price etc. Libraries and database publishers will favour this technology very soon. The factors are holding DVD drives trend towards online and the lack of standardization in this technology. The Web, as, the latest and earliest tool for delivery of information will take the prominent past, but, CD/DVD –ROM technologies will have a place in libraries.

Darmoni[26] carries a study comparing centralized CD-ROM and decentralized intranet access to MEDLINE .The purpose of this study was to evaluate the efficacy of a decentralized intranet access in each medical department as opposed to centralized unique MEDLINE in the medical library. A decentralized Intranet access to MEDLINE increased the number of searches and knowledge of this bibliographic database. MEDLINE Intranet access modified the purpose and the methods of searching. Meera[27] talked about Optical Storage Media. CD-ROM dealing with optical storage media that includes read only optical discs, write once read only optical discs, write once read many optical discs and erasable optical discs. It defines the concept of optical storage and describes the physical character of optical disc and its characteristics in terms of durability, high storage and portability. Read only optical discs are discussed in detail. Highlights the CD-ROM discs, their physical character and manufacturing process. Singh[28] talked about optical storage media which is a viable alternative to online searching in which he discussed the need for the change of library tools and techniques under the changing environment. He describes the role of optical storage media i.e. CD-ROM, its capacity, capability and limitations. He provides a comparison of CD-ROM with online as a viable and economic alternative to online search service. He explains the application of CD-ROM databases in libraries for different kinds of jobs like acquisition, cataloguing public access catalogue, inter library loan (ILL), reference works, indexes and abstracts and document delivery, etc. He examined the use of CD-ROMs in selected libraries of Delhi.

Ramesh, Seth and Sahu[29] discussed about the use of digital information. A study of CD-ROM and ON-LINE databases, deals with the benefits of CD-ROM databases. Hardware and software requirements for both CD-ROM as well as on-line systems are given. Some of the major differences between on-line and CD-ROM searches are discussed. Use of CD-ROM and on-line databases in Library and Information Services are highly influential. Chakravarti et.al.[30] discussed the "Technology Watch about CD-ROM" attempt to cover all objectives of Technology Watch. From the analysis presented, it may be concluded that CD-ROM and their applications are going to be the biggest growth markets in the information technology in the next five years and India must plug into this global market. India must also encash on its comparative strength through: -

*   Its relatively low cost data capturing capabilities tied- up with international CD-ROM producer and publishers.
*   In premastering including software development.
*   In preparing CD-ROM's of India, music, handicrafts, fashion, and garments jewellery designs using proper CAD tools and marketing abroad.

*   In creating its own CD-ROM databases on cultural heritage, tribal arts, archeology, herbal and medicinal plants, traditional medicines and the like.

Samal and Gupta[31] discuss about the use of CD-ROM POPLINE Database in NIHFW and provided an overview of CD-ROM POPLINE. They describe some aspects of use of the CD-ROM POPLINE database maintained by John Hopkins University in the light the experience and exposure gained of the National Documentation Centre of the National Institute of Health and Family, Welfare, New Delhi, India. This database, no doubt, is a tool to provide immediate and urgent specific answers to queries from the functionaries, agencies, and research scholars in the field of population studies and related aspects. Feldman[32] talks about turn of the tide- a new age in multimedia publishing and discussed the evolution of CD since 1982. It has traditionally been mainly a text- only medium. It is a digital medium so it can store anything that can be digitized. Vishwanathan[33] deals with the aspect of growing of library as an organism and discusses about the use of CD-ROM databases in libraries. Electronic library is likely to become a reality in about 50 years time. We see glimpses of the coming electronic libraries in CD-ROMs. Increasingly information is being published on CD-ROMs instead of printed forms. Even existing printed books are being copied on to CD-ROMs and CD-ROM Databases are emerging for compact storage and easy transportability. One may visualize the future library with stalks full of CD-ROMs and reading tables with having a computer with a CD-ROM drive. A user may pick a CD-ROM from the shelf and place it in his computer and read. Today a single CD-ROM disk can hold about 50 books. Today, a sophisticated multi user system that can assure reasonable responses time supports a maximum of sixteen users. The density of storage in CD-ROMs is also likely to increase, with the result the number of users on the system will ever be less than the number of books on the CD-ROM. Thus the technology seems to have limitation in meeting even the rudimentary facility that a library offers today.

Subbarao and Rajalakshmi[34] study libraries in 21st century in India and his study deals with the aspects of information technology. The use of IT is dominating the libraries the librarian's skill in the application of this technology is becoming the deciding factor for the efficiency of services provided by a library. This is obvious from the point that the number of journals available in electronic media (CD-ROMs, floppies, etc.) are increasing day by day. The libraries are using computers, telecommunications etc. for document delivery systems.

There are main pointed out some reasons for acquiring CD-ROMs, they are:

*   It saves the shelf space and reduces the maintenance cost.

*   It is easy to handle and at the same time less expensive compared to other machine-readable databases.

In-house use of the databases on compact discs is comparatively cheaper than providing on-line hosts service because it eliminates connect charges.

Siddiqui[35] discusses the importance of CD-ROM in his paper "Can CD-ROM Replace Online?" While discussing the applications of CD-ROM databases, he says that initial development of CD-ROM databases were for different audiences, such as marketing/finance, law, education, scientific/engineering, medical/health, and library professions, etc. A broader number of CD-ROM applications have broad appeal so those user categories cannot be identified clearly. These may be classified as general reference, which include catalogues, dictionaries, directories, encyclopaedias, and other general reference work. Further he discusses user studies, benefits such as; access through personal computers, enhanced retrieval capabilities, multimedia capability, easy and unlimited access, controllable costs and psychological advances. Krull[36] discusses the role of the service bureau in multimedia diversification. He says that CD-ROM as a mass storage device can be used for word searching of abstracts. Connected with an online system it can request information on newly written abstracts, order copies of articles, or even submit articles and abstracts. McPherson, Harrap, and O'Reilly[37] discuss enhancing search results by editing, analysis and packaging. They say that need and expectations of clients for search output vary widely, and require different information responses form the searcher. The types of information package that may be provided to the client include a single integrated bibliography, a report organizing search results into a problem-solving sequence, and a searchable downloaded computer file. Smith[38] discusses the evaluation of CD-ROM products. He discusses the need for evaluation along with the criteria of evaluation.

Maintenance of Databases

Singh, Jambhekar and Gautam[45] discuss about Authority control and its requirement for maintaining quality in Indian bibliographic databases. The authority control is used to establish standardized/authorized key access points and references to ensure effective access to library catalogue/database. The effective and efficient retrieval of information from bibliographical database calls for maintaining consistency and quality while entering the data as per the accepted format, standards, and related tools. Authority file, its type for manual and automated libraries for efficient and quantitative service has importance. They deal with national and local level requirements for creating authority file in India, with special reference to MARC 21 Format of authority data. Rajashekhar[46] says that database production is an expensive operation. Expenditures include staff, acquisition of publications, computers costs and keyboarding (data entry) for database production, validation, processing, typesetting, printing and dispatch for the printed products, and processing and dispatch for the electronic products. Database production also includes tasks such as maintenance of authority lists for authors, institutions, publishers, etc. thesauri and classification systems, cataloguing rules and formats, etc. These costs increase each year not only because of the inflation (affecting, for e. g., cost of acquisition), but also because of the increase in the number of information items (e.g., documents) to be indexed. Tell[47] discusses the implementation and maintenance of information system. He says that plan must set targets and time limits. Assigning these time limits to each planning step will give an opportunity to estimate how much time is available, rather than how much is required to complete each step of plan. He gives an idea of developing of a capability to tap foreign databases. For this kind of task, he suggests a project type of solution that involves SDI-ON-LINE service.

Graham[48] states that in online searching, no one database satisfies all needs. Since many databases cover similar information material, we need improved system for grouping duplicates. He emphasizes on providing unduplicated and non-repeated information. Thorpe[49] mentions that most international services are now able to supply machine-readable versions of their databases on magnetic tape. Currently, companies active in the design of high-tech products are confronted with a number of, often conflicting, challenges. Not only do they have to develop increasingly complex products in ever-shorter amounts of time but they also have to produce them cheaply for the local as well as global markets. In order to manage these conflicting trends adequately, companies need to have high quality information at the right moment and at the right location. This serves as the motivation in which various databases within the product life cycle are examined. Due to the fact that unanticipated information plays a more and more dominant role, especially in highly innovative business processes, attention is focused on textual databases since textual databases offer the best possibility to handle unanticipated free-formatted information. Also their treatment in the literature has thus far been scant. These databases have a huge potential for valuable information. Further, an analysis tool, data mining that could be used to analyse these textual databases so that we could extract information from them quickly and hence be able to access them at the right time when needed, is presented. Some of the difficulties are faced often when analyzing textual databases. Thus with the right information from the textual databases and the tools to deliver this information at the right time companies, would definitely be able to shorten development times and hence gain a competitive edge.

Mixed-Format Databases

Mixed-Format databases are those which combine two or more of the other database types. For example, a mixed-format database might contain both the full-text of articles and their accompanying illustrations.

Derivative Databases and New Data-driven Research and Capabilities

The ethos in research is that science builds on science. The creation of derivative databases not only enables incremental advances in the knowledge base, but also can contribute to major new findings, particularly when existing data are combined with new or entirely different data. The importance for research and related educational activities of producing new derivative databases cannot be overemphasized. The vast increase in the creation of digital databases in recent decades, together with the ability to make them broadly and instantaneously available, has resulted in entire new fields of data-driven research.

For example, the study of biological systems has been transformed radically in the past 20 years from an experimental research endeavor conducted in laboratories to one that relies heavily on computing and on access to and further refinement of globally linked databases. Indeed, one of the fastest growing disciplines is bioinformatics, a computer-based approach to biological research. New technologies, such as DNA microarrays and high-throughput sequencing machines, are producing a deluge of data. A challenge to biology in the coming decades will be to convert these data into knowledge.

The availability of global remote-sensing satellite observations, coupled with other airborne and in situ observational capabilities, has given rise to a new field of environmental research, Earth system science, which integrates the study of the physical and biological processes of our planet at various scales. The large meteorological databases obtained from government satellites, ground-based radar, and other data-collection systems pose a challenge similar to that mentioned above for biology, but also already have yielded a remarkable range of commercial and non-commercial value. Dissemination of the atmospheric observations in real time or near-real time for "nowcasts" and daily weather forecasts has very high commercial value, which is captured by third-party distributors. Use of these atmospheric observations to develop numerical models that predict the weather accurately, hours or days in advance, adds value in terms of safety and economic benefits to society that are not readily quantifiable. While the economic value of these data can be gauged by the profits of private-sector distributors, how does one measure the value of the lives and property saved by timely and accurate hurricane forecasts and tornado warnings? Once the immediate and most lucrative commercial value is exploited, the resulting data continue to have significant commercial and public-interest uses indefinitely. For instance, these data enable basic research on severe weather and long-term climate trends and provide various retrospective applications for industry. The original databases are archived and made available by the National Climatic Data Center. Derivative databases and data products are distributed under various arrangements by both commercial and not-for-profit entities like the Unidata Program of the University Corporation for Atmospheric Research.

Geographic information systems that integrate myriad sources of data provide an opportunity for new insights about the natural and constructed environment, greatly enhancing our knowledge of where we live and how we affect our physical environment. Important applications include environmental management, urban planning, route planning and navigation, emergency preparedness and response, land-use regulation, and enhancement of agricultural productivity, among many others.

Finally, databases used by researchers and educators also frequently are produced and disseminated primarily for other purposes. For example, a physical scientist studying the complex relationships among geology, hydrology, and biology as they relate to the preservation of species diversity likely would draw on numerous digital and hard-copy databases originally gathered for other purposes. A social scientist studying the characteristics and patterns of urban crime or the spread of communicable diseases likely would do the same. For many scientists, the ability to supplement existing databases with further data collection in a seamless web of old and new data is basic to meeting the needs of their specific investigations.

References

1. Clement, J. B. Increasing Research Productivity through Information Technology: A User-Centred Viewpoint. *International Forum of Information & Documentation*, 15(2), April 1990, p 25-31.

2. Endres-Niggmeyer. A Procedural Model of an Abstractor at Work. *International Forum of Information & Documentation*, 15(4), Oct. 1990, p 3-16.

3. Kar, D.C. and Siddiqui, A.M. Bibliographic database RIZA: design and development using mini/micro CDS/ISIS Version 2.3. *Information Services & Use*, 10, 1990, p 261-274.

4. National Advisory Committee, Washington, D.C. Non-Bibliographic Databases in a Network Environment. *International Information, Communication and Education*, 10(1), March 1991, p 97-100.

5. Behling, G. and Matthies, M. Development of a metadatabase on monitoring environmental programs. *Information Services & Use*, 10, 1990, p 205-214.

6. Choros, Kazimierz, Majewska and Sieminski, Andrzej. Bibliographic Database Compression. *International Forum of Information and Documentation*, 12(1), Jan 1987, p 28-32.

7. Hawkins, Donald T. *Information Services & Use*, 5, 1985, p 199-206.

8. Thorpe, Peter. Agricultural Information Services For the Third World. *International Information, Communication and Education*, 1(2), Sept 1982. p 161-173.

9. Leung, C.H.C. Architecture of an image database. *Information Services & Use*, 10, 1990, p 391-397.

10. Maxon-Dadd, Josephine. Refurbishing an elegant Victorian database- a view from DIALOG. *Information Services & Use*, 10, 1990, p 361-369.

11. Stern, Richard M. and Tarkowski, Stanislow. The need for a unified European environmental health database. *Information services & Use*, 10, 1990, p 5-14.

12. Ydreborg, Berit. Questionnaire based database on occupation and health status. *Information services & Use*, 10, 1990, p 47-51.

13. Jarvis, J. R. Developing an expert system using a PC-based shell. *Information Services & Use*, 9, 1989, p 67-77.

14. Mukhopadhyay, A. Database Management. *International Information, Communication and Education*, 17(2), 1998, p

196-213.

15. Cawkell, A.E. *Information Services & Use*, 13, 1993, p 47-53.

16. Willem, Marc. Presentation of I'M-GUIDE. *International Forum of Information and Documentation*, 18(3-4), Oct. 1993, p 37-39.

17. Philip, G., Crookes, D. and Juhasz, Z. An image database on a parallel processing network. *Information Services & Use*, 10, 1990, p 315-335.

18. International Database on Disability available on diskette. *International Information, Communication and Education*, 8(2), Sept. 1989, p 242.

19. Hasan, Nabi ;Singh, Muktiar and Sharma, Dev Raj. CD-ROM: A powerful media for information packing, retrieval and dissemination. Information Management in e- libraries.

20. Hussain, K.H; Nair, R. Raman and Asari, K. Raveendra. Importance of Search And Retrieval in CD-ROM Full Text Publishing: Experiments Using PDF Documents And NITYA Archival System. *Information Studies*, 8(3), 2002, p 173-180.

21. Mahesh, G. and Das, K. Mohan. Quality Assurance in CD-ROM Based Information Products. *Annals of Library Science and Documentation* , 19(2), 2001, p 167-171.

22. Kavi, Pradeep P. and Jayakant, Francis. Tools For Identification of Duplicate Records Downloaded for Multiple CD-ROM: A Case Study with SPIRS Based Database. *SRELS Journal of Information Management*, 38(4), 2001, p 279-286.

23. Rao, H.R. Achyutha; Ramesh, C.P. and Venkatesh, Y. An Analytical Study on the Use of CD-ROM Databases and other Digital Facilities in Mysore University Library: A case study. Library and Information Networking. *NACLIN 2001*. H.K. Kaul and E. Rama Reddy (ed.).

24. Rathore, R.S. and Kothari, D.V. Compact Disc: A Powerful Information Medium. International Information Communication and Education , 19(2), 2000, p 229-235.

25. Vijayakumar, J.K. and Das, Manju. CD-ROM to DVD-ROM: A New Era in Electronic Publishing of Databases and Multimedia Reference Sources. IASLIC Bulletin, Vol. 45(2); 2000; p. 49-54.

26. Darmoni, Stefan J. A Study Comparing Centralized CD-ROM and Decentralized Intranet Access to MEDLINE. *Bulletin of Medical Library Association*, 88(2), 2000, p 152-156.

27. Meera. Optical Storage Media: CD-ROM. *Annals of Library Science and Documentation*, 45(3), 1998, p 77-83.

28. Singh, Dr. (Mrs.) S.P. Optical Storage Media: A Viable Alternative to Online Searching. *Journal of Library and Information Science*, 22(1-2), 1997, p 16-28.

29. Ramesh, D.B.; Seth, M.K. and Sahu, J.R. Use of Digital Information: A Study on CD-ROM and Online Databases. *Lucknow Librarian*, 28(1-4), 1996, p 1-3.

30. Chakravarti, A.K. et.al. Technology Watch: CD-ROM. *Annals of Library Science and Documentation, 42(1), 1995, p 27-34.*

31. Samal, P.K. and Gupta, Sangeeta. Use of CD-ROM POPLINE Database in NIHFW: A Case Study. *IASLIC Bulletin,* 39(3), 1994, p125-128.

32. Feldman, Tony. Turn of the Tide: A New Age in Multimedia Publishing. *Annals of Library Science and Documentation,* 39(3), 1992, p 86-88.

33. Vishwanathan, T. Object Oriented Database Management System: A New Tool for Information Centres. *Annals of Library Science and Documentation,* 39(3), 1992, p 74-80.

34. Subbarao, A. and Rajalakshmi, V. Libraries in 21st century. *Annals of Library Science and Documentation,* 39(3), 1992, p 89-93.

35. Siddiqui, Moid A. Can CD-ROM Replace Online? *International Information, Communication and Education,* 10(1), 1991, p 40-45.

36. Krull, James S. discusses the role of the service bureau in multimedia diversification. *Information Services & Use,* 9, 1989, p 271-277.

37. McPherson, Malcolm G., Harrap, Chris and O'Reilly, Jan E. Enhancing search results by editing, analysis and packaging. *Information Services & Use,* 9, 1989, p 101-106.

38. Smith, I. W. Evaluation of CD-ROM products. *Information Services & Use,* 9, 1989, p 85-90.

39. Sur, S. N. And Chowdhury, G. G. A Prototype Design of a Bibliographic Database Based on CCF Using Micro-CDS/ISIS. *IASLIC Bulletin,* 38(1), 1993, p17-37.

40. Jarvelin, Kalervo and Niemi, Timo. Simplifying Fact Retrieval through Intermediary Systems: Problems and Requirements. *International Forum of Information & Documentation,* 15, (2) April 1990, p 8-15.

41. see 18.

42. Association of Information and Dissemination Centers 1984 Fall Meeting. *Information Services & Use*, 5, 1985, p 49-56.

43. See 23.

44. Bhattacharya, G. Computer Readable Databases and The Future of Information Service. *IASLIC Bulletin*, 26(2), 1981, p 49-58.

45. Singh, Shivpal; Jambhekar, Ashok and Gautam, J.N. Authority control: Its requirement for maintaining quality in Indian Bibliographic databases. *SRELS Journal of Information Management*, 39(4), 2002, p 395-408.

46. See 1.

47. See 13.

48. Graham, M. H. Information services as a corporate resource in Exxon. *Information Services & Use*, 5, 1985, p 207-212.

Chapter 5
Information Retrieval From Databases

Almost instantly, the computer was applied to the age-old problem of information storage and retrieval. After all, by World War Two, information was already accumulating at rates beyond the space available in publicly supported libraries. And besides, it seemed somehow cheap and tawdry to store the entire archives of "The Three Stooges" in the Library of Congress. Information was seeping out of every crack and pore of modern day society. Thus, the first attempts at information storage and retrieval followed traditional lines and metaphors. The first systems were based on discrete files in a virtual library. In this file-oriented system, a bunch of files would be stored on a computer and could be accessed by a computer operator. Files of archived data were called "tables" because they looked like tables used in traditional file keeping. Rows in the table were called "records" and columns were called "fields".

The "flat file" system was a start. However, it was seriously inefficient. Essentially, in order to find a record, someone would have to read through the entire file and hope it was not the last record. With a hundred thousands records, user can imagine the dilemma. What was needed, computer scientists thought (using existing metaphors again) was a card catalog, a means to achieve random access processing, that is the ability to efficiently access a single record without searching the entire file to find it. The result was the indexed file-oriented system in which a single index file stored "key" words and pointers to records that were stored elsewhere. This made retrieval much more efficient. It worked just like a card catalog in a library. To find data, one needed only search for keys rather than reading entire records. However, even with the benefits of indexing, the file-oriented system still suffered from problems including:

* Data Redundancy - the same data might be stored in different places

* Poor Data Control - redundant data might be slightly different such as in the case when Ms. Lalita changes her name to Mrs. Lalita and the change is only reflected in some of the files containing her data

* Inability to Easily Manipulate Data - it was a tedious and error prone activity to modify files by hand

* Cryptic Work Flows - accessing the data could take excessive programming effort and was too difficult for real-users (as opposed to programmers).

Basic Searches

A. Keyword Search

Controlling how the computer interprets the search

There are some standard ways of retrieving information from any electronic database, be it an online library catalog (GIL), a periodical database (GALILEO), or an Internet database.

Keywords are the words that describe the topic of research. These can be individual words or a phrase. These keywords can be chosen from the sentence user creates to define the research topic. Once user chooses the significant words, he can then come up with synonyms, or words with similar meanings. All of these can be keywords to use in forming the search.

Generally, when user submits a keyword search to a library catalog or periodical database, the title, subject, and abstract fields are the only parts of the record searched. These fields are called the Basic Index.

Keyword searching is available in almost all databases. Many databases require user to explicitly describe the relationship between keywords using special connectors to associate the keywords in various relationships.

Example: User's chosen the topic "alternative fuels" for a research paper. To help user focus this rather broad topic, user put it into the form of a question or sentence:

What are the types of alternative methods for searching information or developed for online systems?

Usually, the nouns and adjectives in the sentence or question will give user a good idea of what the keywords will be. In this case, the phrase **"alternative methods for searching information"** and **"online systems "** are the significant keywords.

From these keywords make a list of synonyms to use as alternatives. Since different writers will describe the same thing using different words, it's good to arm with a variety of keywords so user doesn't miss important information.

B. Boolean Search

And / Or / Not

This is an algebraic concept. Boolean connectors are all about sets. There are three little words that are used as Boolean connectors:

*　　and

* or
* not

Think of each keyword as having a "set" of results that are connected with it. These sets can be combined to produce a different "set" of results. One can also exclude certain "sets" from the results by using a Boolean connector.

1. AND is a connector that requires both words to be present in each record in the results. Use AND to narrow the search.

Search Term	Hits
Library	999 hits
Society	876 hits
Library and Society	123 hits

The words 'library' and 'society' will both be present in each record.

2. OR is a connector that allows either word to be present in each record in the results. Use OR to expand the search.

Search Term	Hits
Library	97 hits
Information	75 hits
Library or Information	172 hits

Either ' Library ' or ' Information ' (or both) will be present in each record.

3. NOT is a connector that requires the first word be present in each record in the results, but only if the record does not contain the second word.

Search Term	Hits
Indexing	423 hits
Abstracting	652 hits
Indexing not Abstracting	275 hits

Each record contains the words 'Indexing', but not the word ' Abstracting'.

C. Natural Language Search

Using plain language to enter the search

This type of search is the easiest to understand, but many databases don't offer it as a function. A natural language search is a search using regular spoken language, such as English. Using this type of search user can ask the database a question or user can type in a sentence that describes the information user are looking for. The database then uses a programmed logic to determine the keywords in the sentence by their position in the sentence.

The Internet search service Ask Jeeves offers natural language searching.

Database Indexing

All of these kinds of database can take advantage of indexing to increase their speed, and this technology has advanced tremendously since its early uses in the 1960s and 1970s. The most common kind of index is a sorted list of the contents of some particular table column, with pointers to the row associated with the value. An index allows a set of table rows matching some criterion to be located quickly. Various methods of indexing are commonly used; B-trees (tree data structure that keeps data sorted and allows insertions and deletions in logarithmic amortized time), hashes, and linked lists are all common indexing techniques.

Relational DBMSs have the advantage that indexes can be created or dropped without changing existing applications making use of it. The database chooses between many different strategies based on which one it estimates will run the fastest. In other words, indexes are transparent to the application or end user querying the database; while they affect performance, any command will run with or without indexes existing in the database. Relational DBMSs utilize many different algorithms to compute the result of an statement. The RDBMS will produce a plan of how to execute the query, which is generated by analyzing the run times of the different algorithms and selecting the quickest. Some of the key algorithms that deal with joins are Nested Loops Join, Sort-Merge Join and Hash Join. Which of these is chosen depends on whether an index exists, what type it is, and its cardinality.

When user submits a query to a database using query language, the database will consult its data dictionary and access the tables user has requested data from. It will then put together a "view" based upon the criteria user have defined in the query. A "view" is essentially a dynamically generated "result" table that is put together based upon the parameters user has defined in the query. Similarly, a view could be composed of the results of a query on several tables all at once (sometimes called a "join"). Thus, user might create a view of all the employees with a salary of greater than 50K from several stores by accumulating the results from queries to the EMPLOYEES and STORES databases. The possibilities are limitless. By the way, many databases allow user to store "views" in the data dictionary as if they were physical tables.

Basics of the database Query

A "query" is a structured request to the database for data. Or, in more specific terms, a query is a simple statement (like a sentence) that requests data from the database. Much as is the case with English, a query statement is made up of subjects, verbs, clauses, and predicates.

Let's take a look at the statement made above. In this case, the subject is "hey user database thing". The verb is "give me a list". The clause is "from the CLIENTS table". Finally, the predicate is "who live in the 213 area code."

The above statement might look like in query:

SELECT * FROM CLIENTS WHERE area_code = 213

*   SELECT = VERB = give me a list
*   FROM CLIENTS = CLAUSE = from the CLIENTS table
*   area_code = 213 = PREDICATE = who live in the 213 area code

Data Types

Before going into the details of database queries, it is important to understand about database structures. Specifically, most databases store their data in terms of data types. Defining data types allows the database to be more efficient and helps to protect the user against adding bad data to the tables.

There are several standard data types including

Type	Alias	Description
CHARACTER	CHAR	Contains a string of characters. Usually, these fields will have a specified maximum length that is defined when the table is created.
NUMERIC	NONE	Contains a number with a specified number of decimal digits and scale (indicating a power to which the value should be multiplied) defined at the table creation.
DECIMAL	DEC	Similar to NUMERIC except that it is more proprietary.
INTEGER	INT	Only accepts integers
SMALLINT	NONE	Same as INTEGER except that precision must be

		smaller than INT precisions in the same table.
FLOAT	NONE	Contains floating point numbers
DOUBLE PRECISION	NONE	Like FLOAT but with greater precision

It is important to note that not all databases will implement the entire list and that some will implement their own data types such as calendar or monetary types. Some fields may also allow a NULL value in them even if NULL is not exactly the correct type.

Query Language

A query language is a language in which a user requests information from a database. These are typically higher-level than programming languages. A complete query language also contains facilities to insert and delete tuples (finite sequence, also known as an "ordered list" of objects, each of a specified type. A tuple containing n objects is known as an "n-tuple) as well as to modify parts of existing tuples.

Queries can be of following types:

* **Procedural**, where the user instructs the system to perform a sequence of operations on the database. This will compute the desired information.

* **Nonprocedural**, where the user specifies the information desired without giving a procedure for obtaining the information.

* Creating Longer Search Statements

One may need to issue several search statements until user has a result set that contains a high percentage of relevant records. As the user becomes proficient, he or she may find to reduce the number of search statements that he/she issues to obtain that result set. The user can do this by specifying additional terms and operators in a single search statement. It is possible to use (practically) as many operators and as many search terms as the user would like in a search statement.

Creating longer search statements is explained as following:

1. Operator Precedence : As user build longer search statements, user should be aware of the order in which the operators are executed in a search statement. When more than one operator is used in the same search statement, an operator with a higher precedence will execute before an operator with a lower precedence. The precedence order, from highest to lowest, is as follows:

adj, near (highest precedence)

with

same

and, not, not same, not with, not near, not adj

xor

or (lowest precedence)

When two operators have equal priority (such as **adj** and **near**), the operator that is encountered first (moving from left to right) will be processed first.

1_: library and information adj services

1_: (INFORMATION ADJ SERVICES) AND LIBRARY 20 RECORDS

In this example, **information adj services** was executed first, because **adj** has a higher priority than **and**. The retrieved records were placed into an internal, intermediate result set. The records in that internal result set were then processed to see which contained occurrences of the word **library**. Records that contained **library** were then placed into the final result set. The parentheses were inserted to help explain the results of the search.

Overriding Precedence by Nesting Search Terms

User can refine search statements by using

parentheses to nest search terms and override the precedence rules. To specify which portion of the search statement user wants executed first, place (or nest) that portion in parentheses. User can use up to **15** nests within a single search statement.

1_: (information or data) same retrieval

1_: RETRIEVAL SAME (DATA OR INFORMATION) 67 RECORDS

In this example, **information or data** was evaluated first, with the retrieved records placed in a temporary result set. The second part of the search statement (same retrieval) places into the final result set those records from the temporary result that contain the term **retrieval** when it occurs in the same field as the term **information** or in the same field as the term **data**.

Sometimes a complex search strategy requires more than one set of parentheses.

1_: computer same (data with (security or protection)) or encryption

1_: ENCRYPTION OR (COMPUTER SAME (DATA WITH (SECURITY OR PROTECTION))) 3 RECORDS

In this example, the search statement within the inner parentheses was processed first, followed by keywords contained in the outer parentheses. Finally, these results were processed with the terms outside the parentheses.

Using Nesting to Make the Not Operators Exclusive

The NOT ADJ Operator, the NOT NEAR Operator, The NOT SAME Operator and The NOT WITH Operator. These operators are not exclusive because if the condition were satisfied somewhere in the record, the record would be retrieved even if it contained a condition that the operator was not supposed to retrieve. User can, however, construct a search statement that would implement an exclusive search. To use the **not same** operator as an example:

1_: classification   not   same   cataloguing
1_: CLASSIFICATION NOT SAME CATALOGUING —— 9 RECORDS

2_: (classification not same cataloguing) not (classification same cataloguing)

2_: (CLASSIFICATION NOT SAME CATALOGUING) NOT (CLASSIFICATION SAME CATALOGUING) —— 73 RECORDS

In this example, the user first retrieved all records in the database that contain fields that discuss **classification** but do not mention the **cataloguing**. But since this is not an exclusive search, some of these records may actually contain **classification** and **cataloguing** in the same field. The second search is exclusive because it also specifically excludes records that do contain **classification** and **cataloguing** in the same field.

*   **Searching for Plurals**

The plural form(s) of a word are automatically searched for. The following description will show the working:

1_:		wolf
wolf	45	RECORDS
wolfs	4	RECORDS
wolves	12	RECORDS

1_: wolf 56 RECORDS

In this example, the user performed a search on the word **wolf**.

If user does not want a search for plurals, place an exclamation point (!) at the end of the term in question.

1_: wolf!

1_: wolf 45 RECORDS

2_: (wolf and fox)!

2_: wolf and fox 34 RECORDS

In this example, the user first placed an exclamation point at the end of a single-term search statement. Then the user qualified a nested search statement with an exclamation point. Both actions temporarily overrode the default behavior for plurals

Truncation / Wildcards

Searching for multiple forms of a word

Some databases allow certain symbols to be used for searching different forms of a word (such as plurals) or different spellings.

Plurals — a symbol added to the end of a word to instruct the database to search for plural as well as singular forms of words. The symbol used in many databases is a plus (+).

Example: catalogue+ retrieves catalogue or catalogue s

Truncation — a symbol added to the end of the root of a word to instruct the database to search for all forms of a word. The asterisk (*) is used in many databases for truncation.

Example: catalog* retrieves catalog, catalogue, or catalogues, cataloguing

Wildcards — a symbol used to represent any character. Wildcards can usually be used at the end of a word or within a word. The pound symbol (#) is used in many databases as a wildcard. One can use this symbol to search variant spellings of a word and can use more than one pound sign to stand in for more than one character. Each pound sign represents 0-1 characters.

Using Wildcard Characters in a Search Term

Using Wildcard Characters: user can let a wildcard character represent one or more characters in a search term.

Different Wildcard Characters

There are three kinds of wildcard characters, which can be used in a search term.

$ Matches zero or more continuous characters.

$n   Matches between zero and n continuous characters.

?   Matches a single character.

Specifying a Wildcard at the End of a Search Term

User can specify a wildcard character to represent letters at the end of a word.

1_: psychia$

PSYCHIA$

PSYCHIATRIC 3 RECORDS

PSYCHIATRIST 4 RECORDS

PSYCHIATRISTS 13 RECORDS

PSYCHIATRY 1 RECORD

1_: PSYCHIA$ 19 RECORDS

In the above example, the user retrieved 19 records. Each record contains a word beginning with **psychia**. The dollar symbol (**$**) represents any combination of searchable characters. In the databases, all characters, are searchable.

Specifying a Wildcard at the Beginning of a Search Term

User can specify a wildcard character to represent letters at the beginning of a word.

1_: $mites

1_: RESULT 12 RECORDS

In this example, the user retrieved 12 records that contain words ending in **mites**. Some databases will not let user perform wildcard searches when user places the wildcard character at the beginning of the word.

Embedding Wildcard Characters in a Search Term

User can specify a wildcard character to represent the letters in the middle of a word.

1_: comp$tion

1_: RESULT 375 RECORDS

In this example, the user retrieved 375 records that contain any word that begins with **comp** and ends with **tion**.

Specifying the Maximum Number of Characters to Match

User can specify the maximum number of characters that the wildcard symbol can match in order to retrieve a record.

1_: psychia$4

PSYCHIA$4

PSYCHIATRIC 23 RECORDS

PSYCHIATRY 61 RECORDS

1_: PSYCHIA$4 44 RECORDS

In this example, the user specified a numeric parameter (**4**) to the wildcard character. This permits records to be retrieved only if they contain the word **psychia** and between zero and four additional characters. In this example, 44 records were retrieved

Amount of Time Needed to Perform Wildcard Searches

User can place wildcard characters at the end, at the beginning, or in the middle of a search term. User can even use more than one wildcard character in a term. As user varies the number and the position of wildcard characters in a single search term, user may notice a difference in the amount of time it takes for database to complete the search.

Wildcards at the end of the word will result in the

fastest search times. Since some database has a reverse dictionary, a wildcard at the beginning of the word will be equally fast. However, if user specifies wildcard characters at the beginning, at the end, and in the middle of the word, the search time will increase.

Using a Wildcard Character as a Literal

What if user wanted to use a wildcard character in one of the search terms? User would want the character to be interpreted as a literal and not as wildcard character. The back-slash escape character (\) tells BRS to interpret the next character as a literal.

1_: $3

	$3
A	17 RECORDS
AA	21 RECORDS
AAA	5 RECORDS
BBA	2 RECORDS
...	
...	

1_: $3   945 RECORDS
2_: $\33

13	71 RECORDS
133	99 RECORDS
143	34 RECORDS
...	
...	

2_: $\3 432 RECORDS

In this example, the user demonstrated how to use the escape character. At the first prompt the search statement ($3) was interpreted as an instruction to retrieve records that contain one, two, or three-letter words. However, what if user wants to retrieve records that end in the number three? To do that, the user placed the escape character in front of the number **3** in search statement 2. This tells BRS not to interpret the **3** as a qualifying parameter, which is the default, but rather as a literal.

*   Searching for Numeric Data

Searching for a Number as User Would Search for a Word

If a searchable text field contains a number (Arabic, Roman, ordinal, cardinal, etc.), user can retrieve that record by simply issuing that number in a search statement. This technique works for all searchable fields in the most of the databases.

Let's say user is looking for records that mention the year 1966.

1_: 1966

1_: RESULT 210 DOCS

In this example, the user retrieved 210 records that contain one or more occurrences of **1066**. There is no guarantee, however, that every occurrence refers to the year **1966**. If a record contains the address **1966 Park Avenue**, that will also be retrieved. A number may also be enclosed in quotation marks.

1_: 1966

1_: RESULT 210 DOCS 3_: "1"

3_: RESULT 634 DOCS

In this example the user retrieved 210 records that contain one or more occurrences of **1966**. The second statement shows that a number may be enclosed in quotes.

Searching for a Publication Date

If user wants documents published up to (**and including**) 1994, user may use **1994** as the **thru** date in the boxes on the search input screen, since the date used in the search in this case is actually 12/31/94, which is really what user want. If user wants documents published from (**and including**) 1991, user may use **1991** as the **from** date in the boxes on the search input screen, since the date used in this case is actually 00/00/91, to include all dates in 1991.

Using Search Operators

To use the search engine, user may use more than one search term combined with search operators.

Search Term

A search term is a number, word, or phrase that user wants to appear in the records to be retrieved.

Search Operator

Search operators are special words that connect one search term with another.

The various search operators are listed below:

1. The ADJ Operator : User can retrieve records that contain the search terms when those terms are found in the same sentence, in the order that user specifies them in the search statement, and with a maximum number of searchable words between the search terms. This is the most precise search statement user can specify on the sentence level.

1 _: president adj3 sharma

RESULT 6 RECORDS

2 _: president (3W) sharma

RESULT 6 RECORDS

3 _: president pre/3 sharma

RESULT 6 RECORDS

In this example, the user retrieved records that mention **President Sharma** in a sentence in any one of the four forms in which his name is likely to appear: **President Shankar Dayal Sharma**, **President Dr. Shankar Dayal Sharma**, **President S D Sharma**, or **President Sharma**. The numeric parameter (3) assigned to the **adj** operator lets user retrieve a record even if there are up to **n** -1 (or two, in this case) searchable words between the search terms. The second and third searches illustrate alternate notations for the **adj** search operator.

ADJn The adj search operator is used to retrieve records in which the second search term is found in the same sentence as the first. The order in which user specifies the search terms is the order in which the terms must be found in the record. User can modify the number of records retrieved with this operator by specifying the maximum number of searchable words that can occur between the search terms in a sentence. It should be remembered that the value of n is one more than the number of words allowed between the two search terms.

The operators **(nW)** and **pre/n** serve as alternate symbols for the **ADJn** operator.

term ADJ[n] term

where **n** = a number which is used by the search engine to compute the maximum number of searchable words (n - 1) that can separate the search terms in the same sentence. The value of **n** can be between 1-99. The use of **n** is optional. In some databases default value for **n**, if omitted, is 1.

Term is defined as the search terms on either side of the operator.

The AND Operator

The **and** search operator is used to retrieve records that contain both of the specified search terms. This operator places no condition on where the terms are found in relation to one another; the terms simply have to appear somewhere in the same record.

term AND term

where **term** is the search terms on either side of the operator.

The ampersand **(&)** may be used as an alternate symbol for the **and** operator.

The NEAR Operator

One can retrieve records that contain the search

terms when they occur in the same sentence, though not in any specific order, and where user can specify the maximum number of searchable words that can occur between the search terms. This lets user specify more precise positional information within a sentence than user can via the **with** operator.

    1_: Ram near1 mohan

RESULT 6 RECORDS

    2_: Ram (A) mohan

RESULT 6 RECORDS

    3_: Ram w/1 mohan

RESULT 6 RECORDS

In this example the user retrieved records that contain the Ram in a sentence. This search statement will retrieve records that contain **mohan** and **Ram** in the same sentence, regardless of the order in which the terms occur. Since this operator will only retrieve records when there are no searchable words between the terms in the same sentence, this search statement would not have retrieved records that contain **mohan** and **Ram** if any searchable words occurred between them. The second and third searches illustrate alternate notations for the **near** search operator.

The operators **(nA)** and **w/n** serve as alternate symbols for the **NEARn** operator.

NEARn

The near search operator is used to retrieve records in which the second search term is found in the same sentence as the first. The order in which the terms appear in a sentence is unimportant.

User can modify the number of records retrieved with this operator by specifying the maximum number of searchable words that can occur between the search terms in a sentence. It should be noted that the value of **n** is one more than the number of words allowed between the two search terms.

term NEAR[n] term

where **n** = a number which is used by the search engine to compute the maximum number of searchable words (**n** - 1) that can separate the search terms in the same sentence. The value of **n** can be between 1-99. The use of **n** is optional.

Term is the search terms on either side of the operator.

The NOT Operator

User can retrieve only those records that contain the first search term and that do not contain the second.

A word or name may be common to many topics. For example, if user searches for the name **Delhi** in an encyclopedia database, user would retrieve many records (encyclopedia articles) on a variety of topics. If users are sufficiently familiar with the text of the relevant records, users should be able to retrieve those records by using other positional operators. For instance, if user is interested in records about **New Delhi** but don't want to retrieve records that mention **Old Delhi**, user might use the search statement **Delhi and History**. This will reduce the chances of retrieving records about **Old Delhi**. However, there is another way to retrieve records that contain a common word or name and to exclude records that contain an unwanted term.

5_: Delhi not old

RESULT 7 RECORDS

In this example, the user retrieved seven records that mention **Delhi** but do not contain the word **Old**. It is possible that relevant information exists in records that were not retrieved. Just because a record contains an undesired term does not mean that it cannot contain information user do want!

NOT Use the **not** search operator to retrieve records that contain the first search term user specify but not the second term.

term NOT term

Where t**erm** is the search terms on either side of the operator.

The NOT ADJ Operator

User can retrieve records that contain the first search term and that satisfy one of the following conditions for the second term:

*   Not in the database
*   In a different record than the first search term
*   In a different field or subparagraph than the first search term
*   In a different sentence of the same field or subparagraph as the first search term
*   In the same sentence as the first search term but the second term precedes the first
*   In the same sentence as the first search term and with the first search term preceding the second search term but with more than **n** -1 searchable terms between the two search terms, where **n** is the value appended to the **adj** operator.

One of the terms user may want to use in the search statement may commonly appear in the same sentence with another word. Furthermore, user may know the maximum number of searchable words that appear between these words. There may be occasions when user want to retrieve records by specifying that the second search term not be found in the same sentence as the first or if found in the same sentence, that the record be retrieved only when there are more than a specified number of searchable words between the first and second terms. The order of the terms in the search statement is the order in which the terms must be found in the record in order for the record to be retrieved.

l_: president not adj3 sharma

RESULT 6 RECORDS

In this example the user retrieved records in which **Sharma** does not satisfy the **adj** condition for **President**.

As with the not same and not with operators, this is not an exclusive operator; if the **not adj** condition is satisfied anywhere in a record, that record will be retrieved even if the **adj** condition is also satisfied in the record.

NOT ADJ

Use the **not adj** search operator to retrieve records in which the second search term does not satisfy the **adj** condition for the first search term.

term NOT ADJ[n] term

Where **n** = a number which is used by the search engine to compute the maximum number of searchable words that can separate the search terms in the same sentence. The value of **n** can be between 1-99. The use of **n** is optional.

Where **term** is the search terms on either side of the operator.

The NOT NEAR Operator

User can retrieve records that contain the first search term and that satisfy one of the following conditions for the second term:

*   In a different record than the first search term
*   In a different field or subparagraph than the first search term
*   In a different sentence of the same field or subparagraph as the first search term
*   In the same sentence as the first search term with more than **n** -1 searchable words between the two search terms, where **n** is the value appended to the near operator.

One of the terms user may want to use in the search statement may commonly appear in the same sentence with another word. Furthermore, user may know the maximum number of searchable words that appear between these words. There may be occasions when user want to retrieve records by specifying that the second search term not be found in the same sentence as the first or if found in the same sentence, that the record be retrieved only when there are more than a specified number of searchable words between the first and second terms. As long as the minimum number of searchable words exists between the search terms, the order in which the terms occur in the sentence does not matter.

1_: ram not near2 mohan

1_: RESULT 56 RECORDS

In this example. the user retrieved records in which **Mohan** does not satisfy the near condition for **Ram**.

As with the **not same** and **not with** operators this is not an exclusive operator. If the **not near** condition is satisfied anywhere in a record, that record will be retrieved even if the **near** condition is also satisfied in that record.

NOT NEARn

Use the **not near** search operator to retrieve records in which the second search term does not satisfy the **near** condition for the first search term.

term NOT NEAR[n] term

Where **n** = a number which is used by the search engine to compute the maximum number of searchable words that can separate the search terms in the sentence. The value of **n** can be between 1-99. The use of **n** is optional. The SPI default value for **n**, if omitted, is 5.

Where **term** is the search terms on either side of the operator.

The NOT SAME Operator

User can retrieve records that do not contain the second search term in the same field or subparagraph that contains the first search term.

1_: translation service not same documentation service

RESULT 24 RECORDS

In this example, the user retrieved 24 records that mentioned **Translation service** in a field and either mentioned **Documentation service** in another field or not in the record at all.

This is not an exclusive operator. The condition that user want satisfied is a field that contains the first word and that does not contain the second word. However, elsewhere in that same record, those terms may occur in the same field. If the not same condition is satisfied anywhere in a record, that record will be retrieved even if the two terms do appear in the same field elsewhere in the record. As in this example, if **Translation service** was found in a field that did not contain **Documentation service**, then the **not same** condition would have been satisfied and the record would be retrieved. But if the term **Documentation service** does appear elsewhere in the record and in a field that also happens to contain the term **Translation service**, the record would still be retrieved.

NOT SAME

The **not same** search operator is used to retrieve records that contain the first search term in a field or subparagraph but that do not contain the second term in the same field or subparagraph. It should be noted that in standard fields, the **not same** operator applies to the entire field; in full-text fields, the **not same** operator applies to each individual subparagraph in turn.

term NOT SAME term

Where **term** is the search terms on either side of the operator.

The NOT WITH Operator

User can retrieve records that do not contain the second search term in the same sentence as the first search term.

1_: Delhi not with mogul
RESULT 1 RECORDS

In this example, the user retrieved one record that contains an occurrence of **Delhi** but not **Mogul** in the same sentence.

This is not an exclusive operator. The condition that user wants to be satisfied is a sentence that contains the first word and that does not contain the second word. However, elsewhere in that same record, those terms may occur in the same sentence. If the **not with** condition is satisfied anywhere in a record, that record will be retrieved even if the two terms do appear in the same sentence elsewhere in the record. As in this example, if **Delhi** was found in a sentence that did not contain **Mogul**, then the **not with** condition would have been satisfied and the record would be retrieved. But if the term **Mogul** does appear elsewhere in the record and in a sentence that also happens to contain the term **Delhi**, the record would still be retrieved.

NOT WITH

Use the **not with** search operator to retrieve records that contain the first search term in a sentence but do not contain the second search term in the same sentence.

term NOT WITH term

Where **term** is the search terms on either side of the operator.

The OR Operator

User can retrieve records that contain one or more synonymous or related terms. Consequently, the result set that user create may require further qualification.

3_: training or apprentice
RESULT 791 RECORDS
4_: training | apprentice
RESULT 791 RECORDS

In this example, the user retrieved 791 records that

contain the words **training** and/or **apprentice**. The second search statement shows that instead of typing the or operator user can use the vertical bar (**|**).

OR : The **or** search operator is used to retrieve records that contain one or both specified search terms. This operator places no condition on where the terms are found in relation to one another; one or both terms simply have to appear somewhere in the same record.

term OR term

Where **term** is the search terms on either side of the operator. The vertical bar (**|**) serves as an alternate symbol for the **or** operator.

The SAME Operator

User can retrieve records that contain the search terms somewhere in the same field or subparagraph. By focusing the search to the field or subparagraph level user make the searches more precise than record-wide searches.

1_: translation service same documentation service
RESULT 2 RECORDS

2_: translation service (L) documentation service
RESULT 2 RECORDS

3_: translation service (P) documentation service
RESULT 2 RECORDS

4_: translation service w/seg documentation service

RESULT 2 RECORDS

In this example, the user retrieved two records that mentioned **Translation service** and **Documentation service** in the same field or subparagraph. The second, third, and fourth searches illustrate alternate notations for the **same** search operator.

SAME The **same** search operator is used to retrieve records that contain the second search term in the same field or subparagraph as the first search term. It should be noted that in standard fields, the same operator applies to the entire field; in full-text fields, the same operator applies to each individual subparagraph in turn.

term SAME term

Where **term** is the search terms on either side of the operator.

The operators **(L)**, **(P)**, and **w/seg** serve as alternate symbols for the **same** operator.

The WITH Operator

User can retrieve records that contain the search terms when they occur in the same sentence. The terms user specifies do not have to appear in any particular order. The number of searchable words that appear between the search terms is also unimportant. By focusing the search to the sentence level user makes the searches more precise than record-wide or field-wide searches.

WITH : The **with** search operator is used to retrieve records in which the second search term is found in the same sentence as the first term.

1_: Delhi with mogul

RESULT 21 RECORDS

In this example the user retrieved 21 records that contain **Delhi** and **Mogul** in the same sentence.

The XOR Operator

User can retrieve records that contain one of the search terms user specify but not both. On occasion, user may need to retrieve records based on two terms that are mutually exclusive. That is, both of the terms never appear in the same record.

2_: old xor Delhi

RESULT 7 RECORDS

In this example, the user retrieves records that mention **Old** and records that mention **Delhi** but retrieved no records that mention both **Old** and **Delhi**.

XOR : The **xor** search operator is used to retrieve records that contain either the first search term or the second term, but not both.

term XOR term

Where **term** is the search terms on either side of the operator.

Summary of Search Operators This section gives user a summary of how operators will retrieve records based on the terms user specify.

YES = will retrieve record.

xor

YES if second term is in different record or not in database

NO otherwise

not

YES if second term is in different record or not in database

NO otherwise

not same

YES if second term is in different record or not in database

YES if second term is in different field or subparagraph

NO otherwise

not with

YES if second term is in different record or not in database

YES if second term is in different field or subparagraph

YES, if the second term is in a different sentence in the same field or subparagraph

NO otherwise

not near

YES if second term is in different record or not in database

YES if second term is in different field or subparagraph

YES if the second term is in a different sentence in the same field or subparagraph

POSSIBLY if the second term is in the same sentence

not adj

YES if second term is in different record or not in database

YES if second term is in different field or subparagraph

YES if the second term is in a different sentence in the same field or subparagraph

POSSIBLY if the second term is in the same sentence

or

YES if second term is in different record or not in database

YES if second term is in different field or subparagraph

YES if the second term is in a different sentence in the same field or subparagraph

YES if the second term is in the same sentence

NO otherwise

and

NO if second term is in different record or not in database

YES if second term is in different field or subparagraph

YES if the second term is in a different sentence in the same field or subparagraph

YES if the second term is in the same sentence

same

NO if second term is in different record or not in database

NO if second term is in different field or subparagraph

YES if the second term is in a different sentence in the same field or subparagraph

YES if the second term is in the same sentence

with

POSSIBLY if the second term is in the same sentence

NO otherwise

near

POSSIBLY if the second term is in the same sentence

NO otherwise

The above list shows whether a record will be retrieved when the first term is found in that record and depending on the position of the second search term and the operator user use. For example, if user uses the NOT ADJ operator, and the second search term is found in a different sentence in the same field, the record will be retrieved.

Using Operators as Search Terms

User cannot search for words like not, and, or that are search operators, if these words are part of the stopword list of the database.

Something special about Proximity Operators

Some database can use any one of four proximity operators. The use of one term "next" to another is such a powerful clue to concepts that user should have a variety of ways to search for one term "next" to another. Sometimes it may be useful to think of proximity within words, within sentences, and within fields. The operators for proximity within words are ADJ and NEAR. Order matters with ADJ; it does not matter with NEAR. The operator for proximity within a sentence is WITH. The operator for within a standard field or within a subparagraph of a fulltext field is SAME.

Problems Related with Databases

Arenas[1] points out shortcomings of online searches such as:

1. Homonym problem
2. First-author problem
3. Journal quality problem
4. Citation lag problem
5. Institutional address problem
6. Abstract/index coverage problem

All relevant data fields can be made searchable. Many data manipulation can be added to the database in particular, data from several literature databases can be combined. Match-key can be defined that contain the minimum amount of information necessary to identify a particular publication and that may be assumed to appear in all correct bibliographic specifications of that 'publication'. Tell[2] discusses the problems for the future. He discusses the problems of databases services and says that un-integrated information is problem for database publication. The new technology is uneatable in many instances. Scientific and technical encyclopaedia in the form of databases can be currently updated. Electronic publishing is both now cheaper and faster than the corresponding publication in printed form. The e-mail is also cheaper and faster than traditional postal service. Jarvelin and Niemi[3] mention some key problems in the development of intermediary systems for fact retrieval, such as:

1. Interface simplification through an object-oriented and independent user data model.
2. Query generation for databases of any data model and conventional or recursive processing requirements.

3. Specification of imprecisely presented queries
4. Distributed database selection
5. Care for compatibility of data from different sources.
    Further they discuss several arguments for focusing
on the problems such as;
1. They are sufficiently many-sided and different to
    prevent straightforward solutions based on the
    development of existing systems.
2. These problems are characteristic of fact retrieval
    and do not emerge in text or bibliographic retrieval.
3. There are relevant methods and systems in the
    context of bibliographic retrieval for solving the
    problems related to the task domains not listed in
    the tabulation.
4. The processing of free natural language and
    interpretation of query results in general are so
    difficult domains, not being the critical core of
    intermediary systems for fact retrieval, that it is
    better to defer their treatment until the other
    problem areas are well understood.

Subject Headings

Search Using "Controlled Vocabulary"

As user looks through the results of an initial search
user will see that the article citations have subject
headings or descriptors. Articles that have similar content
will have the same subject headings even if the authors
of the articles used different terms to describe the topic.
For example, one author may use the phrase "catalogue"
and another "cataloguing." The subject heading on both
records will be the same. This is called a controlled
vocabulary. By searching using that subject heading user
will retrieve records where either term is used. Sometimes
these subject headings are hyperlinked and user can link
to other articles with similar content. Other databases
do not offer this function and so user would have to do a

new search using the terms user have discovered.

Clement[4] says that IT (the complex of computing and communication technologies used in obtaining, storing, organizing, manipulating, and exchanging information) has transformed the conduct of scientific, engineering, and clinical research. He presents a report and it argues for a user centred viewpoint in addressing them. The document with an examination of opportunities for collaboration between specialists and research users in creating information managing tools and in developing large-scale information managing collaborations, themselves potential primary sources for research. According to him, the management of information consists, of course, of much more than the existence of databases. Systems for locating, organizing and accessing the information are required in a given database. Access to data is restricted by tradition and management is reviewed as a community effort, in most areas of research the original collector retains rights of first access at least until he or she has published results from the data. The same constraints inhere to reading data and integrating them with other datasets. Further he says that quality control over data remains a matter of individual responsibility. Proposals have been advanced for the creation and maintenance of what are known as evaluated databases, in which information has been verified by independent assessment. He mentions the problems of bibliographic databases. Searching databases is currently a task for information specialists. Databases are incomplete, and information of interest to one discipline or problems area may be stored in more than place. Different databases are organized differently, and search methods are idiosyncratic and cannot be generalized. Access to information of all sorts suffers from lack of institutional supports. There is an urgent need in some areas for more efficient forms of data storage.

According to Bhattacharya[5] India's problems lie not

so much in the organizational set up in the government for furthering IT developments, as in the lack of financial resources, the rate of obsolescence of computing equipment, the rate of a standardized system all over the country, and the liability of the communication infrastructure to meet the growing demand from industry and information. Matsumura and Tamika[6] discuss the Japanese information scene in context of today and tomorrow. She discusses the use and production of databases and the mode of use. Hawkins[7] discusses library networking at AT&T, new information needs and technologies in a competitive environment. He states that AT&T faces many new challenges. He describes the effect of the challenges, which are cost sensitivity, increased use of electronic technology, and the development of new information products. He suggests enhancements and improvements to online systems and databases and mentions the requirements for marketing and promotion of in-house services.

Griffith[8] categorizes problems associated with local databases in to 6 types such as:

1. **Managerial:** Question of responsibility for technical and non-technical aspects; user interaction; cost recovery; non-standard working;

2. **Hardware Interconnection:** Non-standard working; lack of advice on which hardware to use, or control of what is obtained;

3. **Software Related:** The same questions as for hardware;

4. **Data Communication:** Inadequate national telecommunications; high tariffs; physical movement of tapes, micro-cassettes and floppy disks;

5. **Micro-Computer Related:** The variety leads to incompatibilities, and there are insufficient skilled staff available;

6. **Marketing Management:** All the services are under-
    used, hence the need for more effort in promotion;
    promote as a total service, i.e. including document
    delivery.

Refining / Fine-tuning the Search

Making the search more specific based on the results

After completing the initial search, read through
any full-text documents and note any aspects of the topic
that user might not have considered. Also make note of
the subject headings or descriptors attached to the
results. User might be able to use these for further
searches. If user gets too many results from the search,
try limiting it in some way. User can restrict a search to a
certain range of dates or try a different type of search
(Boolean, natural language, proximity operators).

Auld[9] points out two major barriers to the use of
electronic delivery have been cost and ease of use.
Technology has advanced sufficiently to remove some of
the ease-of-use barriers and has certainly had an impact
on the cost factor. Clark[10] shares that unfortunately
structural deficiencies both in the mineral industry and
in data available have seriously impeded the development
of both the required data files and the information
systems. A partial resolution of the major problems
resulting from inadequate mineral resource data is being
to some extent achieved by a large number of specialized
data files being developed by various nations and/or
international organizations. Wateringh[11] states that our
bonds with the large mainframe computers will be
loosened, although we will always continue to use them
for the very large databases. Further he says, it is difficult
to identify the real user needs in information processing.
Therefore, we intend to look out for so-called 'gate-keepers'
in every division of the laboratory, persons with a clear

interest in automation that can advise and stimulate their colleagues in this area. The future of information is much vaguer. An important development i.e., advent of new version of DECO, the Unilever retrieval system, will enable us to setup databases.

Full-text searching

There are two major components that exist in full-text searching (FTS):

* **Indexing Component :** This is responsible for the initial population of the full-text index and the subsequent update of this index when the data in the full-text indexed tables is modified.

* **Query Component :** This accepts a full-text predicate from SQL Server, transforms the predicate into a command tree, and sends the command tree to the Microsoft Search service.

Commonly Used Full-Text Search Terms

A full-text index stores all the full-text words and their locations for a given table. A full-text index must be defined on a base table; it cannot be defined on a view table, a system table, or a temporary table. A full-text index definition includes

* A column that uniquely identifies each row in the table (primary or candidate key) and does not allow NULLs.

* One or more character string columns covered by the index.

Full-text indexes and regular SQL indexes differ in the following ways:

Regular SQL Indexes	Full-text Indexes
* Stored under the control of the database in which they are defined.	* Stored in the file system, but administered through the database.
* Several regular indexes per table are allowed.	* Only one full-text index per table is allowed.

* Updated automatically when the data upon which they are based is inserted, updated, or deleted.	* Addition of data to full-text indexes, called a population, can be requested through either a schedule or a specific request, or can occur automatically with the addition of new data.
* Not grouped.	* Grouped within the same database into one or more full-text catalogs.
* Created and dropped using SQL Server Enterprise Manager, wizards, or Transact-SQL statements.	* Created, managed, and dropped using SQL Server Enterprise Manager, wizards, or stored procedures.

Full-text indexes are contained in full-text catalogs. A catalog cannot belong to multiple databases and each catalog can contain full-text indexes for one or more tables.

Population

A population is the addition of data from the full-text indexed table to the full-text index. There are three types of populations:

- **Full Population :** If a full population is requested for a full-text catalog, index entries are built for all the rows in all the tables covered by the catalog. If a full population is requested for a table, index entries are built for all the rows in that table. A full population typically occurs when a catalog or index is first populated; the indexes can then be maintained using change tracking or incremental populations.

* **Change Tracking Population :** Maintains a record of the rows that have been modified in a system table and propagates the changes to the full-text index. When using change tracking, user also

specify when the changes are taken from the history table and populated in the full-text index. (This does not exist in SQL Server 7.0.)

* **Incremental Population :** Only adjusts index entries for rows added, deleted, or modified after the last population. This feature requires that the indexed table has a column of the timestamp data type. If the table does not have a timestamp column, only full or change tracking populations can be performed. Requests for incremental populations on tables without timestamp columns result in a full population operation.

Implementing a Full-Text Search

Implementing FTS in a database involves the following tasks:

1. Identify the tables and columns that are to be registered for FTS.
2. Index the data in the registered columns and populate full-text indexes with the nonextraneous words.
3. Issue queries against the registered columns for populated full-text indexes.
4. Ensure that subsequent changes to the data in registered columns get propagated to the index, thus keeping the full-text index synchronized with the data.

Integration of Distributed Data to Broaden Access and Potential for Discovery

In seeking new knowledge, researchers may gather data from widely disparate sources. A significant advantage arising from the abundance of digitized data now accessible through both private and public networks is the potential for linking data in multiple (even thousands of) databases. The ability to link sites on the World Wide Web is one type of integration that could result in more data being available overall to users. Another is the merging of databases of the same or complementary content. It is now possible to maintain a site with continuously verified links to related information sites for use by subscribers or members of a specific group; an example is the Engineering Village of Engineering Information, Inc. Yet another type of integration occurs in the connection of distributed databases such that different parts of a single large database may reside on different computers in geographically dispersed locations throughout the country or the world. With a common structure, data can be located in a physically distributed network and accessed as if they were in one database in one computer in one location. The cost can thus be distributed and the value of each contributory database increased. Still other databases are automatically created from other databases. For example, data are routinely mined and collected by "knowbots" and "web crawlers" (software employing artificial intelligence and rule-based selection techniques) on the Internet throughout the world and retrieved for processing and further use. One such data-mining activity in the area of biotechnology was described and discussed at the committee's January 1999 workshop.

With a capability to integrate information in multiple databases comes the potential for exploiting relationships identified in the information and developing new knowledge. In many scientific fields, the initial investment by the database rights holder may not produce the greatest value until it is integrated with the investments of others. For example, while protein sequence data are valuable in their own right, their value is greatly enhanced if associated x-ray crystallographic data are also concurrently available. It is possible to use the combined data to understand the way in which protein chains are folded and, in the case of an enzyme, the way in which various nonsequential residues, or even residues on separate protein chains, combine to form an active site.

References

1. Arenas, Judith Licea De. Online Databases and Their Impact on Bibliometric Analysis: The Mexican Health Science Research Case. *International Forum of Information and Documentation,* 18(1), Jan 1993, p 18 -19.

2. Auld, Dennis. Information on Vu/text –an experiment. *Information Services & Use,* 5, 1985, p 107-111.

3. Jarvelin, Kalervo and Niemi, Timo. Simplifying Fact Retrieval through Intermediary Systems: Problems and Requirements. *International Forum of Information & Documentation,* 15(2) April 1990, p 8-15.

4. Clement, J. B. Increasing Research Productivity through Information Technology: A User-Centred Viewpoint. *International Forum of Information & Documentation,* 15(2), April 1990, p 25-31.

5. Bhattacharya, G. Databases and Information Service. IASLIC Bulletin, 34(2), 1989, p 49-58.

6. Auld, Dennis. Information on Vu/text –an experiment. *Information Services & Use,* 5, 1985, p 107-111.Hawkins, Donald T. Information Services & Use, 5, 1985, p 199-206.

7. Judge, Peter J. The Marketing of Information Services- A Regional Workshop and its Context. *International Forum of Information & Documentation,* 9(3), 1984, p 16-20.

8. See 6.

9. Clark, A. L. Mineral Resource Information Systems, *Information Services & Use,* 3, 1983, p17-27.

10. Wateringh, C. van de. From card-tray to resource management: the influence of computing on information processing in a large international company. *Information Services & Use,* 2, 1982, p305-318.

Chapter 6

Growth and Development of Databases

Need of Information Planning

Rajshekhar[1] studies "Production and Utilization of Electronic Databases: Some options and strategies". He states that a database producer has to consider a few primary factors before embarking on any database production such as motivation for database production (in-house use, external use and commercial, not-for-profit or free); target users (customers) and purpose (research, business, market intelligence or document delivery); content of database (subject/target area, information source types to be covered- bibliographic, institutions, experts, full text, image, etc; geographic coverage, volume-both prospective and retrospective, details to be stored in each information item, value addition in terms of indexing, abstracting etc.). Hartevelt[2] states that information management (IM) is divided into administrative or business-related information and subject-related information in his study "Information Management in International Development as an Area for Information Services with a Case in the Field of Health

Care in Ghana". The development and implementation of IM requires cooperation between different areas of expertise. Arguments are presented to justify the positioning of IM activities within an information services department instead of creating a separate staff function, or integrating them at an automation department or an organization department. While discussing Health Management Information System, he says that data classification can be done with the help of databases for diminishing the spent time.

O'Docherty, et. Al.[3] discuss the "design and implementation of a multimedia information system with automatic content retrieval". They say that traditional database use simple types chiefly numbers and strings- to represent information such as payroll records or scientific data. The natural successor to traditional databases are multimedia information system which use richer data types- images, text, sound and so on. They explain an introduction to multimedia information system and related fields and describes in detail a pilot system with automatic content built by the multimedia group at Manchester University. Nagarajan, Sangameswaran and Jain[4] in his study "Distributed DataBases: Plan for Interaction and Online Search" state that India is polyglot country. Different kinds of languages and communication channels are recognized. With the improved techniques of information processing and dissemination, it has been possible to organize data of all kinds, sort them out and computerize them for retrieval. In the rapidly changing environment, the information sought has to be relevant and up to date. Since the information centres are scattered in different parts of the country, there is need to have a linkage system. So for the integration, distributed database system must be applied.

Pratap Lingam[5] in his study "Towards a Methodology for Developing a Mechanism for Business Environmental Scanning" discusses methodology for developing a mechanism for business environmental scanning and points out the place of environmental scanning in the overall corporate or business planning and the need to take environmental factors and main characteristics of environment of industrial concerns which make it more complex and uncertain. To reduce this complexity and uncertainty, an attempt is made to analyze and understand the environment as a continuous process. Auld[6] studies "The future of Database Information Services" and stresses on the technology that due to it the most successful database information services in our industry are those that are vertically integrated. Vertically integration allows the provider to control all levels of the product offering. It has proven to be the best way of capitalizing upon the opportunities presented to us.

Whereas it is important for database publishers to take advantage of cost-saving technology and procedures, their greatest effort has to be aimed at the revenue side. Not only do the technological advancements mention come into play, but the economic, legislative and sociological factors as well. Sociological factors, such as business peoples' acceptance of new methods to access information, stand as the greatest, and most elusive issue to assess.

Need of Indigenous Information

Dosa[7] works on "Technological Development as a Learning Process" and says that information professionals face a wide range of new challenges posed by development plans and strategies. The environment of these challenges varies from isolated rural areas to newly developing countries (NDCs) with intensive trade activity in imports and exports. Industry is involved in a continuous research for and evaluation of foreign technology, a process in which contacts with foreign buyers and sellers are of great importance. At the same time scientists and governments are looking for ways to build domestic R&D

infrastructures, which depend on integration into and communications with the international scientific community. In both scientific and technological development, the utilization is on the rise. The information system in any environment is a form of learning tool. Balancing an organization's policies for the protection of proprietary information with policies for participation in broad development related information services would enhance the organization's role in technology development. It is a mistake to think that enterprises need only technical information for their success. In societies where local participation in development brings indigenous vision, experiences and multiple ethnic perspectives into play, generalized models of innovation may be seen as alien abstractions. Industrial or social innovation can hardly succeed without local adaptation. Case studies of development assistance programs conducted in Asia indicate that the management mode of 'learning' by adjusting to local needs worked well in both the public and private sectors.

Bankapur[8] suggests separate "National Data Bank for the indigenous Farm-Management-Information-Technology". In his study 'Need of National Databank for the Indigenous Farm-Management-Information-Technology, he emphasizes the need to start exclusively and utilization of information ass the coverage of agricultural literature either in Agris database or in "Indian Science Abstract" is not up to the mark.

Indigenous Databases: Importance for National Information Accessibility

Gour[9] shares the address of Prof. M. A. Gopinath as he says that the coverage of Indian interest and about India, are only 15% relevant to India. International standards mean too much of processing. CFTRI in Mysore has developed indigenous databases and has access to foreign databases but the communication process is rendering it difficult. Ranganathan Research Circle for the design of thesaurus, Classaurus students can be absorbed on contract basis. In knowledge mapping and use, many statistical formulas are proving useful. Many relationship and clusters are becoming evident in knowledge mapping and hence fields of specialization are identified. Can we link these results with a design for information system? How LIS techniques are workable though we do research? Publications cost are prohibitive. Research is going on in pattern recognition, subject recognition as applied to the sequences of MCs and BCs. Rajshekhar(1994)[10] says that it is now well accepted that electronic databases hold the key to improving information accessibility – the ease and quickness with which our scholars, technologists, business, trade and industrial establishments can access relevant information. Currently there is a wide gap in the information accessibility of both actual and potential information users in our country compared to those in developed countries. He mentions several factors like social, economic, political and technological responsible for this situation. He emphasizes on two important factors i.e., production of our own databases and improved utilization of existing databases responsible for narrowing this gap. He mentions that production of international databases may be limited to areas where there is no competitive, established, international database. Efforts for national level; database production should come from libraries and information centres operating at national level possessing the required information sources (e. g. INSDOC, DESIDOC, National Medical Library, DBT information centres).

National Database

Singh, and Chaddha[11] talk about creation of a national database on Science and Technology and describe the computerization of Indian Science Abstracts, which will reduce the processing time and bring out the final output on target. It is contemplated to create a machine readable, searchable, national database of Indian Scientific and technical. Zadka[12] discusses databases on environmental and health information systems of Israel. She discusses the model for a national environmental and health databases. A national model for a metadatabase that would legally confirm to confidentiality laws has to take into account the fact that personal databases can be made available to the public only under the restriction that no person can be identified.

According to Tell[13] the national database should collect information about articles in national newspapers and journals, technical reports, government prints, and documentation about on-going projects. He suggests that the database should be established by using international standards, e.g. the common communication format.

He informs about the expected outputs from national databases such as:

1. Application of a common machine-readable bibliographic format
2. An integrated national approach to subject access to information generated in the country by sharing indexing and abstracting functions and exchange of data
3. Bibliographies, indexes, abstracts of documents produced in the country
4. Union catalogue of periodicals
5. SDI or current awareness services

The establishment of a national database is necessary in order to transform and adapt the information that is received from abroad to local needs, there has to be awareness and understanding about what is done and available inside the country itself. For this purpose a national database should be crated, to begin within a chosen priority areas. He suggests the creation of a union

catalogue of periodicals with the help of CDS/ISIS. He
states the participation of other libraries for input of
information in order to locating the periodical. He suggests
the establishment of a national database. In order to
transform and adapt the information, which is received
from abroad to local needs, there has to be awareness
and understanding about what is done and available
inside the country itself. For that a national database
should be created, to begin within a chosen priority basis.
In view of the present high costs of telecommunications
between most developing countries and the countries in
which on-line databases are located, the establishment
of local databases may be worthy of consideration. Such
an approach could possibly offer developing countries a
cost-effective alternative to telecommunication-linked
networks and, perhaps even more importantly, stimulate
the development of certain sectors of a local information
industry. This, for instance, is the approach pursued by
Brazil. Copies of many databases are available on
magnetic tapes, which can be mounted on local
computers. This, possibility may become all the more
suitable as the price of hard ware decreases; but at
present, the cost of large computers capable of handling
a major bibliographic database is still rather high, and
there are very few computer programme that will perform
effective bibliographic searches on small computers.
Another possibility is that of using an existing computer
installation for access to databases, provided that spare
capacity is available. Technical problems may arise as to
the compatibility of the various uses, but nevertheless,
this might be a step towards the gradual introduction of
a locally operated database service.

Lahiri and Singh[14] discuss about the development
of Indian bibliographic databases and networks. They
describe objectives behind development of Indian
databases such as: to organize national or nationally
produced information; to create databases in narrow

subject areas relevant to national socio-economic situation; and to develop indigenous capabilities for databases creation and utilization. Further describing the organization of national information, they inform about the advantages to be gained by the user community and also finance-vise. They explain various features of the Indian National Bibliography, National Union Catalogue of Scientific Serials in India, National Citation Index and Union Catalogue of Social Science Periodicals. While describing the indigenous databases on narrow subject areas, NISSAT programmes are mentioned as new ventures of indigenous databases. They also discuss the problems in developing indigenous databases such as technology and compatibility, standardization, vocabulary control, software standardization and software marketing.

New ventures on Indigenous Databases have emerged. Under the NISSAT programme, a major thrust was given to development of indigenous databases by the sectoral information centres set on machine tools at the central Machine tools institute (CMTI), Banglore, leather at Central Leather Research Institute (CLRI), Chennai, food at Central Food Technology Research Institute (CFTRI), Mysore, drugs and pharmaceuticals at Central Drug Research Institute (CDRI), Lucknow, textiles at Ahmedabad Textiles Industry Research Association (ATIRA), Ahmedabad, chemicals at National Chemical Laboratory, Pune, on advanced ceramics at Central Glass and Ceramics Research Institute (CGCRI), Kolkata. The objectives have been such as, to dwell on areas for which in-depth treatment is lacking in global databases. For example, realizing that the COMPENDEX does not adequately cover machine tools information. CMTI has started the creation of a bibliographical database covering periodical articles, books, reports, etc. It has now about 50000 records, and the database is steadily growing, to cull out information from the existing databases, supplement these with Indian Information, and create a product- specific database. For example, a product 'leather' demands handling from multidisciplinary angles. A comprehensive database is also not available internationally. It is in this context that the Leather Science Abstract (LESA) endeavours in CLRI assume greater importance and to create databases for areas in which local information has the more importance over the international information. For example, there is no dearth of databases on textile. However, these are heavily oriented towards machine handling of cotton, its derivatives and synthetics. Where as, in the Indian context, the handloom sector has overwhelming importance. Besides, natural fibers like jute tends to get overlooked in international database at ATIRA are therefore obvious.

Databases

Singh[15] mentions that IIT Kharagpur, library had created databases for books, bound volumes of periodicals, current periodicals, reports, theses/dissertations, and microfilms/microfiches. Under house keeping jobs, the library is using computer for acquisition, circulation etc. Library databases are accessible through IIT/LAN and WAN. Tanabe[16] gives details of "JOINT" which is a significant database on Japanese economic and business information. She discusses the JOINT Index Magazine and discusses various challenges in the information industry. Ramachandran[17] advocates the creation and updating of databases and making them accessible to not only experts but also common users. Tell[18] discusses paperless communication. He mentions the current status of database development and says the one specific feature of database is that we need four factors to characterize them. These factors are to a great extent independent of each other that are producers; users; contents; and types. Lupovici[19] discusses a full electronic information system at INIST. He discusses various aspects of PASCAL database, its multidisciplinary, general and multilingual nature and qualities. He reflects document delivery service, including collections, digitization and digital storage, automated order management system, electronic document delivery. He discusses further copyright problem and AGADES, an integrated information system.

Tiamiyu[20] discusses about the pragmatics of developing information resource management system in government organizations in developing countries. Hossain[21] emphasizes the importance of on-line databases in the age of scientific literary explosion. He attempts to show the application of on-line in the field of mathematical literature-search. He explains that most representative databases are searchable on-line which cover mathematical subject in terms of their on-line versions. Dugal and Brown[22] present a brief description of the Institute of Paper Chemistry (IPC), and a more detailed account of three of its Information Services Division groups: Library, Editorial & Publications, Abstracting-Indexing in their study "The Future of a small technical database". There follows a discussion of IPC's reasons for automating its abstracting-indexing operations. They outline the factors, which have a bearing on the success-and even on the survival-of a small database. One of these is size itself, since the larger producer can more easily adapt to changing circumstances. Quality, appropriate coverage and convenience are important properties of a file, certainly so for as users are concerned today. The authors' list certain 'negative influences' against which a small database must contend, and conclude with a presentation of the priorities enunciated by the recently formed Paperchem users' group. They discuss the database automation and survival in IPC. They discuss the database management and importance of vocabulary control in database.

Liddle[23] states that digital patent database is the

major component affecting the system architecture. It will contain two types of data; text or character data, and image or facsimile data. Further he mentions that commercial databases will continue to be used and will be accessible through the system but there are no plans to duplicate any of these databases which are accessed via commercial systems, such as the chemical registry, scientific and technical abstract, and similar databases by patent examiners. Lucker (1985)[24] informs about a recent innovation that has been the utilization of computerized databases as a routine function in reference and information services. Computer terminals have been located at reference and information desks in all major library units and librarians utilize them to respond to information requests ranging from specific facts to bibliographic citations, from citation verification to printouts of brief bibliographies. Further he mentions that among the functions expected to be provided by the libraries are: access to the online catalogue with search capability by author, title, subject and keyword; document delivery of books, reports, journal articles, etc. using the network as an electronic mail system; an online reference network whereby patrons can send queries to the librarians that will be routed to the appropriate staff member; access to external sources of information including bibliographic and numerical databases. One of the potential long-range benefits of such a system will be the ability to identify, and to make available, locally created data files. The library's role as identifier, cataloguer, and communicator of availability of such information becomes a natural extension of traditional and newly evolving responsibilities of research libraries. She further states that research libraries play an essential role in the dissemination of information, both bibliographic and numerical, including acquisition, processing, cataloguing, retrieval, and document delivery. Most of these functions have been affected dramatically by the application of computer and other technology. Various printed tools and online services in genetic engineering and biotechnology are available to research libraries. The retrieval of periodical literature from print and online services is an essential aspect of bibliographic control. He says that Massachusetts Institute of Technology library services have evolved in the light of new technology, and will continue to change and the libraries become as integral part of an evolving campus-wide computer and information network. Ramanenko(1982)[25] discusses the INIS database, its brief history of development and type of database as distributed database.

Growth and Development of Databases

Rashid[26] discusses the application of CD-ROM technology in database development. He discusses the advantages of CD-ROM databases over to online databases. He says that there was the opportunity with CD-ROM to offer users a database on a yearly subscription basis, which then gave the chance to use it as much as they wished without incurring any cost. He shares the application of CD-ROM to developing countries. According to him, although some criticism has been leveled at the currency of the databases on CD-ROM, they are in fact a considerable improvement on the printed versions of indexes and abstracts, which are usually sent overseas. He emphasizes that some CD-ROM databases offered, have been a selection of databases, which together try to address the total subject requirements of specific group of users by giving example of OSHROM file from Silver Platter.

Database Society of India (DSI)[27] has been formed with the following main objective:

1. To develop a National Policy for India on database development and distribution;

2.   To plan and identify the areas for developing database in India;

3.   To promote and train database manpower in the areas of systems development, information analysis, quality control and data distribution. The headquarters of DSI shall be located at Bangalore, with local chapters in major Indian cities.

McFadden and Hoffer[28] discuss that many observers of trends in business believe that the organizations that will excel with the help of databases. The databases have become the standard technique for structuring and managing data in most organizations today. Database management is designed as an introductory course on the subject. Such a course is usually required as part of an information systems curriculum in business schools, computer technology programmes and applied computer science departments. Design and use of databases have been stressed in meeting the business information needs. Tell[29] estimates that in the world, foremost in the US and Europe, there are around 3,000 databases of open access by means of terminals and telecommunications. The number of bibliographic databases is now growing slowly; instead the non-bibliographic databases containing data are increasing rapidly. Data, as usually understood in physics and chemistry, are numerical representation of the magnitudes of various quantities. If we further include basic qualitative data, i.e. specific, but non-numerical scientific facts, such as the chemical and geometrical structures of molecules, it is not unrealistic to say that "data" make up a substantial and important fraction of scientific knowledge. Further he compares the properties of printed and displayed information. According to him, the main positive features of printed information are agreeable presentation, legibility, portability, reading comfort, and the possibility of surveying a number of documents simultaneously. On the other hand, the strength of computerized system is information handling.

Remote access by users simultaneously, and intelligent help support to the user.

Quinn[30] discusses the Australian and New Zealand databases in 1988. She discusses the survey carried out during 1987/88 in Australia and New Zealand. She presents data on the characteristics of databases, their producers and vendors, access costs, subject's coverage, and associated publications and products. Sathyanaraya[31] states the growth of databases and impact on drug and pharmaceuticals. Bandyopadhyay[32] tells some steps to be followed to design an information system. Cuadra[33] discussed about Growth in online databases, which throws light upon the use of online databases. The number of online databases available to the public has grown more than 500% in the past 5 years. Nearly three new databases are being added every business day. According to King Research[34] Inc., development in communication and education are enormous and continually progressing. Keenan[35] discusses that a logical development is the production of hybrid databases that combine the bibliographic record with data contained in the original document, together with indexing, abstracting and classification. In effect, these files combine factual information and data from the original document coupled with the bibliographic references. This means that the information worker will have the conventional elements in the machine-based record such as bibliographic record, index terms and classification codes together with factual data, table, graphs, and illustrations. With the increasing number of data banks available, the information worker is increasing use of software packages, which allow for computerization and manipulation of data.

Man Power and Development

Chakrabarty[36] analyses the demand for library and information workers during 1988 as advertised in five national dailies. He stresses the need for training suitable manpower by laying greater emphasis on information technology and information management to meet present day needs. Pitroda[37] stresses on manpower as an important asset to India which must be put to maximum utilization. Working Group on Information and Library Network, UGC, New Delhi[38] proposed that database of projects/institutions/specialists in an integrated information system. Besides handling bibliographic information, there should also cover non-bibliographic information about ongoing and completed projects related with Information and Library Network (INFLIBNET).

Kemparaju[39] identifies and throws focus on the trends in the job market for library and information manpower in special library and information sector. He analyses Trends in Manpower Development in Special Library and Information Centres in India pragmatically. He analyzes and scans the advertisements from leading national English newspapers and compiles to consider trends in manpower requirements and presents with different manifestations. He identifies number of anomalies and projects by comparative observation of different aspects. The data is viewed in relation with the job market and the present curriculum and also considered to bring out compatibility between job requirements and course contents. The programmes of placements and liaison with prospective employers are suggested to bring amendments to lack of proper job descriptions. Courrier[40]discusses the problems connected with training in the use of the new technologies. He says, as in many fields, training in information science raises acute problems in most developing countries have reliable institutions which provide university-level training, and are now beginning to produce a body of skilled professions. But they are not in majority. The second difficulty derives from the quantitative and qualitative evaluation of training needs. Some developed countries have still not found an answer to the basic question of

who are the potential employers of the specialists being
trained. He suggests that attention should be paid to the
institutional aspects of information services. It is true
that in many situations, large and expensive information
technology equipment with potential use in major national
and university libraries and national documentation
centres are out of reach; training should therefore be
adapted to such situations. He discusses last problem of
the level of training sought. Needs are immensely varied.
Prospective candidates may have acquired experience on
the job; they may have been trained in university, either
recently or some times ago; or they may be specialists
trained in the best schools of the developed countries.

Training Strategies

Courrier[41] mentions various training strategies such
as;

1. A tradition of awarding fellowships for high-level
    training with a recognized status in developed
    countries.
2. Ad Hoc international courses of limited duration at
    UNESCO.
3. Traveling course

He tells the advantage of the second strategy that
the human and material resources of a developed country
are made available to students from developing countries
for specific subjects at less cost than by awarding
fellowships.

Online Information, Databases and Gateways

Nederhof[42] works on delimitation of a medical
research topic: A comparison of Online Databases and
shows that online databases may differ substantially in
the coverage of literature. Sayers and Bawden[43] compared
six databases on the retrieval of review articles in a
biomedical area. Only two of the six databases allowed

retrieved of more than 50% of the relevant material. Boykheva[44] talks upon Online Access to Japanese information in engineering comparative analysis of the JICST-E, INSPEC and COMPENDEX databases and presented them as information sources for Japanese documents in engineering. Six search topics representing the most advanced engineering fields in Japan are used in this study. The 1977 references retrieved from the three databases are analyzed for contribution to each database and duplication of references of journal articles. Also the speed of bringing online the references of Japanese scientific and technical documents in engineering is compared.

Arenas[45] finds in varied results in a comparison of bibliographic and citation databases those measured bibliometrically Mexican health sciences research in her study "Online Databases and Their Impact on Bibliometric Analysis: The Mexican Health Science Research Case". She states different types of setting in emergence and accessibility of online databases. She recommends cautions when attempting bibliometric studies, since databases serve different purposes and have different objective. Bibliographic databases may say something about the scientific effort of entities being assessed but citation databases highlight mainstream research, hence the need to combine publication counts with other partial indicators, such as citation counts. Panda[46] discusses some basic issues about online databases and provides an insight into how online databases brings numerous advantages than printed counterparts. He highlights some of the basic issues relating to Online database which include its growth and development; conceptual framework; classification; steps involved; searching device; supporting technologies; merits and pitfalls from user's standpoint. It shows that the inherent limitations possessed by the conventional IR system and printed indexes can be minimized, if not eradicated by online system. It puts together the results of some of the recent published studies on the various aspects of online databases. Dou, et. al.[47] discuss advanced interface to analyze the automatically online databases set of answers. They say that the use of database, which contains an increasing number of references leads to a new concept in online retrieval. Because the number of answers increases with time.

Rao[48] discusses the online bibliographic services in academic libraries and said that with the accelerating growth of information produced by research, it has become necessary to evolve ways to retrieve the required information successfully and speedily. Online services help users to search large bibliographic databases and retrieve relevant information within minutes. These services are of immense importance in academic libraries, in, serving the needs of faculty, researchers, and other scholars. Cuadra[49]discusses various aspects of the directory of databases through international online services and gateways such as its accurate and comprehensive coverage, use and accessibility, display of access points, updating online version and other else. He discusses access to online information especially Japanese Business Information in his study in various segments such as increase in online databases covering Japan, how English language is playing role, New and Defunct databases etc.

Cuadra[50] discusses online databases and services. How growth slow down and how new gateways emerged, have been discussed. He gives an year-vise account of growth of online databases. Marx[51] works on the 'Online databases'. He also discussed 52% of the databases are factual ones, 35% are only bibliographic, which are more frequent in mathematics, physics and equal to other types in materials science. According to him in other fields factual data are more frequently produced: Numeric data for chemistry, textual, numeric for bio and medicine.

Directory type data are more frequent for databases in progress in the life sciences and earth, ocean, and space sciences.

Role of Govtenrment

Kaula[52] says that dissemination and conservation of the work of foreign scholars on Indian thought require the establishment of the National Book Museum, role of government is important while developing and networking of databases, Networking and government efforts are necessary

Role and Importance of Databases

Databases[53] emerged as early as the 1960's for solving management problems in various types of enterprise and organization. Their sphere of application soon extended, however to cover other tasks, in particular, data storage and handling in science and technology. In the future, with the emergence of an international computerized information milieu and improvement of the methods for data analysis and processing, such systems will constitute an important addition to the conventional means and forms of information exchange, such as books, periodicals, etc. The use of databases allows the user to receive the same information as was previously accessible by conventional means, but in a more efficient way faster, fuller and more convenient, e.g., along with a communication line on to a personal computer display. In addition, databases provide opportunities for new kinds of services that did not exist previously. These include complex processing of large sets of data and the communication of the results of such processing to any user in the most convenient form.

Goswami[54] informs about the application and importance of databases in the library services in his study 'Application Information Technology in Library Services'. Siddiqui[55] states that in every academic institution it is essential to acquaint the users with the collection available in it. Due to explosion of knowledge, increasing number of users and higher levels of research on complex topics it is obligatory on the part of library personnel to regulate satisfaction of its users. Vijayakumar and Das[56] discuss the aspects of application of DVD technology in electronic publishing of reference sources and databases. According to them, there is a trend towards publishing reference sources and bibliographic databases in DVD format instead of CD-ROM. Due to its high storage capacity of 17 GB, high quality of data, diminishing price etc. libraries and database publishers will favor this technology very soon. The main factors holding DVD back is the delayed availability of DVD drives, trend towards online and lack of standardization in this technology. They mention the library application of this new technology in areas such as large full-text database, mixed database, quick reference database, high quality multimedia help, archival purposes, cost effective mass storage for networking and training application. Samal and Gupta[189] provide an overview of CD-ROM POPLINE in their study 'Use of CD-ROM POPLINE Database in NIHFW'. They describe some aspects of use of the CD-ROM POPLINE maintained by John Hopkins University in the light of the experience and exposure gained of the National Documentation Center of the National Institute of Health and Family Welfare, New Delhi, India. This database is a tool to provide immediate and urgent specific answers to queries from the functionaries, agencies and research scholars in the field of population studies and related aspects. Further they state the importance of CD-ROM technology. According to them, it has become a viable medium for the distribution of data. Due to the qualities of it, here is a tremendous growth in user demand and production of CD-ROMs.

      Pinelli et. al.[57] study the electronic transfer of

information and aerospace knowledge diffusion. According to them, increasing reliance and investment in information technology and electronic networking systems presupposes that computing and information technology will play a major role in the diffusion of aerospace knowledge. Little is known, however, about actual information technology needs, uses, and problems within the aerospace knowledge diffusion process. The authors state that the potential contributions of information technology to increased productivity and competitiveness will be diminished unless empirically derived knowledge regarding the information-seeking behavior of the members of the social system-those who are producing, transferring, and using scientific and technical information-is incorporated into a new technology policy framework. Research into use of information technology and electronic networks by U. S. aerospace engineers and scientists, collected as part of a research project designed to study aerospace knowledge diffusion, is presented in support of this assertion. Further state that both in-house and commercial databases are used in connection of networking for information retrieval. The rate of use for maturing technologies (e.g., electronic databases) was relatively high.

Weiske[58] discusses the use and popularity of databases for chemistry information in West Germany. Khan and Carroll[59] discuss the role of NTIS in acquisition and dissemination of industrial and technological information. He informs about the handling of information and databases as bibliographical information, once input to the NTIS database, remains accessible almost 24 hours a day through a variety of database distributors, such as DIALOG and BRS. Sathyanaraya[60] discusses the impact of information technology on drugs and pharmaceutical information systems. He states the growth of databases and impact on drug and pharmaceuticals. Further he discusses the online access to these databases. Operating philosophy of an online system such as:

1. Instant access: Calling the services whenever it is required.
2. Pay by use: No need to own the information source, pay only when it is used and for what is used.
3. Interactive: Establishing a dialogue with the system, put questions, get answers. Based on answer received, refine or redefine your questions.
4. User-friendly: Major thrust on making the system comfortable for users.

Large[61] discusses downloading data from online searches and the ways in which such data can be re-used. He looks in particular at the re-use of downloaded records in local databases. One software package "FILTER" has been examined which reformats records and which can be used to convert records downloaded from an online search into a format suitable for an in-house database. He mentions that in a short period of time, downloading from bibliographic and later full-text and numerical, databases passed from being a rare event to an everyday occurrence in many organizations. This is explained by three developments: the appearance of cheap and relatively powerful microcomputers with increasingly large backing stores; higher data transmission speeds; and a growth in the number of bibliographic databases. Howell[62] states that the concept of creating database is a good one. His study indicates the IDRC program is not only practical but also that it is perhaps the only way that a large data base of citations and abstracts of development literature on the Third World might be created that is, first building the file at the national level, then transferring the data to the regional and international level as it is needed. This approach is confirmed by the findings in the study, which indicates that Morocco has a distinct development profile, traceable in the citations that appear in both small databases devoted to development literature and large

databases that only incidentally include development
literature. The future studies might concentrate on the
merging of online files from various sources, national,
international to produce a single file of each developing
country. The creation of such a file would require the co-
operation of managers of commercial databases, as well
as the help of officials of both the national and
international level Wood and Smith[63] says that scientific
databases are proving to be cost-effective research tools
for scientists, engineers and technicians due to their
capability and benefits. Their ready online availability with
standard terminals and telecommunication channels,
combined with their ease if use is making accessibility
progressively easier both nationally and internationally.
Jones[64] discusses the citizen's rights to information and
the role of Government. She says that the core of the
challenge confronting us is to create the information
resources and delivery systems dedicated to the principal
information needs of citizens and consumers. Only then
we can determine the exact extent to which these new
technologies can best serve these needs. In order to do
this we actually need to develop specific data bases geared
to the most important information needs of citizens and
consumers, and we need to develop demonstration models
of how communities can use the new technologies to link
the citizen/consumers with the existing community
services already available to serve them. Many of the
databases required to meet the information needs of
consumers simply do not exist.

Thorpe[65] discusses the problems, developments and
prospects of agricultural information services for the third
world. He emphasizes the assistance through databases
that database can be divided into a number of separate
bulletins. SDI services are offered through databases and
this is another way in which the database may be broken
up into smaller sections more relevant to a specialized
centre's needs. Most international services are now able

to supply machine-readable versions of their databases on magnetic tape. Further he states the help from database publisher in ways such as inclusion of informative abstracts in the publication and provision of a document delivery or photocopying service. He discusses the importance of databases while mentioning CAB databases in agriculture field.

References

1. Rajashekhar, T.B. Production and Utilization of Electronic Databases: Some options and strategies. *International Information Communication and Education*, 13(2); 1994; p 181-191.

2. Hartevelt, J.H.W. Van. Information Management in International Development as an Area for Information Services with a Case in the Field of Health Care in Ghana. *International Forum of Information and Documentation*, 18(3-4), Oct 1993, p 32-37.

2a O'Docherty, M.H. et. Al. The design and implementation of a multimedia information system with automatic content retrieval. *Information Services & Use*, 11, 1991, p 345-385.

3 Nagarajan, S., Sangameswaran, S. V. and Jain, H. C. (Ed.). Distributed DataBases: Plan for Interaction and Online Search. New Delhi: Informatics Publications, 1989.

4 Pratap Lingam, P. Towards a Methodology for Developing a Mechanism for Business Environmental Scanning. *IASLIC Bulletin* 31(3), 1986, p 83-96.

5 Auld, Dennis. The future of Database Information Services. *Information Services & Use*, 3, 1983, p 11-15.

6 Dosa, Marta. Technological Development as a Learning Process. *International Information, Communication and Education*, 13(2), Sept 1994, p 162-170.

7 Bankapur, M. B. Need of National Data Bank for the Indigenous Farm-Management-Information-Technology. *IASLIC Bulletin* 31(4), 1986, p 177-182.

8 Gour. Prof. M. A. Gopinath's Address. Ranganathan Research Circle. *Herald of Library Science*, 34(1-2), January-April, 1995, p 83.

9 See 1.

10 Singh, Hukum and Chaddha, O.N. Towards Creation of a National Database on Science and Technology. *Annals of*

Library Science and Documentation, 37(1), 1990, p 20-27.

11   Zadka, Pnina. Environmental and health information systems: Israel. *Information Services & Use,* 10, 1990, p 243-250.

12   Tell, Bjorn. Implementation and Maintenance of Information System. *International Information, Communication and Education,* 9(1), March 1989, p 5-18.

13   Lahiri, Abhijit and Singh, B.G. Sunder. Bibliographic Databases and Networks. *International Information; Communication and Education,* 8(1), March 1988, p 79-105.

14   Singh, S. P. Collection Development and Reader's Services at IIT Library (Khraragpur): User's Assessment. *IASLIC Bulletin,* 44(3), 1999, p 97-110.

15   Tanabe, Noriaki. JOINT: Significant Database on Japanese Economic and Business Information. *International Information, Communication and Education,* 15(1), March 1996, p 95-98.

16   Murthy, S S. International Conference on Bibliographic Databases and Networks, *International Information, Communication and Education,* 9(1), March 1990, p104-106.

17   Tell, Jorn B. Paperless Communication. *International Information, Communication and Education,* 9(2), Sept. 1990, p156-163.

18   Lupovici, Christian. Towards a full electronic information system at INIST. *Information Services & Use,* 15, 1995, p 229-236.

19   Tiamiyu, Mutawakilu Adisa. Pragmatics of Developing Information Resource Management Systems in Government Organizations in Developing Countries. *International Information, Communication and Education,* 12(2), Sept 1993, p 201-212.

20   Hossain, Kazi Kabir. Online Databases for Mathematical Literature. *IIASLIC Bulletin* 31(2), 1986, p 51-54.

21   Dugal, H. S. and Brown, C. L. The future of a small technical data base. *Information Services & Use,* 5, 1985, p 157-165.

22   Liddle, L. Patent Information System. *Information Services & Use,* 5, 1985, p 113-119.

23   Lucker, Jay. K. Research Libraries and the Dissemination of Information in Genetic Engineering and Biotechnology. *Information Services & Use,* 5, 1985, p131-142.

24   Ramanenko, A.G. *International Information, Communication and Education,* 1(1), March 1982, p 85-92.

25   Rashid, Abdul. Application of CD-ROM Technology. *International Information, Communication and Education,* *14*(1), March 1995. p 15-31.

26   Database Society of India. Notes and News. *Herald of Library Science,* 34(1-2), January-April 1995, p 171.

27   McFadden, Fred R. and Hoffer, Jeffrey A. Database Management. 3rd ed. CA: Benjamin/Cummings Publishing Co., 1991.

28   See 18.

29   Quinn, Sherry. Australian and New Zealand databases in 1988. *Information Services & Use,* 9, 1989, p 3-14.

30   Sathyanarayana, N. V. Impact of Information Technology on drug and Pharmaceutical Information System. *International Information, communication and Education,* 7(2), Sept. 1988, p 148-154.

31   Bandiupadhaya, N. Designing an Information System *International Information, Communication and Education,* 6(2), Sept. 1987, p 177-185.

32   Cuadra, C.A. Growth in Online Databases. *International Information Communication and Education,* 14 (2), 1985, p 179-180.

33   King Research Institute. Development in Communication and Education. *International Information, Communication and Education,* 14(2), 1985, p 173-176.

34   Keenan, Stella. Re-use and repackaging of Information: the Information Worker's View. *Information Services & Use,* 3, 1983, p1-6.

35   hakrabarty, Bipul Kumar. Information Manpower- Strategic Issues for Development. *IASLIC Bulletin,* 38(2), 1993, p 67-72.

36   Murthy, S S. International Conference on Bibliographic Databases and Networks. *International Forum of Information and Documentation,* 9(1), March 1990, p104-106.

37   A Summary of the Report of the Inter Agency Working Group. *International Forum of Information and Documentation,* 9(1), March 1990, p 68-96.

38   Kemparaju, T. D. A Pragmatic Analysis of Trends in Manpower Development in Special Library and Information Centres in India. *IASLIC Bulletin,* 33(2/3), 1988, p 45-51.

39   Courrier, Yves. Information Technology Training Needs, Strategies and Objectives for the Developing Countries.

International Forum of Information & Documentation, 12(3), July 1987, p 32-37.

40   See 47.

41   Nederhof, A.J. Delimitation of a Medical Research Topic: A Comparison of Online Databases. *IASLIC Bulletin,* 13(1), 1994, p 14-22.

42   Sayers, W. and Bawden, L. Information retrieval in databases. *Information Services & Use,* 4, 1984, p 11-16.

43   Boykheva, I. Online Access to Japanese Information in Engineering: Comparative Analysis of the JICST-E, INSPEC, and COMPENDEX Databases. *Information Services and Use,* 14, 1994, p 25-35.

44   Arenas, Judith Licea De. Online Databases and Their Impact on Bibliometric Analysis: The Mexican Health Science Research Case. *International Forum of Information and Documentation,* 18(1), Jan 1993, p 18 -19.

45   Panda, Krishna C. Online Database: Some Basic Issues. *National Policies and Programmes. IASLIC, p. 57-70.*

46   Dou, Henry, Hassanaly, Parina, Tela, La Albert and Quoniam, Luc. Advanced interface to analyze the automatically online databases set of answers. *Information Services & Use,* 10, 1990, p 135-145.

47   Rao, D.N. Online Bibliographic Services in Academic Libraries. *Lucknow Librarian,* 21(1), 1989, p 11-14.

48   Cuadra, Carlos. Expansion of Access to Online Japanese Business information. *International Information, Communication and Education,* 8(1), Mach 1989, p 117-132.

49   Cuadra, Carlos. Online Databases and Services. *International Information, Communication and Education,* 7(1), 1988, p 92-102.

50   Marx, Bernard. Online Databases. *Information Services,* 7(1), 1987, p 77-83.

51   Kaula, P. N. Dissemination and Conservation of the Work of Foreign Scholars on Indian Thought and The Need for Establishment of the National Book Museum. *International Information, Communication and Education,* 17(1), March 1998, p 18-26.

52   Rumble, J. R. and Hampel, V. E. (ed.). Database Management in Science and Technology. A CODATA Source Book on the Use of Computers in Data Activities. New York: Oxford, 1984.

53   [oswami, Anjana. Application of Information Technology in

Library Service. *Herald of Library Science*, 40(1-2), 2001, p 36-42.

54 Siddiqui, Asif Fareed. Use of Library Collection in the Jawahar Lal Nehru University Library, New Delhi. *IASLIC Bulletin* 46(4), 2001, p 184-196.

55 Vijayakumar, J. K. and Das, Manju. CD-ROM to DVD-ROM: a new era in electronic publishing of Databases and Multimedia Reference Sources. *IASLIC Bulletin,* 45(2), 2000, p 49-54.

56 Samal, P. K. Gupta, Sangeeta. Use of CD-ROM Popline Database in NIHFW: A case study. *IASLIC Bulletin,* 39(3), 1994, p 125-127.

57 Pinelli, Thomas E., Bishop, Ann P., Barley, Rebecca O. And Kennedy, John M. The Electronic Transfer of Information and Aerospace Knowledge Diffusion. *International Forum of Information & Documentation,* 17(4), Oct 1992, p 8-16.

58 Weiske, Christian. Chemistry Information in West Germany. *Information Services & Use,* 11, 1991, p 23-31.

59 Khan, Rahaman A. and Carroll, Bonnie C. Industrial and Technological Information: The Role of NTIS in Acquisition and Dissemination. *International Information, Communication and Education,* 9(2), Sept. 1990, p 139-152.

60 See 31.

61 Large, J. A. The Re-Use of Online Information. *International Forum of Information & Documentation,* 13(4) Oct. 1988, p 18-25.

62 Howell, John Bruce. Online databases as Source for the literature on Developing Countries. *International Forum of Information and Documentation,* 11(2), April 1986, p22-34.

63 Wood, Gordon H. and Smith, Elmer V. Scientific Numeric Databases: Their Useful and Accessibility. *International Forum of Information and Documentation,* 11(4), Oct. 1986, p3-9.

64 Jones, Mary Gardiner. Citizens' Rights to Information: the Role of Government. *Information Services & Use,* 5, 1985, p37-47.

Chapter 7
Linguistics in Databases

Neelameghan[1] discussed an online glossary for a multilingual database and the use of terms of non-English language transliterated into Latin script in the database and by users of the database in this search expression. The need for provision of vocabulary aids to assist users is mentioned and describes an online glossary and its use while pre-using records retrieved from the database. ECHO[2], the European Commission Host Organization offers Greek Enquirer the possibility to access a number of databases in Greek. Receiving text from data network in non-Latin characters requires some modification of the normal procedure. ECHO is providing a separate Network User Address (NUA) for special linguistic character sets.

Indexing in Databases

Minecci, and Hodge[3] mention the BIOSIS' approach to machine-aided indexing is detailed from a production point of view. In their study 'Machine-sided indexing: productivity and organizational implications' emphasize upon computer support for indexers and on problems encountered with this approach. They explore future consideration, particularly an interactive online system for indexers. They discuss the potential impacts of such a system on training, indexing, quality control and the indexers themselves, as well as other organizational concerns and possible benefits. They mention that natural language terms are the most keywörds and phrases in the BIOSIS database. While explaining the comforting staff with online activities, use of PREVIEWS database for solving indexing problems has been discussed. They emphasize on improving the relevancy of the scientific content of indexed and databases for supporting online indexing.

Validity and Improvement of Data

Granick[4] discusses assuring the quality of information dissemination and responsibilities of database producers. He compares the database producers' responsibilities for the quality (self-defined) of their products and their responsibilities to the user community and a new quality scale (other–defined). Among the responsibilities of producers are what users want; consistency; coverage/scope; timeliness; accuracy/error rate; accessibility/ease of use; integration; output; documentation/customer support and training and guidelines by database type. Briggs[5] discusses the data improvement in his study "Establishing an environmental information system for the European Community", the experience of the CORINE Programme. According to him the need is to improve the supply of new environmental data; and to improve the consistency of the data, which already exist. Cuadra[6] discusses better text management. He says that selecting a software package for in-house management of text databases can be difficult and downright scary. He discusses the specialties about handling text in databases such as data validities, repeating fields, automatic indexing, text searching features, management tools, and generating reports for text databases etc.

Tuomisto and Savolainen[7] discuss the background

information. They examine the database of Finland that they are limited in accuracy, scope, and availability. Voigt, Benz and Matthies[8] discuss the need of improved information system in their study "Information system on environmental chemicals: databank of data sources for environmental chemicals. Graham[9] questions the quality of databases. He discuss the rating of online databases for quality, both of the product and of the structure of database itself. He says that files are updated but none checks to ensure that every bit is loaded. He gives importance to ways for organizations of users to develop ongoing system of checks and feedback to database producers and vendors. He further questions validated data. Clark[10] states that separate and apart from the problem of insufficient data, which may reflect either lack of collection or simply that the data are not available for a variety of other reasons, is the problem of validity of the data that do exist. Few if any problems relative to data exchange are as complex as or more difficult to resolve than ascertaining the validity of the data within an exchange program.

Updating Information in Databases

Information Access Company (IAC)[11] assures its newsletter databases updating daily to provide current and most updated information. Complete Newsletter Database now Available LEXIS-NEXIS Services. UNIDO[12] has updated its database of Industrial Statistics. Schmidt[13] states that frequency of updates as well as Nature and frequency of use are the deciding factor. Frequent updates eliminate CD-ROM as a practical medium as does its show response time. King Research Inc[14] mentions about the interest have been taken in updating and improving upon the assessment of the value of energy information services and products and in learning about:

1. The effect comprehensiveness of the energy databases has on value of energy information
2. The effect timeliness of primary and secondary information has own value of energy information
3. The contribution that intermediary services such as libraries and information analysis centers make to the value of energy information.

Searching of Databases

Thandavamoorthy and Kumar[15] discuss the quality in digital information retrieval. They inform about the importance of OPACs in using the databases. They say that users will have the facility to access the library housekeeping operations; especially circulation facility and it will also facilitate the users to access the machine-readable bibliographic database of the library directly. According to Schmidt[16], access mode for CD-ROM versus online is a critical issue. Rajshekhar[17] discusses that a database may be delivered in one of the two forms such as flat file consisting of a sequence of records or packaged form, accompanied by retrieval software. The first form is useful if the database purchaser is interested in uploading the information into a database that already exists on a computer. Flat files can also be conveniently delivered over using e-mail and using more powerful file transfer protocols. In second form, information items are organized into searchable database files and delivered on media like diskettes and CD-ROM, along with search and retrieval software. Further he says that a major cost factor in producing such packaged databases is the retrieval software which may be internally developed or a third party, proprietary software which will involve payment of royalty for every copy of the database supplied.

Boni, Geiss and Penning[18] discuss the ECDIN database for chemicals in the environment. They inform about the users of database (world wide) due to its online availability. Jarvelin, and Niemi[19] discuss the problems of fact retrieval form modern distributed and heterogeneous fact databases. In order to simplify retrieval, analogous to those for bibliographic retrieval, is needed. An imaginary example of distributed fact retrieval process, based on current tools and systems, is analyzed in order to clarify the requirements of such an intermediary system. They have described the retrieval process as supported by as intermediary system for fact retrieval and the properties of such a system. They have introduced key problems in and approaches to the simplification of fact retrieval.

Linguistics and Full-text searching

The full-text searching (FTS) allows user to retrieve specific text data from columns in a database. It does this by first indexing those columns, and then providing user the ability to query the indexes that were created. User may now be asking, Why can't I use the LIKE T-SQL predicate to do this? Well, the FTS feature gives user the following advantages over the LIKE predicate:

* *With FTS user can perform a linguistic search of character data.* A linguistic search can operate on words and phrases unlike a LIKE predicate.

* *With FTS user can weigh how well the results that are returned rank in comparison to the original search condition.* This is not possible with a LIKE predicate because it only returns the results that contain the query term.

* *With FTS user can remove noise words (such as "and," "or," etc.) from the search criteria.* This makes the search more effective, and it is not possible with the LIKE predicate.

* *With FTS user can conduct language-specific searches.* This is not possible with the LIKE predicate.

* *FTS is more effective at searching large tables (greater than 1 million rows) because it uses a precomposed*

index. In comparison, a LIKE predicate must search for the string through the whole table at query time.

* *FTS can be used to index and query certain types of data stored in image columns.* It uses one of several supported filters to interpret the data and extract the text data for indexing and querying. SQL Server provides filters for the .doc, .xls, .ppt, .txt, and .htm file extensions. User can create custom filters for full-text indexing of additional file types.

Jarvelin, and Neimi[20] analyze the problems of fact retrieval from modern distributed and heterogenous fact databases and intermediary systems for distributed fact retrieval is proposed as the solution. They discuss several possible approaches, representation formalisms and methods, including object-oriented database systems, data model integration, recursive query languages, semantic networks and the frames representation, abstract data types and information resources dictionaries. They evaluate these features for solving the problems of intermediary systems and implementing them. For Data Model Integration various steps have been given such as: Integration of the Hierarchical and the Relational Data Model and A High Level Recursive Query Language. While discussing High-level recursive query language, they say that databases users understand the idea of recursion and often have information needs that require recursive processing, formulating correct recursive queries is often very difficult for them. However, having only a large binary relation, the query is difficult to formulate for a non-specialist. It requires two possibilities:

1. The base case: the node is a bottom node; there are no connections from in it the binary relation. The node is part of the result and this path of recursion terminates.

2. The recursive case: the node is not a bottom node, i.e., there are further connections in the binary

relation. The node is part of the result and each of the connected nodes must be considered recursively.

They discuss an entity based query system for single site database also. While developing DBMS, high-level representation of database is an essential factor. It is highly desirable from the user's point of view that the representation is structured in a way corresponding to the structure of real world complex objects, their attributes and relationships. Such a representation scheme should be able to represent complex objects, their attributes, classes and their hierarchical and other relationships structurally and to encapsulate the details of their implementation. While discussing entity types, instances and relations; and entity-based queries they give an overview of entity query processing. They discuss the semantic networks and frames: their structure and their working. Ruge and Gregor[21] give an overview of the hyperterm system REALIST (retrieval aids by linguistics and statistics). REALIST is a prototype of a search and indexing help for free-text databases, combining linguistic and statistical techniques. REALIST is a part of a larger text analysis project, where natural language processing software is being developed for the treatment of large amount of textual data. In their study, they find out that full-text databases of a hundred MBs up to a GB of text taken from any application area, a REALIST version can be built within some weeks. All REALIST processing components work in a fully automatic way. They also mention about the TINA (Text-Inahlts-Analyse: Text content analysis) project, which is a long-range project with the aim of providing natural language access facilities for large amounts of textual data.

Ingwersen and Wormell[22] focus on communication and they propose practical solutions to key problems in online information retrieval, in particular concerned with ill-defined information requirements, concept representation in searching and text representation in indexing. The study stresses on the relationships between different information retrieval techniques and characteristic type of information problem, and points to feasible natural language methods and principles of representation adaptable to in-house information systems. While discussing Boolean Logic and Probability, they state that some probability model exist which are able to identify important term dependency. This feature limits the calculations. He finds that most bibliographic databases are believed to be used for providing physical and bibliographic access to the recorded knowledge of mankind. They mention three types of information problems or need, which are verificative information problems, conscious typical information problems and muddled topical information problems. Further they suggest design solutions. Salton[23] says about the increasing amount and variety of available machine-readable databases. He discusses various technologies to handle this large amount of data. New approaches have also been considered for processing the stored information and the use of expert system techniques to control the user-system interactions. His work provides an evaluation of the new information processing technologies, and of software methods proposed for information manipulation.

Fox[24] discusses the testing of applicability of intelligent methods for information retrieval. He discusses two complementary efforts at Virginia Technical undertaken for advanced retrieval method evaluation. Gopinath[25] gives a set of criteria involved in the design and development of information retrieval system. He analyses the value of facet analyses technique in the knowledge representation process. He gives the complete idea of information retrieval system as what are the basic features of information retrieval system, information processing language, and how it can be made efficient. He discusses facet analytic approach in this context, applied to design database. He gives a detailed example of database for motor vehicle engineering. Further he emphasizes on the basis of knowledge representation language for an intermediate lexicon. He discusses features of intermediary system. He says that development of conceptual structure, classification structure, and the knowledge structure representation techniques indicates the varieties of ways in which concept modeling can proceed towards developing basic taxonomy for information processing and modeling for use in information retrieval systems. Kasiveswanadham[26] discussed about Role of Commercial Databases in Information Retrieval Systems. He studies CA Search Database using CAN/SDI Package and aims at various aspects of commercial databases being used in libraries and information centres for information retrieval services. The sources of these databases and the tape services offered by multinational or national information systems have been dealt with. The various aspects of computer, such as, hardware and associated software and processing these databases either offline or online, have been described.

Jucquois-Delpierre[27] states that the reality of the office situation, the heart of every institution or enterprise, can be extraordinary lively: everything has to be planned so that everyone, whether information specialist or not, can obtain the correct information at the most suitable time and at the most appropriate place within the office. Further he states, an information system is a kind of information system where the user utilizes programs managing data, communication programs and programs for information processing, the data: database and set of files. He suggests that the user does not necessarily need to be aware of the complexity of the system before him, but rather should be carried along and guided through the paths laid out by the designers of the system. Further he says that we find that more and more people are becoming convinced of the necessarily of archiving and retrieval. Special text database software is being developed and integrated in the set of office automation procedures. Mauldin, Carbonell, and Thomason[28] state that present retrieval systems use the presence or absence of keywords to determine whether a document is relevant to a user's query. Although some systems do sophisticated statistical weighing and word-stem extraction, or exploit a hierarchical controlled vocabulary, all suffer from the same basic limitation; their inability to represent relational information among primitive concepts. Research in artificial intelligence and natural language processing has produced richer representations of texts and techniques for reasoning about these representations. In their work, they describe the frame-based knowledge representation methods as they apply to information retrieval, including research in user interfaces and automatic document classification. While describing natural-language interface, they mention about that generation of appropriate frames to match the document databases shows the establishment of a point into the database. They stress on the applications of frames to information retrieval. The output of the standard retrieval is a list of relevant documents. With frames the result is a list of semantic representations, which can be used by the computer to do more·that just retrieve documents. Further they inform about the considerable progress made for knowledge representation in electronic form.

Kaul[29] states that most academic scientists are aware of the existence of computerized databases but only a small fraction use them. Those who do are, finding that the development of machine-readable databases has revolutionized the process of information retrieval, especially for locating published scientific literature. In 1990s the use of these databases is likely to increase dramatically as scientists have more experience with the excellent results obtaining from online literature searching. The work attempts that online searching in all its broader perspective with elaborate discussions on its advantages and use. Further he says that online information retrieval will be indispensable to productive research. Newton[30] gives an informal description of a general-purpose database and a database management system. He proposes to improve the latter's abilities in terms of extending the set of requests concerning information stored in the database. In an attempt to justify the concept of the intelligence with the help of the Turning test, he asserts that intelligence consists primarily in the ability to conduct a dialogue with a computer correctly. He emphasizes on making the database as a subsystem to assist users. Ebinuma and Takahashi[31]discuss different aspects of information retrieval in their study "Different Effect of Subject Key Schemes on Retrieval Efficiency in the INIS On-line Search". They classify methods of document retrieval as:

1.   One using natural terms (free terms)
2.   One using control terms (descriptors)
3.   One using both of the above two.

Further they discuss the formulation of queries. By giving examples they explain different types of methods. These methods are

(i)   Free term method,
(ii)   Descriptor method and
(iii) Keyword method.

The choice of search term is easier by the descriptor method than by the free-term method and consecutively one can obtain better search results, if an appropriate term or its analogue term is found among descriptors. It has been experienced also with other search topics. Almost queries use any comprehensive term in the case of the descriptor method. In the case of free-term method, the comprehensiveness is enhanced by means of the truncation function. However, comprehensive terms in the descriptor method are superior to the above function from the point of view of elevation of comprehensiveness. In the cases where comprehensive term worked as descriptor, the descriptor method and the keyword method are hardly discriminated in their abilities. Nevertheless, one can say that an experienced searcher would prefer the descriptor method, though both methods are equally easy to handle. This is because correspondence between the questioning concept and the search term is clearer in the descriptor method. The free-term method or the keyword method assures high precision ratio and good recall ratio equally. Moreover, formulation of queries is easier than the case of the descriptor method. They state that trained searcher will choose either descriptor method or keyword method considering whether appropriate terms are available among descriptors. On the contrary, untrained searchers will prefer the keyword method rather than descriptor method and they can still expect rather high retrieval effectiveness. While discussing the 'title search', they say that title search would meet online users desiring high precision ratio, shortening of the search time and expansion of the search region (search on multiple databases). If a database size were more than five years used for a retrospective search, one would obtain the considerable number of hits. In cases where an appropriate term is not available among descriptors, a related descriptor is found by carrying out the search with free terms. Here, free terms are not necessarily extracted from the abstract. Free terms in the title may be rather adequate, because they give less output but high precision ratio; thus one can find samples of hit documents quickly. They suggest that it would be best for online system to introduce the descriptor method and the keyword method containing free terms from the title and abstract. If it is difficult to realize, one should request at least a system supplying the keyword method with free terms from the title besides the descriptor method.

Gibson, Shepard and Kunkel[32] present end-user needs for online system, in the context of the structure, function and mission of the General Motors Research Laboratories Library. They present statistics showing the systems, databases, and query types for the 1984 "model" year. They describe procedures used in end-user interfaces and search example. Problems identified with respect to the baud rates for online searching, availability of 'gray literature, limiting search output, combining search results (and sorting them), document delivery and uniform access protocols. Graham[33] states that online access to information is the way of life in our facilities. He mentions the continuing SDI. Mikhailov[34] considers the influence of new information technology on information users while discussing information in a developing world. He describes inner mechanisms of information handling in a scientific community. Displays and terminals of information systems ensuring direct access to machine-readable databases are provided in the first place to managers and leading specialists. This situation is temporary. He argues, "don't we recognize de facto the priority of information service? Don't we try to substantiate indirectly new information ethics according to which information users should not enjoy equal opportunities in accessing information?"

Wilde[35] states that innovation is extremely chancy. Innovative ideas are like frog eggs: of a thousand hatched, only one or two survive to maturity. Because early researchers into the nature of technology transfer did embryonic transfer centres a failure. Today, innovation is better understood, and more mature centres with its unique multiple database approach are routinely documenting that scientific information does aid innovation. While discussing multiple sources he gives example of his information centre, which makes use of worldwide sources. There are at least 200 commonly available machine-readable files. In contrast multiple database approach is designed to maximize the member handling each user question automatically accesses all appropriate databases, ensuring that no relevant information is missed. Questions can be answered with retrospective or current-awareness searches, or both. This allows the user to find out what has been done in an area and then to keep up-to-date. He further discusses the attempt made to answer all user questions, independent of subject or difficulty. The users expect relevant citations to articles and reports that will help them solve their problems.

CSIR[36] developed database containing bibliographic information of more than 30,000 Indian Patents published during 1978-92, called INPAT. This database provide search facility available on: applicant's name, inventor's name, catch words, Indian/international patent classification, patent number, application number, and publication date. The information supplied comprises patent number, publication date, applicants' name and title. Cambridge Scientific Abstracts (CSA)[37] has combined new user software with a stacked MultiDisc drive unit to produce the CSA MultiDisc Drive system. The system makes searching large database and multiple years easier.

References

1.   Neelameghan, A. Online Glossary for Multilingual Database. *Information Studies*, 5(2), 1999, p 83-98.

2.   ECHO Offers Greek Database. Digest and Notes. *International Information, Communication and Education*, 14(2), Sept. 1995, p 292-3.

3.   Minecci, Catherine M. and Hodge, Gail. Machine-sided indexing: productivity and organizational implications. *Information Services & Use*, 8, 1988, p 133-138.

4.   Granick, Lois. Assuring the quality of information dissemination: responsibilities of database producers. *Information Services & Use*, 11, 1991, p 117-136.

5.   Briggs, David J. Establishing an environmental information system for the European Community: the experience of the

CORINE Programme. *Information Services & Use*, 10, 1990, p 63-75.

6.   Cuadra, Carlos A. Better text management. *Information Services & Use*, 10, 1990, p 305-314.

7.   Tuomisto, Jouko and Savolainen, Kai. Background information for a European metadatabase on environment and health information sources: Finland. *Information Services & Use*, 10, 1990, 233-241.

8.   Voigt, K., Benz, J, and Matthies, M. Information system on environmental chemicals: databank of data sources for environmental chemicals. *Information Services & Use*, 10, 1990, p 215-222.

9.   See 102.

10.   Clark, A. L. Mineral Resource Information Systems, *Information Services & Use*, 3, 1983, p 17-27.

11.   Digest and Notes. *International Information, Communication and Education*, 15(1), March 1996, p 147.

12.   Digests and Notes. *International Information, Communication and Education*, 13(1), March 1994, p 147.

13.   See 55.

14.   see 34.

15.   Thandavamoorthy, K. and Kumar, S. Quality in Digital information Retrieval. *University News*, 40(6), Feb. 2002, p 6-9.

16.   See 55.

17.   See 1.

18.   Boni, M., Geiss, F. And Penning, W. The ECDIN database for chemicals in the environment, *International Information, Communication and Education*, 10, 1990, p 83-86.

19.   See 88.

20.   Jarvelin, Kalervo and Neimi, Timo. Simplifying Fact Retrieval Through Intermediary System. *International Forum of Information and Documentation*, 15(4), Oct. 1990, p 16-31.

21.   Ruge, Gerda, Schwarz and Gregor Thurmair. A Hyperterm System Based on Natural Language Processing. *International Forum of Information and Documentation*. 15(3), July 1990, p 3-8.

22.   Ingwersen, Peter and Wormell, Irene. *International Forum of Information and Documentation*, 14(3), July 1989, p 17-22.

23.   Salton, Gerard. Thoughts about modern retrieval technologies. *Information Services & Use*, 8, 1988, p 107-113.

24. Fox, Edward A. Testing the applicability of intelligent methods for information retrieval. *Information Services & Use*, 7, 1987, p 119-138.

25. Gopinath, M. A. Design of Concept Codes in information Retrieval. *International Information, Communication and Education*, 24(4), Dec. 1987, p 226- 234.

26. Kasiveswanadham, S. Role of Commercial Databases in Information Retrieval Systems. *Annals of Library Science and Documentation*, 34(1), 1987, p 1-11.

27. Information Retrieval in the Office Environment. *International Forum of Information & Documentation*, 12, o.3, July 1987, p15-22.

28. Mauldin, Michael, Carbonell, Jaime and Thomason. Beyond the keyword barrier: knowledge-based information retrieval. *Information Services & Use*, 7, 1987, p 103-117.

29. Kaul, B. K. Online Searching in Information Retrieval. *IASLIC Bulletin* 31(2), 1986, p 43-49.

30. Kuznetsow, S. A. Informatics 7: Intelligent Information Retrieval. *International Forum Information and Documentation*, 11(2), April 1986, p 44-47.

31. Ebinuma, Yukio and Takahashi, Satako. Different Effect of Subject Key Schemes on Retrieval Efficiency in the INIS On-line Search. *International Information, Communication and Education*, 4(1), March 1985, p 14-19.

32. Gibson, Robert W. Jr., Shepard, Margaret and Kunkel, Barbara. GMR Online. *Information Services & Use*, 5, 1985, p 213-220.

33. See 102.

34. Mikhailov, A. I. Information in a developing world. *International Forum of Information & Documentation*, 9(3), 1984, p 1-2.

35. Wilde, Daniel U. Scientific Information as an Aid to Innovation. *Information Services & Use*, 2, 1982, p 81-91.

36. INPAT Database. Digest and Notes. *International Information, Communication and Education*, V 15, N 1, March 1996, p 146.

37. Practical Application of MultiDisc Searching of CD-ROM Databases. Digests and Notes. *International Information, Communication and Education*, 9(2), 1990, p 254.

Chapter 8
Marketing of Information and Databases

Wong and Freitas[1] conduct a study on marketing an information service in OECS Economic Affairs Secretariat Documentation Centre. In their case study, they present a methodology for marketing an information service, which focus on including information users in the strategic marketing planning process. They describe an attempt to rationalize development of services and to deepen and broaden the base of information products and services offered, beginning with preparation for market growth through analysis, and subsequent limitation, of user groups. An approach to a marketing planning process is identified and the stages in this process- analysis of the environment, information audit, information needs assessment, market opportunity analysis, tactical marketing programme, and evaluation – are described. They find out the exercise, simple and inexpensive to implement and therefore a good choice to try out the methodology developed. Sharma and Murthy[2] discuss consumer orientation. They emphasize on identification of consumer and diagnosis of user's information needs. Needs' can be identified in terms of quantity, time, quality and cost. They also emphasize identification of information formats. According to him, information must be provided in the form, language, coverage and volume, which appeals or suits the user most. The medium of presentation is also very important. For planning and input agencies information may be given in floppies or tables. Further they state that we should develop and mount new research projects to generate required information. It is needed to answer all the questions, and gauge future needs.

Langerman[3] discusses the marketing a database in the social sciences; description of an experience and its result. She describes a marketing project for a bibliographic database in the social sciences. It states the reasons which prevent the potential users of the databases from using it. The marketing of information products and services is now viewed as an essential part of the management of databases and of information system. She describes a planned effort of marketing the services of a national bibliographic database in the social sciences in Israel, its stages – market segmentation, market positioning, marketing program- and its result. Kalseth[4] discusses the strategic uses of information – challenges for the information services department. He says that market orientation demands a professional attitude, not only to the way we perform responsibilities and complete out tasks, but professionally with in management is also must. A stronger customer relationship is important in order to link new ideas towards consumer requirements and to obtain feedback on the quality of services rendered.

Ryan and Barbara[5] discuss the customer services and marketing at the Defense Technical Information Center. They give some idea of the development of the customer services and marketing programs; how they came to be; some of the vision and objectives of the future; and in general, how the organizational structure is geared to meeting customer needs. Center's customer services and marketing program has been discussed in light of the historical perspective of marketing in the federal government environment and the emergence of customer services issue in information services. Kinyon and Jackson[6] discuss the marketing problems through producer/user collaboration. They say that databases and indexes created and maintained by producers and publishers make the job of every reference librarian easier. While users benefit greatly from these products, libraries feel that information publishers do not always get sufficient input from the users. Additional input often could make products much more user-friendly and thus more marketable. Librarians can let producers know what is important to users out in the market, and producers can let librarians know what is important to them in developing, creating, and marketing the product. Further they discuss the information that users (librarians) can supply to producers such as: need, suitability of format, cost, equipment and plans for the future. They inform about the ways in which users and producers can help each other such as: field testing of databases, provide copies for trial, make review copies available. They highlight the ways in which producers can help users such as: support, manuals, search software, frequent updating and point of use instruction guides.

Sharp[7] discusses business information services and implications for Australian corporate libraries. He says that corporations in the US have become sophisticated in the exploitation of online databases for business applications. He intends to describe what is happening in the US and to suggest ways in which corporate libraries can be promoted with in Australia and elsewhere. Haravu[8] states that it is not only recently that librarians, even in the free market economies of the west, have begun to talk of marketing of their products and services. Growing interest in applying marketing concepts to library and information products and services is on account of the increasing threat from the emerging information industry comprising profit-based companies that distribute, repackage or improve access to information. The potential of information products and services itself is speedily expanding given the fact that all sections of society are involved in increasingly complex and multidimensional exchanges and require more and more information to fulfill their purposes and objectives in an environment that is being continually reshaped by new forces. According to him, there is a clear need for libraries to woo back their patrons by eschewing their passive ways and adopting a more proactive approach to the provision of services. This is evident that libraries have not fully exploited the comparative advantages that they possess in relation to private sector information agencies. These and other factors, such as rising cost, declining support and funds to libraries and a crisis of identity have made it necessary for Librarians to reconsider their position and to utilize some of the tools that have made it possible for profit organization to operate efficiently, and profitably. One is the tools is marketing. The report[9] of Association of Information and Dissemination Centers 1984 Fall Meeting mentions that BRS and Saunders have formed a joint venture to deliver medical information to end-users. 'Colleague' is a conventional bibliographic database containing items from books, journals and newspapers. Early pilot experiences with 'Colleague' show that users become sophisticated rapidly. End-users and librarians interact well, as the librarians becoming a search consultant. In one arrangement, the librarians log on to the service, and then allow the requesters to do their own searching and to retrieve their own data. New features planned for 'Colleague' are an accounting system, and a method for librarians to block access to selected databases, such as expensive ones. Training is by computer-aided instruction accompanied by a manual.

Database producers[10] and online hosts have been keen to exploit the end-user market for bibliographic databases as well as for a whole range of databases.

According to Griffith[11] the local databases are of two categories, as:

1. Databases of national scope aiming at serving national institutions or covering topics of specific significance for the country;

2. Databases of regional or international scope covering topics of interest to a large group of countries.

In the first 'national', category she puts a variety of databases with library applications, and on topics such as ongoing research, science and technology, testing facilities, statistics, industry and commerce and other items specific to individual countries. She also finds that as so many of the definitions which confuse discussion about information matters, the term 'local databases' can mean different things to different people: information about local holdings, or locally generated information, or databases accessible locally.

Auld[12] says that the marketplace has been significantly influenced by a number of volatile factors, first, technology's evolution and presentation into organizations of all types and sizes; second, the managerial awareness of what is taking place. The evidence is that companies are spending money for these technological innovations. Third, database publishers are aware of the new environment of opportunities and challenges.

Pricing, Costing

Rajshekhar[13] discusses that who should fund the production of databases. Should the information services to end-users be subsidized? These questions are of great significance today in the rapidly evolving liberalized economy in the country. Since the government-supported institutions are the largest information repositories in the country, these institutions should have the major stake in database production. He visualizes the catalytic role that should be played by professional societies and associations in actively promoting database production. Industries (both government and private) in the concerned area are other major sources of funding. He suggests that for achieving wider reach and cost recovery, there have to be tie-ups with commercial sector. Working with international print publishers like Elsevier, Pergamon, etc., may also become essential, particularly for resolving royalty issues. Tell[14] analyses the aspects of the present cataloguing routines in the light of an online environment. His experiences of teaching cataloguing in a developing country have brought about some speculations concerning the need for future changes in training in cataloguing by taking more advantage of the potential of microcomputers. The regulative role of Anglo-American Cataloguing Rules 2 is discussed. According to him, short entry forms should be introduced to allow for cataloguing by not fully trained staff, which could make more use of a book's inherent attributes. He argues that the present conventions of the Western countries hamper a creative development in the Third World, and that international organizations should lend prestige to a change. Holms[15] discusses an experiment in pricing mechanisms for online information retrieval. He describes an experiment with a two part-time and volume based- tariff structure, which is felt to have advantages over present time-based tariffs for searching within online information retrieval system. The nature of the experiment, tariff of online use, and some problems concerning the proposed tariff are discussed. According to the report[16] of Association of Information and Dissemination Centers 1984 Fall Meeting, it might be concluded that information is a 'quasi-commodity' and thus the market of information can be defined as a 'quasi-market' on the basis of economic investigations using different approaches. The dangers of an enormous inflation in the information sector must be eliminated, but a library system, which is based only on state subventions and provides services free or almost free of charge, cannot be efficient. King Research Inc[17] discusses the study of the Library and Information Services Division of the National Oceanic and Atmospheric Administration. Library operations have been indicated as an example of areas that might be contracted out, and many Federal libraries are now faced with the prospect of conducting reviews. It mentions three phases:

1. **Phase I:** Conduct a management effectiveness study (MES) of the present organization and method of performance of the function by the govt. employees for the purpose of determining the most effective organization (MEO).

2. **Phase II:** Prepare a Performance-oriented Work Statement (PWS) for the accomplishment of that activity, ready for advertisement that includes an explicit Quality Assurance Surveillance Plan.

3. **Phase III:** Prepare an estimate of Govt. cost to perform the function as an in-house activity according to the PWS and utilizing MEO established by the management study.

Auld[18] discusses the challenges the marketplace imposes upon database publishers. According to him pricing is a critical challenge. Pricing will have to be determined by evaluating such diverse factors as volume of data downloaded, re-use of the information, royalties paid for derivative information products, speed of downloading, etc. If pricing is too high, publishers will lose customers because of their inability to pay high costs, or if too low, revenue will be insufficient to keep the publisher in business. Further he says that the variety of potential products made possible through the sophistication of the user and the equipment involved, will cause database publishers to incorporate multiple use pricing in addition to the single use of pricing schemes currently employed. Keenan[19] says that the database producers need to generate adequate income to maintain their services and the information worker is anxious to purchase as cost effectively as possible, information tailored to meet user needs. To use a simpler analogy, the information worker would like to acquire the database producers' products in a form that can be used repeatedly. A dictionary, once purchased, can be used over and over again by many different users. The growing availability and increased use of data banks adds another problem to the economic debate. While it is possible to charge for the use of the bibliographic file based on a royalty charge levied for each reference used, the use of a data bank creates a need for a different method of charging-possibly by time, number of characters, etc.

Professional Attitude

Manjunatha and Shivalingaiah[20] comment that the librarians do have some concerns on application of marketing techniques to library services as they consider library as a service organization and not as a business house. They often believe that marketing is concerned with selling, advertising, industrial products and profit-motivated. Further they do not conduct end user-survey. They believe that "whatever the service we provide is essential and best in interest of users". This indicates the lack of visualization of marketing concepts in its totality. They emphasizes on an orientation towards the marketing approach, desirable to give the clear picture of marketing approach.

They discuss marketing of library and information services as the subject of growing interest among the library professionals. Developments in information technology particularly CD-ROM, Internet and communication media have challenged the concept of traditional library at one place. Librarians no longer would like remain as custodian of books. Rather they visualize themselves as resource persons for knowledge and information dissemination. They analyze the attitude of librarians towards the concept of marketing, level of understanding on nature of library business, and its products/services and the methods adopted to understand the customers' needs. Hartevelt[21] says that the role of information manager will primarily comprise the analysis and determination of information needs, the development of procedures which can structure information channels and ensure quality control, the design of information 'carriers' (input-output concepts, registration forms, tally sheets, etc.) and the development of databases, including access methods.

Graham[22] states that with ongoing changes in the format of the reference materials and handbooks, information professionals cannot be barriers to users directly accessing the information they need. The role of professionals are changing, knowing end-user programming, serving as hot lines to help end-users, keeping abreast of new and updated databases and handling the complex questions and analysis that will continue to be. He says that stature of professionals will increase and their recognition will be greater. The report[23] of Association of Information and Dissemination Centers 1984 Fall Meeting mentions that present vendors must become innovative in serving a fragmented market; new vendors must prove that they know the market. Market research will become more important and new features are introduced. For the database producer, this means lower profits, print products subsidizing online products, and the necessity to find alternate means of delivering information. Users are demanding more satisfaction, tailored services, more access to information, easier-to-use systems, and more relevant information. Auld[24] emphasizes on the use of e-mail to reach to market, which has been getting a great deal of attention lately. He says that unfortunately gathering of customer information is not as easy for the majority of bibliographic database producers who traditionally have used the services of vendors providing public access to their files. Database producers must utilize expensive methods to develop awareness and analysis of their marketplace. Because of this and other factors, this recent trend of vertical integration is accelerating. Primary publishers are developing databases, databases developers are constructing their own delivery systems, and online vendors are developing databases. To what extent this evolution will carry on is certainly going to occupy much time and thought over the next few years.

Users Attitude and Behaviour Related to Databases

According to Jarvelin and Niemi[25], user's problems are as following:

1. Is there relevant data available in the database?
2. Is it appropriate necessary or useless to acquire such information?
3. Are equivalent data available in some other types of source?
4. Which databases contain relevant data?
5. Is it necessary to search several databases?
6. How are connections established with each database?
7. How are the data named and represented in different databases?
8. Is it possible to execute the query in different databases and what does it require?
9. How is the query executed in different databases?
10. How do the data from different sources fit together–how can they be fitted?

The concept of object, property and relationship are essential in structuring the user interface of an intermediary system for fact retrieval. The properties of an object structure the information describing the object- e.g. price, weight and color of a product or a domain of a variable. It is natural to analyze the contents of fact databases into information concerning objects, their properties and their relationship. It is essential that these concepts be not tied to any conventional data models: users can analyze their environments and information needs with these concepts without having to pay attention to principles of data storage at the same time. Note, especially, that databases based on the relational data model- and those applying their normalization theory. In particular-incorporate several decisions related to data storage and processing, which are clearly at a more technical level than objects, their properties and relationships. The relational data model is known for the physical data independence it provides. Further more normalized relations are, however, often not the clearest or most natural way of structuring information.

Graham[26] states the necessity of ability of using resources in electronic form that they use traditionally in print form. He mentions front-end packages developed for end-users. Once an end-user becomes somewhat familiar with searching, these packages will ultimately be found wanting. Packages with the required flexibility are tailored more for the intermediary than for the real end user, as he/she will not be searching every day. According to the United Nations Centre on Transnational Corporations (UNCTD) documentation[27] although users of online-databases are more likely to find information about business and science-related topics than about social or consumer oriented topics, a steady stream of new on-line databases is becoming available, including consumer oriented and general news databases, which will help to correct the present imbalance. The demand of on-line information is growing, and as the demand increases, potential database producers, such as publishers of print products, are very likely to respond by putting more information on-line. This process can be accelerated and can lead to the inclusion of the type of material that is of particular relevance to users in developing countries, once these users make their needs and demands known. There is an interim possibility for users in developing countries to gain immediate access to on-line database services from established search centres in information-rich countries. Such search centres would be geographically close to on-line services, have easy access to telecommunication networks, and be able to receive prompt help-desk-type assistance. Another alternative would be for a developing country to use information brokers located in the countries of interest, although the cost would need to be carefully assessed. Perhaps, a consortium of developing countries with similar interests could establish such linkages, not only to help with the database access problem, but also to expedite delivery.

Smith[28] states that the relationship between users, librarians and suppliers of information products has been a relatively stable one, with librarians acting as mediators in the delivery of information form suppliers to users. The emergence of electronic databases linked to users by ("free-of-charge") communication networks tends to threaten two sides of this "Golden Triangle". Some commentators have forecast the end of libraries, anticipating a future in which users satisfy all their – indeed from electronic databases, without recourse to traditional libraries or librarians – indeed, the "virtual libraries" may not be run by librarians at all! This threat extends beyond libraries to the suppliers themselves. The appearance of networked electronic journals, with no print equivalents, may herald the start of a trend towards bypassing traditional publishing methods and traditional publishers. Continually, and steeply, rising periodical prices can only serve to exacerbate the problem.

Suggestion for Databases

Auld[29] suggests for databse publishing as following:

1. A database publisher can look at the feasibility of publishing a database of citations, citations and abstracts or full text.

2. Capturing key stroked and utilizing pre-composition software has allowed economic processing for both print and electronic versions.

3. Technologies such as optical character recognition have come quite a way in the last few years.

4. Likewise, utilizing terminals in place of typewriters for direct input subsequent to editorial review is also economically feasible now.

5. Database producer should carefully evaluate the requirements of his marketplace in regard to producing a citation only, citation and abstract, or a full-text file.

6. Although auto-indexing methods have proven to be consistently bad, there is progress, which holds hope for the future. Better and cheaper composition software and hardware are also much more prevalent now.

Feedback from Users

King Research Inc[30] Technical Information Center took the assessment of value of energy information and information services and products. They collected data by user survey. Auld[31] emphasizes on technology that it has certainly provided us with the tools to deliver information electronically, but it has also given us the opportunity to determine how it benefits the recipients and what these benefits are. The area needing the most analysis today is that of the information user. Good feed back mechanisms can greatly aid the providers of information in determining what to deliver and how to deliver.

User Education: Searching

INSPEC[32] organized training time to time. Tell[33] states that there is a need for professional training of highly knowledgeable specialists related not only to scientific and technical information systems but also to general information systems. For the successful implementation and operation of scientific and technical information systems in the future, a new training system for information specialists should be established. Specialists engaged in specialized tasks in scientific information systems might be broadly classified into three categories: those engaged in information dissemination services, information collection and provision and database creation. Freeman[34] describes following guidelines regarding the efficient implementation of data systems.

1. The aspects of implementation covered include parallel operation with existing systems; the criteria for change-over;

2. Hardware and software deployment;

3. User training and documentation;

4. The delineation of new system savings and resource requirements and savings.

5. The training for users includes instructions regarding the overall operation of the new system.

6. Detailed delineation of how particular subsystems operate, guidance on the operation of computer hardware.

7. Hands on practice in the actual operation of the system.

8. Developing easy-to-understand user manuals that provide information relative to various other matters i.e. operation of terminals and printers.

9. Functioning of and entering information into screen displays.

10. Retrieving information from databases.

11. Formats of reports provided by the new system etc. Meadow[35] discusses his interest in languages, user behavior. Many people could not or would not take time to learn a complex language, but was intrigued by a simple one. This leads to a trade-off these users are not always aware of: trading ease and simplicity of learning for ability to accomplish work. This trade-off is at the root of the decision to create such systems as Knowledge Index. The intelligent user will rationally choose between system power and simplicity. The uninformed will not recognize that a choice is being made, and may opt for simplicity instead of the complexity that might be needed to solve certain problems.

Tschudi[36] says that training online searchers in not an easy task, for several reasons. First of all, new searcher comes from a wide variety of backgrounds with very diverse levels of skills. We also have vastly different learning rates as well as different career goals and interest. None of us will ever use all of the 1,200 plus databases that now exist are the thousands that are expected to exist in the near future. Which ones do you teach and to whom? He places secondly this field's own jargon. The file is "up"; the system is "down"; the word is "double posted"; you "string search"; you "neighbor"; you "root"; you "AND", you "OR", and you "NOT". Ordinary everyday English words that don't mean what they used to. The third reason is the difficulty to train online searcher is the natural human resistance to the new and unfamiliar. Most people think 'change' is a dirty word. Younger generation won't have this particular problem. He emphasizes on the necessity of training. It's the time library schools as a whole accepted online searching as a fully legitimate tool of librarianship. Its time that most library schools get out of the rout they are in. Too many schools have been stuck in the rut of teaching traditional librarianship in a non-traditional, rapidly changing world.

They are stuck with some tenured traditional library science professors who are unable and /or unwilling to keep up with the modern technologies that are galloping into the library world. It is imperative that the library schools get their act together while online searching is still an offshoot of librarianship, or they are going on to find someone else teaching online as a tool for some other subject.

Caruso and Caruso[37] discuss the 'Trainer', a computer tutorial for end-users of database services, its context, content and results of use. 'Trainer', computer-mediated learning aid for users of DIALOG or ORBIT retrieval services, is available via TELNET or EDUNET, from Carnegie-Mellon University. Environment of its present user at the Graduate School of Public and International Affairs, University of Pittsburgh, as a major component of computer competence for professionals in specialized knowledge fields. They report an experiment with sixty-one graduate student trainees: the skill level achieved and online training time show positive correlation; non-western cultural backgrounds do not relate to success; age and typing skills correlate with success, but older trainees spend more time online whereas good typists are quicker to complete the training.

Courrier[38] states that constant increase in the amount of information technology introduced into the information and library services of developing countries makes the question of suitable training of the necessary personal extremely urgent. He briefly reviews some problems involved in formulating general training strategies and choosing specific ways and methods of training. The precise determination of the desired training objectives is of great importance, because the objective may vary over a broad range, depending on the local conditions under which information services operate in developing countries. Sperr[39] says that online databases are being made accessible to end users, but often the end users must be taught how to search this information resource effectively and efficiently. He discusses the findings of a survey conducted by the User Education Committee of the National Federation of Abstracting ad Information services to draw a profile of the trainers and their job. According to him, the trainers are key agents in the information transfer chain. They teach users to search for and retrieve information efficiently. Searching databases is a skill.

Future of User

Roy[40] discusses the creation and preparation of the National Index of Translations. It was developed with the help of CDS/ISIS. According to Auld[41] the user will demand more satisfactory answers to his questions. User will demand services more tailored to his individual needs. User will do a great deal more accessing of information, either directly or through intermediaries. The user will demand capabilities of packaging or formatting the information that he draws from external systems, and incorporates it with a more varies use at his end. In sum, more relevant data to user requirements, more specialized and easier-to-use software and greater flexibility of information manipulation at the user's site will be the feature of future. Graham[42] looks into future that in-house database of published information will be downloaded. He says creating internal databases of published information that flow into a large bibliographic utility is difficult due to broad interests. He says that putting much of effort into planning and encouraging cooperation between information professionals and users will help developing databases.

Budgeting

Tiamiyu[43] discusses the budgeting for information management systems. The situation is not helped by vendors of imported technologies who are apt to tout the capabilities of their hardware and general-purpose software and gloss over the protracted nature of staff training and the resource implications of both user training and database maintenance. The cost of staff training and database maintenance though often not adequately recognized, are usually recurring costs.

Funding

Schmidt[44] says that start-up funds for the development of non-bibliographic databases may be available from foundations and through grants, but such projects entail unavoidable operational costs and the determination of access to fees to meet these costs.

Man Power and Development

Chakrabarty[45] analyses the demand for library and information workers during 1988 as advertised in five national dailies. He stresses the need for training suitable manpower by laying greater emphasis on information technology and information management to meet present day needs. Pitroda[46] stresses on manpower as an important asset to India which must be put to maximum utilization. Working Group on Information and Library Network, UGC, New Delhi[47] proposed that database of projects/institutions/specialists in an integrated information system. Besides handling bibliographic information, there should also cover non-bibliographic information about ongoing and completed projects related with Information and Library Network (INFLIBNET).

Kemparaju[48] identifies and throws focus on the trends in the job market for library and information manpower in special library and information sector. He analyses Trends in Manpower Development in Special Library and Information Centres in India Pragmatically. He analyzes and scans the advertisements from leading national English newspapers and compiles to consider trends in manpower requirements and presents with different manifestations. He identifies number of anomalies and projects by comparative observation of different aspects. The data is viewed in relation with the job market and the present curriculum and also considered to bring out compatibility between job requirements and course contents. The programmes of placements and liaison with prospective employers are suggested to bring amendments to lack of proper job descriptions. Courrier[49] discusses the problems connected with training in the use of the new technologies. He says, as in many fields, training in information science raises acute problems in most developing countries have reliable institutions which provide university-level training, and are now beginning to produce a body of skilled professionals. But they are not in majority. The second difficulty derives from the quantitative and qualitative evaluation of training needs. Some developed countries have still not found an answer to the basic question of who are the potential employers of the specialists being trained. He suggests that attention should be paid to the institutional aspects of information services. It is true that in many situations, large and expensive information technology equipment with potential use in major national and university libraries and national documentation centres are out of reach; training should therefore be adapted to such situations. He discusses last problem of the level of training sought. Needs are immensely varied. Prospective candidates may have acquired experience on the job; they may have been trained in university, either recently or some times ago; or they may be specialists trained in the best schools of the developed countries.

Training Strategies

Courrier[50] mentions various training strategies such as;

1.   A tradition of awarding fellowships for high-level

training with a recognized status in developed countries.

2.   Ad Hoc international courses of limited duration at UNESCO.

3.   Traveling course

He tells the advantage of the second strategy that the human and material resources of a developed country are made available to students form developing countries for specific subjects at less cost than by awarding fellowships.

References

1.   Wong, Sue Evan and Freitas, Claudette de. Marketing an Information Service: A case study of the OECS Economic Affairs Secretariat Documentation Centre. *Information Services & Use*, 15, 1995, p 117-130.

2.   Sharma, V. P. and Murthy, Lakshmi. User-Friendly and Complete Packaging: Consumer Orientation and marketing Agricultural Information. *International Forum of Information and Documentation*, 14(2), Sept. 1995. p 173-182.

3.   Langerman, Shoshana The marketing a database in the social sciences; description of an experience and its result. *Information Services & Use*, 11, 1991, p 3-8.

4.   Kalseth, Karl. The strategic uses of information –challenges for the information services department, *Information Services & Use*, 11, 1991, p 63-71.

5.   Ryan, R. paul and Barbara, Colgate. Customer Services and Marketing at the Defense Technical Information Center. *Information Services & Use*, 10, 1990, p 371-379.

6.   Kinyon, William R. and Jackson, Kathy M. Look before you leap: avoiding marketing problems through producer/user collaboration. *Information Services & Use*, 9, 1989, p 279-288.

7.   Sharp, Geoffrey E. Business information services and implications for Australian corporate libraries. *Information Services & Use*, 9, 1989, p 117-126.

8.   Haravu, L. J. Marketing of Library and Information services. *IASLIC Bulletin* 33(4), 1988, p139-147.

9.   Auld, Dennis. Information on Vu/text –an experiment. *Information Services & Use*, 5, 1985, p 107-111.

10. Information System for End-Users: Research and Development Issue. / edited by Micheline Hanock-Beaulieu. London: Graham Taylor, 1992.

11. Judge, Peter J. The Marketing of Information Services- A Regional Workshop and its Context. *International Forum of Information & Documentation,* 9(3), 1984, p 16-20.

12. See 6.

13. See 1.

14. Tell, Bjorn V. Cataloguing Rules on Database Production- Implications for Manpower Training in a Developing Country. *International Forum of Information & Documentation,* 14(1), Jan 1989, p22-27.

15. Holms, P. L. An experiment in pricing mechanisms for online information retrieval. *Information Services & Use,* V 5, 1985, p 269-275.

16. News, Trends and Comments. *Information Services & Use,* 5, 1985, p57-71.

17. See 3.

18. See 6.

19. See 3.

20. Manjunatha, K. and Shivalingaiah, D. Marketing of Library and Information Services: A study of attitude of librarians. *Herald of Library Science,* 40(3-4), July-Oct. 2001, p172-185.

21. See 2.

22. See 10.

23. See 9.

24. See 6.

25. See 8.

26. See 10.

27. Potential relevance of online databases for developing countries. UNCTC/ Transborder data flows. *Information Services & Use,* 1982, p 92.

28. See 6.

29. See 3.

30. See 6.

31. See 27

32. INSPEC Online Training. Digests and Notes. *International Information, Communication and Education,* 12(2), Sept. 1993, p 285.

33. See 18.

34. Freeman, Raoul J. Guidelines for Efficient Implementation of Data Systems. *International Forum Of Information And Documentation,* 13(2), April 1988, p 14-17.

35. Meadow, Charles T. User Education for Online Information Systems. *Information Services & Use,* 3, 1983. p 173-177.

36. Tschudi, C. M. Educating and/or Training the Online Searcher. *Information Services & Use,* V3, 1983, p 179-183.

37. Caruso, Nicholas and Caruso, Elaine. TRAINER- a computer tutorial for end-users of database services: its context, content and results of use. *Information Services & Use,* 3, 1983, p191-198.

38. Auld, Dennis. Information on Vu/text –an experiment. *Information Services & Use,* 5, 1985, p 107-111.

39. Sperr, Inez L. The Trainers of Online Database Users: A Survey. *International Forum of Information & Documentation,* 9(3), 1984, p 27-331.

40. Roy, P. K. Creation of NIT Database Using Micro-CDS/ISIS Package. *IASLIC Bulletin,* 34(1), 1989, p 11-20.

41. Auld, Dennis. Information on Vu/text –an experiment. *Information Services & Use,* 5, 1985, p 107-111.

42. Auld, Dennis. Information on Vu/text –an experiment. *Information Services & Use,* 5, 1985, p 107-111.

43. Tiamiyu, Mutawakilu Adisa. Pragmatics of Developing Information Resource Management Systems in Government Organizations in Developing Countries. *International Forum of Information and Documentation,* 12(2), Sept 1993, p 201-212.

44. See 5.

45. Chakrabarty, Bipul Kumar. Information Manpower- Strategic Issues for Development. *IASLIC Bulletin,* 38(2), 1993, p 67-72.

45. Murthy, S S. International Conference on Bibliographic Databases and Networks. *International Forum of Information and Documentation,* 9(1), March 1990, p104-106.

46. A Summary of the Report of the Inter Agency Working Group. *International Forum of Information and Documentation,* 9(1), March 1990, p 68-96.

47. See 42.

48. Kemparaju, T. D. A Pragmatic Analysis of Trends in Manpower Development in Special Library and Information

Centres in India. *IASLIC Bulletin*, 33(2/3), 1988, p 45-51.

49. Courrier, Yves. Information Technology Training Needs, Strategies and Objectives for the Developing Countries. *International Forum of Information & Documentation*, 12(3), July 1987, p 32-37.

50. See 7.

Chapter 9
Database and Web Application

Database driven web sites are replacing the web site development using static pages. Database driven Web site programming helps organization to provide interactive online information. With the introduction of Internet and World Wide Web now we have free access to information and can do business from any part of the world. For companies and organizations, web is an effective and interactive means of advertising their products, services and for providing information. A web application often uses a database to store information. The web application then uses this data to create web pages for display on the user's browser. The user can enter data to be stored in the database, or the data can be used by the web application to determine how the web application should respond to the user input. This way the page served to the user can be unique to that user. This goes beyond changing background colors, fonts and layouts, all which can be done by JavaScript. A web application can serve up page content according to user input. Web applications are often used for online shops. Any kind of information that can be stored on a computer can be made available over the web in the form of database for better application. There are type of information such as

Text and numerical data like customer, transaction, inventory and a myriad of other details. There can be image, sound or any other kind of files. Things like timestamps, dates, co-ordinates and what have libraries can be stored according to requirement. In fact the short list discussed here encompasses most types of information known to man. Any organization may use a database for web applications. A database makes activities so much easier. All the data is always there at the tip of the fingers. Just let the fingers wander over the keyboard, and voila, users have what they wanted. A database is indispensable for a website doing any of the following:

* Display changing content, like newly arrived documents.

* An online catalogue that wants easily accessible records.

* A mailing list sending things like newsletters to subscribers

* An application allowing certain users, belonging to certain groups, to sign in and do things permitted for that group

* Accept subscriptions from users for any reason

* Allow users to upload content like images, sound files, video, etc.

Web databases vary greatly in function and complexity from collecting visitors' email addresses to storing and retrieving thousands of banking transactions. As the Internet matures, it is becoming apparent, that huge amounts of data and information need to be retrieved and made easily available for an e-business to succeed. A few things Database Applications can do for the organization:

* Online shops with real time secure credit card processing

* Shopping carts for these shops

* Document upload, some to be sold, others to be

displayed as images, etc.

* Download of documents sold after they have been paid for - there is no other way to download these documents

* Selling tickets for events online. Again, secure, real time credit card processing.

* Links pages managed from the database - create and remove links very easily

* Determine which country a user is from and then displaying content for his country

* E-Mail system mailing to subscribers entered into the database. The subscribers have to activate before they will get the actual newsletter. They can also remove themselves by clicking a link in the email.

* The E-Mail gets sent out as both html and text

* Newsletters get saved to the database and can later be viewed by any users

* Subscribers can add themselves and/or the site admin can add them

* Form filled in by users submitted as e-mail to any number of recipients

* Sign in to the web application to be allowed to do certain things. Users can belong to any number of groups each with its own set of permissions

* Run Google Adwords campaigns for users

* Set up site to receive Google Adsense advertisements from which one can make money

* Display newsfeeds on the site. This provides changing content which one doesn't have to manage

* Set up a forum on the site

* Tell how to make the site as visible as possible to search engine spiders, or do it for user

* Display advertisements for pay, other than Google Adsense, on the site

Any database can be accessible over an intranet or the Internet. If the task/project is reasonably big or if heavy use is anticipated, organizations use Java 2 Enterprise Edition applications to access the database. If it already has Microsoft SQL Server then it can use Access forms and reports to connect to the MS SQL Server via an Access Data Project. The new EJB3 specification is out. Database Applications used JBoss to create and serve several EJB3 web applications. Most of the organizations works are EJB3 applications.

Technologies

In the beginning the use of Internet was limited for communication and providing information. In this limited sense it was very difficult to provide information through web sites designed by static pages; because then it needs to change the page every time for new entry. Online web sites with searchable database are gaining popularity now. Programming with new technologies such as ASP, JSP, Servlet, XML has contributed very much for this. Oracle and SQL Server databases have proved its reliability in the web also. Now modern scripting solutions like ASP, JSP, Servlets and PHP have tremendously simplified web applications development. New products are keeping on coming out from great software houses including Sun and Microsoft. Database Applications uses mainly Open Source technologies. Some of the big concerns that use the same Open Source technologies are NASA, Walmart, Google, Optus and many more.

MS Access

Many small and medium sized organizations use MS Access. MS Access is perfectly adequate in many cases. Database Applications can develop and implement the MS Access database. This includes database design, table and query creation, design and creation of forms (for data entry) and reports. Building applications with Access is usually fast.

MS SQL Server

Organizations may find that they have outgrown MS Access. One can use MS SQL Server for them, but keep MS Access as a front end. Staff will then find familiar Access forms for data entry and Access reports in a format they are used to. One can then use any organization can transact SQL stored procedures, which are not available in a pure MS Access application, to extend the usefulness of the application.

Oracle

Oracle Database (commonly referred to as **Oracle RDBMS** or simply as **Oracle**), a relational database management system (RDBMS) software product released by Oracle Corporation, has become a major feature of database computing. An Oracle database system comprises at least one instance of the application, along with data storage. An instance comprises a set of operating-system processes and memory-structures that interact with the storage. Typical processes include PMON (the process monitor) and SMON (the system monitor).

The Oracle RDBMS stores data logically in the form of tablespaces and physically in the form of data files. Tablespaces can contain various types of memory segments; for example, Data Segments, Index Segments etc. Segments in turn comprise one or more extents. Extents comprise groups of contiguous data blocks. Data blocks form the basic units of data storage. At the physical level, data-files comprise one or more data blocks, where the block size can vary between data-files. Oracle Corporation refers to some extensions to the core functionality of the Oracle database as "database options".

1.   Records database
2.   Content database
3.   Database Vault
4.   Data Mining (ODM)

5.   Oracle OLAP

6.   Partitioning

7.   Real Application Clusters (RAC)

Apart from the clearly-defined database options, Oracle databases may include many semi-autonomous software sub-systems, which Oracle Corporation sometimes refers to as features. Such features may include:

1. Automatic Workload Repository: providing monitoring services to Oracle database installations from Oracle version 10. Prior to the release of Oracle version 10, the Statspack facility provided similar functionality.

2. Oracle-managed files: a feature allowing automated naming, creation and deletion of datafiles at the operating system level.

3. Recovery Manager: for database backup, restoration and recovery

4. SQL*Plus: a CLI-based program that allows users to interact with Oracle database(s) via SQL and PL/SQL commands

5. Data Pump utilities: which aid in importing and exporting data and metadata between databases.

6. Data Aggregation and Consolidation

7. Data Guard for high availability

8. Flashback for selective data recovery and reconstruction

9. iSQL*Plus, a web-browser-based interface to Oracle database DML

JavaServer Pages

JavaServer Pages (JSP) is a Java technology that allows software developers to dynamically generate HTML, XML or other types of documents in response to a Web client request. The technology allows Java code and certain pre-defined actions to be embedded into static content.

JSPs are compiled into Java Servlets by a JSP compiler. A JSP compiler may generate a servlet in Java code that is then compiled by the Java compiler, or it may generate byte code for the servlet directly. JSPs can also be interpreted on-the-fly reducing the time taken to reload changes.

The JSP syntax adds additional XML-like tags, called JSP actions, to be used to invoke built-in functionality. Additionally, the technology allows for the creation of JSP tag libraries that act as extensions to the standard HTML or XML tags. Tag libraries provide a platform independent way of extending the capabilities of a Web server.

Reasons to use JSP: JSP is easy to learn and allows developers to quickly produce web sites and applications in an open and standard way. JSP is based on Java,an object-oriented language. JSP offers a robust platform for web development. The following are the main reasons to use JSP:

* Multi platform
* Component reuse by using Javabeans and EJB.
* Advantages of Java.
* One can take a JSP file and move it to another platform, web server or JSP Servlet engine.

JSP and ASP are fairly similar in the functionality that they provide. JSP may have slightly higher learning curve. Both allow embedded code in an HTML page, session variables and database access and manipulation. Whereas ASP is mostly found on Microsoft platforms i.e. NT, JSP can operate on any platform that conforms to the J2EE specification. JSP allow component reuse by using Javabeans and EJBs. ASP provides the use of COM / ActiveX controls.

JSP architecture

JSPs are built on top of SUN Microsystems' servlet technology. JSPs are essential an HTML page with special JSP tags embedded. These JSP tags can contain Java code. The JSP file extension is .jsp rather than .htm or .html. The JSP engine parses the .jsp and creates a Java servlet source file. It then compiles the source file into a class file,this is done the first time and this why the JSP is probably slower the first time it is accessed. Any time after this the special compiled servlet is executed and is therefore returns faster.

Servelets

Servlets are the Java platform technology of choice for extending and enhancing Web servers. Servlets provide a component-based, platform-independent method for building Web-based applications, without the performance limitations of CGI programs. And unlike proprietary server extension mechanisms (such as the Netscape Server API or Apache modules), servlets are server- and platform-independent. This leaves free to select a "best of breed" strategy for servers, platforms, and tools. Servlets have access to the entire family of Java APIs, including the JDBC API to access enterprise databases. Servlets can also access a library of HTTP-specific calls and receive all the benefits of the mature Java language, including portability, performance, reusability, and crash protection.

Today servlets are a popular choice for building interactive Web applications. Servlet containers are available for Apache Web Server, Microsoft IIS, and others. Servlet containers are usually a component of Web and application servers, such as BEA WebLogic Application Server, IBM WebSphere, Sun Java System Web Server, Sun Java System Application Server, and others. It makes it easier to combine fixed or static template data with dynamic content. Even if one is comfortable writing servlets, there are several compelling reasons to investigate JSP technology as a complement to existing work

Database Design and Development Process

Database design is very critical to the scalability and performance of the applications. It is very difficult to make changes to the application when it is completed. If the database is poorly designed it will affect the performance of the application. The whole process of developing a database is called as database development life cycle (DDLC). It includes information gathering to determine user's data needs, database schema (logical structure) design to satisfy those needs, selection of software to support the use of the database development of computer programs to use the database and review of user information needs in context of the development of database. The database design and development process involves the following stages:

* Analyzing organization process and defining business requirements
* Preparing detail design specifications
* Planning the resources available and scheduling timelines.
* Developing initial design/prototype for client's review
* Incorporating the review and developing the database application
* Testing components and integrated system.
* Preparing installation files and final deliverables.
* Providing Technical support/documentation on the final deliverables.
* Maintaining/upgrading the database application based on further business requirements.

Creating Web Based Database Services

With most of the services on the web being powered by web database applications, it becomes important for any web developer to know how bring together the web and databases to build applications. When user browses the Web, he or she uses the web browser to request resources from a web server and the web server responds with the resources. User makes these requests by filling in and submitting forms, clicking on links, or typing URLs into his or her browser. Often, resources are static HTML pages that are displayed in the browser. Following figure shows how a web browser communicates with a web server to retrieve desired home page. This is the classic two-tier or client-server architecture used on the Web.

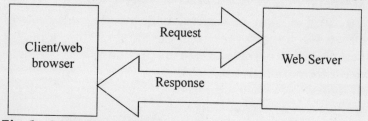

Fig. 1. A two-tier architecture where a web browser makes a request and the web server responds

It is found that a web server is not sophisticated storage software. The complicated operations on data, which are done by commercial sites and anyone else, presenting lots of dynamic data, are to be handled by a separate database. This aspect leads to a more complex architecture composed of three-tiers: (1) the browser is still the client tier, (2) the web server becomes the middle tier, and (3) the database is the third or database tier. Following figure shows requesting of a web browser to a resource that's generated from a database, and the way the database and web server respond to the request.

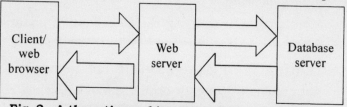

Fig. 2. A three-tier architecture where a web browser requests a resource and a response is being generated from a database

Three-tier Architectures

At the base of an application is the *database tier,* consisting of the *database management system* that manages the data users create, delete, modify, and query. Built on top of the database tier is the *middle tier,* which contains most of the application logic that anybody develops. It also communicates data between the other tiers. On top is the *client tier,* usually web browser software that interacts with the application. Basically, the three-tier architecture is conceptual. In practice, there are different implementations of web database applications that fit this architecture. The most common implementation has the web server (which includes the scripting engine that processes the scripts and carries out the actions they specify) and the database management system installed on one machine: it's the simplest to manage and secure. With this implementation on modern hardware, the applications can probably handle tens of thousands of requests every hour.

For popular web sites, a common implementation is to install the web server and the database server on different machines, so that resources are dedicated to permit a more scalable and faster application. For very high-end applications, a cluster of computers can be used, where the database and web servers are replicated and the load distributed across many machines. Describing web database applications as three-tier architectures makes them sound formally structured and organized. However, it hides the reality that the applications must bring together different protocols and software, and that the software needs to be installed, configured, and secured.

Database Applications and the Hypertext Transfer Protocol

The three-tier architecture provides a conceptual framework for web database applications. The Web itself provides the protocols and network that connect the client and middle tiers of the application: it provides the connection between the web browser and the web server. HTTP is one component that binds together the three-tier architecture. HTTP allows resources to be communicated and shared over the Web. Most web servers and web browsers communicate using the current version, HTTP/1.1.

HTTP example

HTTP is conceptually simple: a web browser sends a *request* for a resource to a web server, and the web server sends back a *response.* For every request, there's always one response. The HTTP response carries the resource—the HTML document, image, or output of a program—back to the web browser. The HTTP request is a textual description of a resource, and additional information or *headers* that describe how the resource should be returned. An example request:

GET /~hugh/index.html HTTP/1.1

Host: goanna.cs.rmit.edu.au

From: xyz@alphabets.com (xyz) User-agent: xyz-fake-browser/version-1.0 Accept: text/plain, text/html

This example uses a GET method to request an HTML page */~hugh/index.html* from the server *goanna.cs.rmit.edu.au* with HTTP/1.1. In this example, four additional header lines specify the host, identify the user and the web browser, and define what data types can be accepted by the browser. A request is normally made by a web browser and may include other headers.

An HTTP response has a response code and message, additional headers, and usually the resource that has been requested.

State

Traditional database applications are *stateful.* Users log in, run related transactions, and then log out when they are finished. For example, in a bank application, a bank teller might log in, use the application through a series of menus as he serves customer requests, and log out when he's finished for the day. The bank application has state: after the teller is logged in, he can interact with the application in a structured way using menus. When the teller has logged out, he can no longer use the application. HTTP is *stateless*. Any interaction between a web browser and a web server is independent of any other interaction. Each HTTP request from a web browser includes the same header information, such as the security credentials of the user, the types of pages the browser can accept, and instructions on how to format the response. The server processes the headers, formulates a response that explains how the request was served, and returns the headers and a resource to the browser. Once the response is complete, the server forgets the request and there's no way to go back and retrieve the request or response.

Statelessness has benefits: the most significant are the resource savings from not having to maintain information at the web server to track a user or requests, and the flexibility to allow users to move between unrelated pages or resources. However, because HTTP is stateless, it is difficult to develop stateful web database applications: for example, it's hard to force a user to follow menus or a series of steps to complete a task. To add state to HTTP, a method is needed to impose information flows and structure. A common solution is to exchange a token or key between a web browser and a web server that uniquely identifies the user and her *session*. Each time a browser requests a resource, it presents the token, and each time the web server responds, it returns the token to the web browser. The token is used by the middle-tier software to restore information about a user from her previous request, such as which menu in the application she last accessed. Exchanging tokens allows stateful structure such as menus, steps, and workflow processes to be added to the application. They can also be used to prevent actions from happening more than once, time out logins after a period of inactivity, and control access to an application

Client and the Three-tier Model

It is given that a web database application built with three-tier architecture doesn't fit naturally with HTTP, then what is the use of model at all? The answer mostly lies in the popularity and standardization of web browsers: any user who has a web browser can use the web database application, and usually without any restrictions. This means an application can be delivered to any number of diverse, dispersed users who use any platform, operating system, or browser software. Web browsers are *thin clients*. This means almost no application logic is included in the client tier. The browser simply sends HTTP requests for resources and then displays the responses, most of which are HTML pages. This thin client model means that users don't have to build, install, or configure the client tier, but that they need to build almost all of their application to run in the middle tier. User can thicken the client tier to put more work on the browser. Using popular technologies such as Java, JavaScript, and Macromedia Flash, he or she can develop application components that process data independently of the web server or preprocess data before sending it to the server. It is found that JavaScript is particularly good for many tasks because it's easy to use, open source, and built into all popular browsers. It's often used to validate data that's typed into forms before it's sent to the server, highlight parts of a page when the mouse passes over, display menus, and perform other simple tasks. However, it's limited in the information it can store and it can't communicate with a database server. Therefore, although user shouldn't depend on

JavaScript to do critical tasks, it's useful for preprocessing and it's another important technology.

The Middle Tier

The middle tier has many roles in a web database application. It brings together the other tiers, drives the structure and content of the data displayed to the user, provides security and authentication, and adds state to the application. It's the tier that integrates the Web with the database server.

Web servers

Essentially two types of requests are made to a web server: the first asks for a file—often a static HTML web page or an image—to be returned, and the second asks for a program or script to be run and its output to be returned. HTTP requests for PHP scripts require a server to run PHP's Zend scripting engine, process the instructions in the script (which may access a database), and return the script output to the browser to output as plain HTML. For example, Apache is an open source, fast, and scalable web server. It can handle simultaneous requests from browsers and is designed to run under multitasking operating systems such as Linux, Mac OS X, and Microsoft Windows. It has low resource requirements, can effectively handle changes in request loads, and can run fast on even modest hardware. It is widely used and tested. The current release at the time of writing is 2.0.48. Conceptually, Apache isn't complicated. On a Unix platform, the web server is actually several running programs, where one coordinates the others and doesn't serve requests itself. The other server programs notify their availability to handle requests to the coordinating server. If too few servers are available to handle incoming requests, the coordinating server may start new servers; if too many are free, it may kill spare servers to save resources. Apache's configuration file controls how it listens on the network and serves requests.

The server administrator controls the behavior of Apache through more than 150 directives that affect resource requirements, response time, and flexibility in dealing with request load variability, security, how HTTP requests are handled and logged, how scripting engines are used to run scripts, and most other aspects of its operation. The configuration of Apache for most web database applications is straightforward.

Web Scripting With PHP

PHP is the most widely supported and used web scripting language and an excellent tool for building web database applications. This isn't to say that other scripting languages don't have excellent features. However, there are many reasons that make PHP a good choice, including that it's:

Open source

Community efforts to maintain and improve it are unconstrained by commercial imperatives.

Flexible for integration with HTML

One or more PHP scripts can be embedded into static HTML files and this makes client tier integration easy. On the downside, this can blend the scripts with the presentation.

Suited to complex projects

It is a fully featured object-oriented programming language, with more than 110 libraries of programming functions for tasks as diverse as math, sorting, creating PDF documents, and sending email. There are over 15 libraries for native, fast access to the database tier.

Fast at running scripts

Using its built-in Zend scripting engine, PHP script execution is fast and all components run within the main memory space of PHP (in contrast to other scripting frameworks, in which components are in distinct modules). The experiments suggest that for tasks of at least moderate complexity, PHP is faster than other popular scripting tools.

Platform- and operating-system portable

Apache and PHP run on many different platforms and operating systems. PHP can also be integrated with other web servers.

A community effort

PHP contains PEAR, a repository that is home to over 100 freely available source code packages for common PHP programming tasks.

Database Applications and the Web - Introducing PHP5

PHP4 includes the first release of the Zend engine version 1.0, PHP's scripting engine that implements the syntax of the language and provides all of the tools needed to run library functions. PHP5 includes a new Zend engine version 2.0, that's enhanced to address the limitations of version 1.0 and to include new features that have been requested by developers. However, unlike the changes that occurred when PHP3 became PHP4, the changes from PHP4 to PHP5 only affect part of the language. Most code that's written for PHP4 will run without modification under PHP5. The following are the major new features in PHP5

New Object Model

PHP4 has a simple object model that doesn't include many of the features that object-oriented programmers expect in an OOP language such as destructors, private and protected member functions and variables, static member functions and variables, interfaces, and class type hints. All of these features are available in PHP5. The PHP5 OOP model also better manages how objects are passed around between functions and classes.

Handles to objects are now passed, rather than the objects themselves. This has substantially improved the performance of PHP.

Internationalization

It has support for non-Western character sets and Unicode.

Exception Handling

New try...catch, and throw statements are available that are aimed at improving the robustness of applications when errors occur. There's also a backtrace feature that user can use to develop a custom error handler that shows how the code that caused an error was called. This feature has been back-ported into PHP4.

Improved memory handling and speed

PHP4 was fast, but PHP5 is faster and makes even better use of memory.

New XML support

There were several different tools for working with the eXtensible Markup Language (XML) in PHP4. These tools have been replaced with a single new, robust framework in PHP5.

The Improved MySQL library (mysqli)

A new MySQL function library is available in PHP5 that supports MySQL 4. The library has the significant feature that it allows an SQL query to be prepared once, and executed many times, and this substantially improves speed if a query is often used.

The Database Tier

The database tier stores and retrieves data. It's also responsible for managing updates, allowing simultaneous (*concurrent*) access from web servers, providing security, ensuring the integrity of data, and providing support services such as data backup. Importantly, a good database tier must allow quick and flexible access to millions upon millions of facts. Managing data in the database tier requires complex software. Fortunately, most database management systems (DBMSs) or servers are designed so that the software complexities are hidden. To effectively use a database server, skills are required to design a database and formulate queries using the SQL language. An understanding of the underlying architecture of the database server is unimportant to most users.

The *MySQL* server, to manage data, has a well-deserved reputation for speed: it can manage many millions of facts, it's very scalable, and particularly suited to the characteristics of web database applications. Also, like PHP and Apache, MySQL is open source software. The first step in successful web database application development is understanding of system requirements and designing databases. The techniques can be developed for modeling system requirements, converting a model into a database. There should be focus on the database tier and introduce database software by contrasting it with other techniques for storing data. There are other server choices for storing data in the database tier. These include search engines, document management systems, and gateway services such as email software.

Database Management Systems

A database server or DBMS searches and manages data that's stored in databases. A database is a collection of related data, and an application can have more than one database. A database might contain a few entries that make up a simple address book of names, addresses, and phone numbers. At the other extreme, a database can contain tens or hundreds of millions of records that describe the catalog, purchases, orders, and payroll of a large company. Most web database applications have small-to medium-size databases that store thousands, or tens of thousands, of records. Database servers are complex software. However, the important component for web database application development is the applications interface that's used to access the database server. For all but the largest applications, understanding and configuring the internals of a database server is usually unnecessary.

SQL

The database server applications interface is accessed using SQL. It's a standard query language that's used to define and manipulate databases and data, and it's supported by all popular database servers.

SQL has had a complicated life. It began at the IBM San Jose Research Laboratory in the early 1970s, where it was known as *Sequel*; some users still call it Sequel, though it's more correctly referred to by the three-letter acronym, SQL. After almost 16 years of development and differing implementations, the standards organizations ANSI and ISO published an SQL standard in 1986. IBM published a different standard one year later!

Since the mid-1980s, three subsequent standards have been published by ANSI and ISO. The first, SQL-89, is the most widely, completely implemented SQL in popular database servers. Many servers implement only some features of the next release, SQL-2 or SQL-92, and almost no servers have implemented the features of the most recently approved standard, SQL-99 or SQL-3. MySQL supports the entry-level SQL92 standard and has some proprietary extensions. For example an user wants to store information about books in a library. He can create a table—an object that's stored in his database—using the following statement:

```
CREATE TABLE books (
    title char(50),
    author char(50),
```

ISBN char(50) NOT NULL,

PRIMARY KEY (ISBN)

);

Then, he can add books to the database using statements such as:

INSERT INTO books ("Web Database Apps", "Rama and Vama", "123-456-N");

Once he has added data, he can retrieve facts about the books using queries such as the following that finds the author and title of a book with a specific ISBN:

SELECT author, title FROM books WHERE ISBN = "456-789-Q";

These are only some of the features of SQL, and even these features can be used in complex ways. SQL also allows updating and deleting data and databases, and it includes many other features such as security and access management, multiuser transactions that allow many users to access the same database without corrupting the data, tools to import and export data, and powerful undo and redo features.

Database Server

There are several reasons that can be explained by contrasting a database with a spreadsheet, a simple text file, or a custom-built method of storing data. We can take spreadsheets for example. Spreadsheet worksheets are typically designed for a specific application. If two users store names and addresses, they are likely to organize data in a different way and develop custom methods to move around and summarize the data. The program and the data aren't independent: moving a column might mean rewriting a macro or formula, while exchanging data between the two users' applications might be complex. In contrast, a database server and SQL provide data-program independence, where the method for storing the data is independent of the language that accesses it.

Managing complex relationships is difficult in a spreadsheet or text file. For example, consider what happens if user wants to store information about customers: he might allocate a few spreadsheet columns to store each customer's residential address. If he had to add business addresses and postal addresses, he'd need more columns and complex processing to, for example, process a mail-out to customers. If he wants to store information about the purchases by his customers, the spreadsheet becomes wider still, and problems start to emerge. For example, it is difficult to determine the maximum number of columns needed to store orders and to design a method to process these for reporting. In contrast, databases are designed to manage complex *relational* data.

A database server usually permits multiple users to access a database at the same time in a methodical way. In contrast, a spreadsheet should be opened and written only by one user; if another user opens the spreadsheet, she won't see any updates being made at the same time by the first user. At best, a shared spreadsheet or text file permits very limited concurrent access. An additional benefit of a database server is its speed and scalability. It isn't totally true to say that a database provides faster searching of data than a spreadsheet or a custom file system. In many cases, searching a spreadsheet or a special-purpose file might be perfectly acceptable, or even faster if it is designed carefully and the volume of data is small. However, for managing large amounts of related information, the underlying search structures allow fast searching, and if information needs are complex, a database server should optimize the method of retrieving the data. There are also other advantages of database servers, including data-oriented and user-oriented security, administration software, portability, and data recovery support. A practical benefit of this is reduced application development time: the system is already built; it needs only data and queries to access the data.

When to use a database server

In any of these situations, a database server should be used to manage data:

* There is more than one user who needs to access the data at the same time.

* There is at least a moderate amount of data. For example, organization might need to maintain information about a few hundred customers.

* There are relationships between the stored data items. For example, customers may have any number of related invoices.

* There is more than one kind of data object. For example, there might be information about customers, orders, inventory, and other data in an online store.

* There are constraints that must be rigidly enforced on the data, such as field lengths, field types, uniqueness of customer numbers, and so on.

* New or consolidated information must be produced from basic, related information; that is, the data must be queried to produce reports or results.

* There is a large amount of data that must be searched quickly.

* Security is important. There is a need to enforce rules as to who can access the data.

* Adding, deleting, or modifying data is a complex process.

* Adding, deleting, and updating data is a frequent or complex process.

When not to use a DBMS

There are some situations where a relational DBMS is probably unnecessary or unsuitable. Here are some examples:

* There is one type of data item, and the data isn't searched. For example, if a log entry is written when a user logs in and logs out, appending the entry to the end of a simple text file may be sufficient.

* The data management task is trivial and accessing a database server adds unnecessary overhead. In this case, the data might be coded into a web script in the middle tier.

The MySQL Server

MySQL has most of the features of high-end commercial database servers, including the ability to manage very large quantities of data. Its design is ideally suited to managing databases that are typical of most web database applications. The difference between MySQL and high-end commercial servers is that MySQL's components aren't as mature. For example, MySQL's query evaluator doesn't always develop a fast plan to evaluate complex queries. It also doesn't support all of the features one might find in other servers: for example, views, triggers, and stored procedures are planned for future versions. There are other, more minor limitations that don't typically affect web development. However, even users who need these features often choose MySQL because it's free. MySQL 4 is a major new release that includes important features that have been added since MySQL 3.23. The current version, MySQL 4.1, supports a wide range of SQL queries, including joins, multi-table updates and deletes, and nested queries. At present it supports most features of the SQL 92 standard, and its aim is to fully support SQL 99. The MySQL server supports several table types that allow a wide range of choice in the applications of locking techniques, transaction environments, and performance choices. It also has good tools for backup and recovery. MySQL is a powerful, fully-featured DBMS that's commercially supported by the company MySQL AB.

The following are the major features of MySQL 4:

Nested query and derived table support

Sub-queries are new in MySQL 4.1. This allows to use the SQL statementsEXISTS,IN,NOT EXISTS, andNOT IN, and it also allows to include a nested query in theFROMclause that creates a derived table.UNIONwas introduced in MySQL 4.0.

Internationalization

MySQL 4.1 now supports Unicode, allowing to develop applications that don't use Western languages.

Query caching

MySQL 4.0 introduced a query cache that stores the most-recent results of queries, and intelligently delivers these as answers to identical future queries.

Transaction-safe InnoDB tables

The InnoDB table type was included as a built-in module in MySQL 4.0. InnoDB supports transactions, and allows deciding whether to commit or rollback a set of writes to the database. It also supports checkpointing, which is used by MySQL to get the database into a known state after a crash or serious error.

Full text searching

MySQL 4 introduced new methods for fast searching of text and a form of search engine-like ranking.

References

1.   Bawden, D. & Robinson, L. (2002). Internet subject gateways revisited. *International Journal of Information Management,* **22**(2), 157-162.

2.   *Beckett, D (2002). Connecting XML, RDF and Web technologies for representing knowledge on the Semantic Web. Paper*

presented at XML Europe Conference 2002, Barcelona, May 2002. Retrieved 2 May, 2004 from http:// www.idealliance.org/papers/xmle02/dx_xmle02/papers/03- 05-07/03-05-07.html

3.   Goldman, R., McHugh, J. & Widom, J. (1999), "From semistructured data to XML: migrating the lore data model and query languages." *in: Proceedings of the ACM International Workshop on the Web and Databases (WebDB'99), 25-30, Philadelphia, Pennsylvania, USA. pp. 25- 30 New York, NY: ACM press.*

4.   Online database application. http://creator.zoho.com/ explore/online-database-application.html

5.   Gruber, T. (1993), "A translation approach to portable ontology specifications." *Knowledge Acquisition,* **6**(2), 199- 221.

6.   Hugh E. Williams & David Lane. *Web Database Applications with PHP and MySQL.* Cambridge: O'Reilly, 2004.

7.   Lu, Shiyong, Dong, Ming and Fotouhi, Farshad (2002) "The Semantic Web: opportunities and challenges for next- generation Web applications." *Information Research* **7**(4), Available at: http://InformationR.net/ir/7-4/ paper134..html www.onlamp.com/pub/a/onlamp/2002/ 04/04/webdb.html -

8.   www.alphasoftware.com

9.   www.ironspeed.com

10. Ankolekar, A., et al., (2001), "DAML-S: semantic markup for web services.", in: *The First Semantic Web Working Symposium,* pp. 411-430, Heidelberg: Springer-Verlag Heidelberg.

11. Custom **Software Development.** http:// www.myprogrammer.com/

12. Berry, M.E. & Browne, M. (1999). Understanding search engines: mathematical modeling and text retrieval. Software, environments, tools. Philadelphia, PA: Society for Industrial & Applied Mathematics.

13. http://www.caspio.com/

14. Thuraisingham, B. (2002). *XML databases and the semantic web.* Boca Raton, FL: CRC Press.

15. www.webbase.com

16. www.mysql.com

17. Stephen Schaub. Creating Database Web Applications with Eclipse. http://www.eclipse.org/articles/Article-EclipseDbWebapps/article.html

18. Barros, F., Goncalves, P. & Santos, T. (1998). "Providing context to web searches: the use of ontologies to enhance search engine's accuracy." *In Journal of the Brazilian Computer Society.* 5(2), 45-55.

Chapter 10
Online Database Services Worldwide

OCLC

Founded in 1967, OCLC Online Computer Library Center is a nonprofit, membership, computer library service and research organization dedicated to the public purposes of furthering access to the world's information and reducing information costs. More than 50,000 libraries in 84 countries and territories around the world use OCLC services to locate, acquire, catalog, lend and preserve library materials. Researchers, students, faculty, scholars, professional librarians and other information seekers use OCLC services such as FirstSearch to obtain bibliographic, abstract and full-text information when and where they need it. OCLC and its member libraries cooperatively produce and maintain WorldCat, the OCLC Online Union Catalog. OCLC's electronic journal archives do more than save library the cost of managing a print collection. OCLC has secured archival rights to journal content, thus ensuring that the library will have ongoing access to the journals it subscribes to through Electronic Collections Online.

Enabled by FirstSearch, the users can find and retrieve materials on almost any research topic. The service delivers bibliographic records and library holdings from WorldCat, electronic journals from Electronic Collections Online, and access to more than 72 databases to give the users a convenient and easy-to-use reference service that is searchable in five languages. The enhanced service provides instant access to full text from 9,000 full-text journals, and more than 4,000 full-image journals online. The FirstSearch base package includes WorldCat and ArticleFirst, which includes all the citations from Electronic Collections Online. Library can easily add access to other databases, such as PAIS International, the premier resource for public policy and world affairs information. New choices are continuously available: Alternative Press Index Archive and Media Review Digest were recently added. Electronic Collections Online enables librarians to assemble, manage, and archive large collections of journals on the Web and make them widely available to their patrons.

FirstSearch

FirstSearch is an online service that gives library professionals and end users access to a rich collection of reference databases. With FirstSearch, materials in the library's collection are highlighted in results from searches in dozens of leading databases. FirstSearch offers seamless electronic access to dozens of databases and more than 10 million full-text and full-image articles. It offers a broad range of databases and full text collections or a select list that fits the needs of the users. FirstSearch's Web-based interface and Z39.50 compatibility make it highly accessible, and its detailed online help, suggestion tools and source and location icons make it highly usable. Users can start and refine searches at one of three different skill levels. Library has the ability to customize many aspects of the experience. FirstSearch easily integrates into the current library resources. The subscription includes everything library needs to start using FirstSearch and promote it to the users. And a variety of support options make it easy to find answers. FirstSearch's purchase options help library stay within budget, and its functionality can be extended to include other OCLC services such as Interlibrary Loan and NetLibrary eBooks. Since its introduction in 1991, FirstSearch has been continuously enhanced based on input from users. These improvements include the use of icons to indicate local holdings in results lists and online usage statistics that help library plan electronic resource purchases.

Direct links to Web information and loan requests

FirstSearch is the convenient way to access the journals available through Electronic Collections Online. FirstSearch provides abstracts and full text for articles in electronic journals to which the library or consortium subscribes. Full-image articles from Electronic Collections Online journals are linked to corresponding citations in databases throughout the FirstSearch service. Users can borrow articles and materials from other libraries using OCLC holdings information and a link to the OCLC Interlibrary Loan service. They can jump to Internet resources from links in a growing number of FirstSearch databases, including WorldCat, FactSearch and Consumers Index.

Electronic Collections Online at a glance

OCLC's Electronic Collections Online, accessible through FirstSearch, provides bibliographic information for a growing collection of more than 5,000 electronic journals from over 70 publishers in a wide range of subject areas, with article citations and full text available through several options. Far more than just an aggregator, Electronic Collections Online enables librarians to assemble, manage, and archive large collections of academic and professional journals on the Web.

Benefits

A single point of access : through FirstSearch for cross-journal searching and browsing

Retain access : to archived journals even if library cancel the subscriptions to them

Save : by subscribing only to the electronic journals library need

Close gaps : in the collection through our powerful archiving solution

Save time and effort : in acquisitions by letting OCLC negotiate fees with individual publishers

Control costs : through data standardization as well as through centralized access and storage

Features

* Users can obtain full text and abstracts of articles in subscribed journals through the FirstSearch interface, and can even look up citations for articles in journals to which library do not subscribe

* Multiple search levels and methods are present, including searches by title, publisher and topic

* Robust archiving solutions provide stable and convenient access to the journals collection

* Tools for collection management are available which include monthly journal-level statistics and matching bibliographic records for the OPAC

* Electronic versions of more than 3,900 print journals are available at no additional cost to existing subscribers through the print subscriber program

* There is strong international content and breadth of subject areas

* Citations in other FirstSearch databases link to full-text articles in Electronic Collections Online

* The library's subscription profile is linked to a centralized access account

Requirements

* Netscape 4.0 or Microsoft Internet Explorer 4.0 (or a higher version of either)
* Adobe Acrobat Reader, version 4.0 or higher (to view full-text articles in PDF format)
* Ingenta's RealPage software, version 2.10 or higher (to view the full-text RealPage-formatted articles)

Options

* Per-article-use purchasing is available
* Purchasing for consortia lets library share access to a common group of journals with other libraries
* It link directly to journals and articles from the library's catalog or Web site as well as from FirstSearch
* One can order journals from OCLC, subscription agents, or the publishers themselves
* It supplements the OPAC with matching bibliographic records for all the electronic journals
* Users can login methods via FirstSearch include IP authentication, WebScript automatic logon scripting or authorization/password
* The inbound linking allows access to the journals from other information service providers

OCLC FirstSearch Service Databases

The OCLC FirstSearch service offers increased visibility for the library's holdings, easier access to full text, including full-image articles, and much more. The users can find information faster than ever. Following are the names of all the FirstSearch databases available from OCLC. One can select any database name to obtain detailed information for that database, including indexes, index labels and examples. Subscription takes place to the FirstSearch Internet distribution list in English, French, or Spanish to receive news about upcoming database changes and enhancements to the service.

* ABI/INFORM
* AGRICOLA
* Alternative Press Index
* Alternative Press Index Archive
* Applied Science and Technology Abstracts
* Applied Science and Technology Index
* Art Abstracts
* Art Index
* ArticleFirst
* Arts & Humanities Search
* ATLA Religion
* ATLA Serials Database
* BasicBIOSIS
* Biological & Agricultural Index
* Biology Digest
* Biography Index
* Book Review Digest
* Books In Print
* Business Dateline
* Business and Industry
* Business Organizations, Agencies, and Publications Directory
* Business and Management Practices
* Chemical Abstracts, Student Edition
* Clase and Periódica
* Consumers Index
* Contemporary Women's Issues
* Disclosure Corporate Snapshots (Disclosure)
* Disclosure Corporate Snapshots (DisclosureS)
* Dissertation Abstracts Online
* Electronic Books
* Electronic Collections Online
* EconLit
* Education Abstracts

*   Education Index
*   Environmental Sciences and Pollution Management
*   ERIC
*   Essay and General Literature Index
*   FactSearch
*   General Science Abstracts
*   General Science Index
*   GEOBASE
*   GeoRefS
*   GPO Monthly Catalog
*   Humanities Abstracts
*   Humanities Index
*   Inspec
*   Index to Legal Periodicals & Books
*   Library Literature
*   Media Review Digest
*   MEDLINE
*   MLA International Bibliography
*   Newspaper Abstracts
*   PAIS Archive
*   PAIS International
*   PapersFirst
*   Periodical Abstracts
*   Philosopher's Index
*   ProceedingsFirst
*   PsycARTICLE
*   PsycBOOKS
*   PsycCRITIQUES
*   PsycFIRST
*   PsycINFO 1887
*   Readers' Guide Abstracts
*   RIPM Retrospective Index to Music Periodicals
*   RILM Abstracts of Music Literature
*   SIRS Researcher

* Sociological Abstracts
* Social Sciences Abstracts
* Social Sciences Index
* Wilson Business Abstracts
* Wilson Select Plus
* WorldCat (The OCLC Online Union Catalog)
* WorldCat Dissertations and Theses (WorldCatDissertations)
* World Almanac
* Worldscope

The OCLC FirstSearch service is a comprehensive reference service with a rich collection of databases supporting research in a wide range of subject areas. It includes bibliographic and full-text databases in addition to ready-reference tools such as directories, almanacs and encyclopedias. At the heart of FirstSearch is WorldCat, containing more than 57 million records representing over 900 million holding locations in libraries worldwide. WorldCat adds value to databases in FirstSearch by linking citations to holdings that helps users find these materials in their own libraries and through the WorldCat Resource Sharing service. Library can also limit the searches to the collections of the own library or library group.

Recent Additions

PsycCRITIQUES : It is updated weekly, this database offers full-text reviews of current books, popular films, videos and software and comparative reviews of books. It also includes a backfile of more than 5,000 reviews dating to 1995.

MLA International Bibliography : Retrospective content from 1926-1962 is available to libraries as part of their current subscriptions for no additional cost. The 160,000 records come from thirty-eight print volumes and all have been reviewed for standardization of names and terms. ISSNs have been addded

WorldCat Dissertations and Theses : It is updated daily, this database contains records for all dissertations and theses, and published materials based on theses, cataloged by libraries in WorldCat. It is available at no additional cost to all existing U. S. subscribers and new purchasers of the OCLC Base Package and OCLC Collection on FirstSearch.

OCLC Databases by Topic

Arts & Humanities

WorldCat
Art Abstracts/Art Index
Arts & Humanities Search
ATLA Religion
ATLA Serials Database
Book Review Digest
Clase and Periódica
Electronic Collections Online
Essay and General Literature
Index
Humanities Abstracts/Humanities
Index
Media Review Digest
MLA International Bibliography
PAIS Archive
PAIS International
Philosopher's Index
RILM Abstracts of Music Literature
RIPM Retrospective Index to Music
Periodicals
Wilson Select Plus

Biography

WorldCat
Biography Index

Features of FirstSearch Database

FirstSearch Database	Suggested Audience by Library Type (may include users, librarians, Item faculty, or staff)	Ordering Options that Own	Links to Libraries OPACs	Links to Local Holdings	Z39.50 Links to Databases	Via Other ILL Link Linking	Full Text Availability		
							Via OCLC URL Text	Via Open Full	Online
1	2	3	4	5	6	7	8	9	10
ABI/INFORM	Academic, Public	Subscription and Per-Search (per-search not available to users outside the U.S. and Canada)	X	X	X	X	X	Inbound Outbound	Articles, JSTOR links
AGRICOLA	Academic	Subscription and Per-Search	X	X	X	X	X	Outbound only	JSTOR links
Alternative Press Index	Academic, Public	Subscription and Per-Search	X	X	X	X	X	Outbound only	Hot links to publisher web sites, JSTOR links
Alternative Press Index Archive	Academic, Public	Subscription and Per-Search	X	X	X		X	Outbound only	JSTOR links

1	2	3	4	5	6	7	8	9	10
Applied Science & Technology Abstracts	Academic, Public	Subscription only	X	X	X	X	X	Outbound only	JSTOR links
Applied Science & Technology Index	Academic, Public	Subscription only	X	X	X	X	X	Outbound only	JSTOR links
Art Abstracts	Academic, Public	Subscription only	X	X	X	X	X	Outbound only	JSTOR links
Art Index	Academic, Public	Subscription only	X	X	X	X	X	Outbound only	JSTOR links
OCLC ArticleFirst®	Academic, Public	Subscription and Per-Search	X	X	X	X	X	Outbound only	JSTOR links
Arts & Humanities Search	Academic	Subscription and Per-Search	X	X	X	X	X	Outbound only	JSTOR links
ATLA Religion	Academic	Subscription only	X	X	X	X	X	Inbound Outbound	Articles, serials, JSTOR links
ATLA Serials	Academic	Subscription only	X	X	X	X	X	Inbound Outbound	Articles, serials, JSTOR links

1	2	3	4	5	6	7	8	9	10
BasicBIOSIS	Academic	Subscription and Per-Search	X	X	X	X	X	Outbound only	JSTOR links
Biography Index	Academic, Public, School	Subscription only	X	X	X	X	X	Outbound only	JSTOR links
Biological & Agricultural Index	Academic	Subscription only	X	X	X	X	X	Outbound only	JSTOR links
BiologyDigest	Academic, Public, School	Subscription and Per-Search	X	X	X	X	X	Outbound only	JSTOR links
Book Review Digest	Academic, Public, School	Subscription only	X	X	X	X	X	Outbound only	JSTOR links
Books In Print	Academic, Public, School	Subscription and Per-Search		X	X		X	Outbound only	Reviews and publisher information
Business Dateline	Academic, Public	Subscription and Per-Search (per-search not available to users outside the U.S. and Canada)		X	X		X	Inbound Outbound	Articles

1	2	3	4	5	6	7	8	9	10
Business & Industry	Academic, Public	Subscription and Per-Search, not available to corporations	X	X	X	X	X	Inbound Outbound	Articles
Business & Management Practices	Academic, Public	Subscription and Per-Search	X	X	X	X	X	Inbound Outbound	Articles, JSTOR links
Business Organizations, Agencies, and Publications Directory	Public	Subscription and Per-Search							Directory
CA Student Edition	Academic	Subscription only	X	X	X	X	X	Outbound only	JSTOR links
Clase and Periódica	Academic, Public	Subscription and Per-Search	X	X	X	X	X	Outbound only	
Consumers Index	Public, School	Per-Search only	X	X	X	X	X	Outbound only	Articles (Hot links to some free full text)
Contemporary Women's Issues	Academic, Public	Subscription and Per-Search	X			X		Inbound Outbound	Articles

1	2	3	4	5	6	7	8	9	10
Disclosure Corporate Snapshots (Brief entries)	Academic, Public	Per-search only		X					Directory only; Financials additional charge
DisclosureS Corporate Snapshots (Full entries)	Academic, Public	Subscription only		X					Directory, Financials
Dissertation Abstracts	Academic	Subscription and Per-Search(per-search not available to users outside the U.S. and Canada)		X			X	Outbound only	
EconLit	Academic	Subscription and Per-Search	X	X	X	X	X	Outbound only	JSTOR links
Education Abstracts	Academic, School	Subscription only	X	X	X	X	X	Outbound only	JSTOR links
Education Index	Academic, School	Subscription only	X	X	X	X	X	Outbound only	JSTOR links
Electronic Books	Academic, Public, School	Subscription and Per-Search	X	X				Outbound only	Links to public domain and

licensed e-book collections

1	2	3	4	5	6	7	8	9	10
Electronic Collections Online	Academic	Subscription, Per-Search, and Per-Article Use Purchase	X	X	X	X	X	Inbound Outbound	Articles (PDF, RealPage, HTML), JSTOR links
Environmental Sci.& Pollution Management	Academic	Subscription only	X					Outbound only	
ERIC—includes thesaurus	Academic, School	Subscription and Per-Search	X	X	X	Link to ERIC,	X	Outbound only	ERIC Digest documents, JSTOR links
Essay and General Literature Index	Academic, Public	Subscription only	X	X	X		X	Outbound only	
FactSearch	Academic, Public, School	Per-Search only	X	X	X	X	X	Outbound only	Articles (Hot links to some free full text), JSTOR links

1	2	3	4	5	6	7	8	9	10
General Science Abstracts	Academic, Public, School	Subscription only	X	X	X	X	X	Outbound only	JSTOR links
General Science Index	Academic, Public, School	Subscription only	X	X	X	X	X	Outbound only	JSTOR links
GEOBASE	Academic	Subscription and Per-Search	X	X	X	X	X	Outbound only	JSTOR links
GeoRefS—includes thesaurus	Academic	Subscription only	X	X	X	X	X	Outbound only	JSTOR links
GPO Monthly Catalog	Academic	Subscription and Per-Search	X	X	X		X	Outbound only	
Humanities Abstracts	Academic, Public, School	Subscription only	X	X	X	X	X	Outbound only	JSTOR links
Humanities Index	Academic, Public, School	Subscription only	X	X	X	X	X	Outbound only	JSTOR links
Index to Legal Periodicals & Books	Academic	Subscription only	X	X	X	X	X	Outbound only	JSTOR links

1	2	3	4	5	6	7	8	9	10
Inspec—includes thesaurus	Academic	Subscription only	X	X	X	X	X	Outbound only	JSTOR links
Library Literature	Academic, Public, School	Subscription only	X	X	X	X	X	Outbound only	
Media Review Digest	Academic, Public	Per-Search only	X	X		X			Articles (Hot links to some free full text)
MEDLINE—includes thesaurus	Academic, Public	Subscription and Per-Search	X	X	X	X	X	Outbound only	JSTOR links
MLA International Bibliography (Includes Directory of Periodicals, Thesaurus)	Academic	Subscription only	X	X	X		X	Outbound only	JSTOR links
Newspaper Abstracts	Academic, Public	Subscription and Per-Search (per-search not available to users outside the U.S. and Canada)	X	X	X		X	Outbound only	

1	2	3	4	5	6	7	8	9	10
PAIS® Archive	Academic, Public	Subscription only	X	X	X	X	X	Outbound only	JSTOR links
PAIS International® (Includes PAIS International subject authority files)	Academic, Public	Subscription only	X	X	X	X	X	Outbound only	Links to web resources and publisher web sites, JSTOR links
OCLC Papers First®	Academic, Public	Subscription and Per-Search						Outbound only	
Periodical Abstracts	Academic, Public, School	Subscription and Per-Search (per-search not available to users outside the U.S. and Canada)	X	X	X	X	X	Inbound Outbound	Articles, JSTOR links
Philospher's Index	Academic	Subscription only	X	X	X	X	X	Outbound only	JSTOR links
OCLC	Academic,	Subscription and						Outbound	

1	2	3	4	5	6	7	8	9	10
Proceedings First®	Public, School	Per-Search						only	
Psyc ARTICLES	Academic	Subscription only	X	X	X	X	X	Inbound Outbound	X
Psyc BOOKS—includes thesaurus	Academic	Subscription only	X	X				Outbound only	X
Psyc CRITIQUES—includes thesaurus	Academic	Subscription only	X	X	X	X	X	Inbound Outbound	X
PsycFIRST—includes thesaurus	Academic	Per-search only	X	X	X	X	X	Outbound only	
PsycINFO_1887—includes thesaurus	Academic	Subscription only	X	X	X	X	X	Outbound only	JSTOR links
Readers' Abstracts	Academic, School	Subscription only	X	X	X	X	X	Outbound only	Guide
RILM Abstracts of School	Public, School	Subscription only	X		X	X	X	Outbound only	JSTOR links

1	2	3	4	5	6	7	8	9	10
Music Literature									
RIPM Retrospective Index to Music Periodicals	Academic	Subscription only	X	X	X		X	Outbound only	
SIRS Researcher	Public, School	Subscription and Per-Search	X	X			X	Outbound only	Articles with images
Social Sciences Abstracts	Public, School	Subscription only	X	X	X	X	X	Outbound only	JSTOR links
Social Sciences Index	Public, School	Subscription only	X	X	X	X	X	Outbound only	JSTOR links
Sociological Abstracts—includes thesaurus	Academic	Subscription only	X	X	X	X	X	Outbound only	JSTOR links
Wilson Business Abstracts	Academic	Subscription only	X	X	X	X	X	Outbound only	JSTOR links

1	2	3	4	5	6	7	8	9	10
Wilson Select Plus	Public	Subscription and Per-Search	X	X	X	X	X	Inbound Outbound	Articles, JSTOR links
World Almanacs	Academic, Public, School	Subscription and Per-Search							Full entries with images (Hot links to some free full text)
WorldCat® (the OCLC Online Union Catalog)—includes thesaurus	Academic, Public, School	Subscription and Per-Search	X	X	X	X	X	Outbound only	
WorldCat® Dissertations and Theses	Academic, Public, School	In U.S.: Subscription only, as part of OCLC Collection or OCLC Base Package. For regions outside the U.S., contact the regional service provider.	X	X	X	X	X	Outbound only	Links to public domain and licensed dissertations and these

1	2	3	4	5	6	7	8	9	10
Worldscope GLOBAL (Brief entries)	Academic, Public, School	Per-search only		X					Directory only; Financials additional charge
WorldscopeS GLOBAL (Full entries)	Academic, Public	Subscription only		X					Directory, Financials

Wilson Select Plus

Business & Economics
WorldCat
ABI/INFORM
Business Dateline
Business & Industry
Business & Management Practices
Business Organizations, Agencies, and Publications
Directory
Disclosure Corporate Snapshots
—Brief Records
Disclosure Corporate Snapshots
—Full Records
Dissertation Abstracts
EconLit Electronic Books
Electronic Collections Online
Wilson Business Abstracts
Wilson Select Plus
Worldscope GLOBAL—Brief Entries
Worldscope GLOBAL—Full Entries

Conferences & Proceedings
WorldCat
OCLC PapersFirst
OCLC ProceedingsFirst

Consumer Affairs & People
WorldCat
Biography Index
Consumers Index
Contemporary Women's Issues
Electronic Collections Online
Newspaper Abstracts

Education
        WorldCat
        Dissertation Abstracts
        Education Abstracts
        Education Index
        Electronic Collections
        Online
        ERIC
        Library Literature
        Media Review Digest

Engineering & Technology
        WorldCat
        OCLC PapersFirst
        OCLC Proceedings First
        Applied Science & Technology
        Abstracts
        Applied Science & Technology Index
        Clase and Periódica
        Electronic Collections
        Online
        Environmental Sciences & Pollution Management
(with abstracts)
        Inspec

General
        WorldCat
        OCLC ArticleFirst
        Dissertation Abstracts
        Electronic Books
        Electronic Collections Online
        Essay and General Literature
        Index
        Periodical Abstracts
        Readers' Guide Abstracts

SIRS Researcher
Wilson Select Plus
WorldCat Dissertations and
Theses

General Science
WorldCat
Applied Science & Technology Abstracts
Applied Science & Technology Index
Chemical Abstracts Student Edition
Clase and Periódica
Electronic Collections Online
Environmental Sciences & Pollution Management
General Science Abstracts
General Science Index
GEOBASE
GeoRefS
Inspec
Wilson Select Plus

Life Sciences
WorldCat
AGRICOLA
Basic BIOSIS
Biological & Agricultural Index
Biology Digest
Clase and Periódica
Electronic Collections Online
Environmental Sciences & Pollution Management

Medicine/Health, Consumer
WorldCat
Consumers Index
Contemporary Women's Issues
Electronic Collections

Online   FactSearch
MEDLINE

Medicine/Health, Professional

WorldCat
Electronic Collections Online
MEDLINE
PsycARTICLES
PsycBOOKS
PsycCRITIQUES
PsycFIRST
PsycINFO_1887

News & Current Events

Alternative Press Index
Alternative Press Index Archive
Business Dateline
Newspaper Abstracts
Periodical Abstracts
Readers' Guide Abstracts
Wilson Select Plus

Public Affairs & Law

WorldCat
Alternative Press Index
Alternative Press Index
Archive
Electronic Collections Online
FactSearch
GPO Monthly Catalog
Index to Legal Periodicals & Books
PAIS Archive
PAIS International

Quick Reference

WorldCat

Book Review Digest
Books In Print
Electronic Books
FactSearch
Media Review Digest
World Almanacs
WorldCat Dissertations and Theses

Social Sciences

WorldCat
ATLA Religion
Alternative Press Index
Alternative Press Index
Archive
Clase and Periódica
Contemporary Women's Issues
Dissertation Abstracts
EconLit Electronic Books
Electronic Collections Online
Library Literature
PAIS Archive
PAIS International
Philosopher's Index
PsycARTICLES
PsycBOOKS
PsycCRITIQUES
PsycFIRST
PsycINFO_1887
Social Sciences Abstracts/Social
Sciences Index
Sociological Abstracts
Wilson Select Plus

Customizing the FirstSearch Databases

Library can use the FirstSearch administrative module to customize FirstSearch for the users and integrate FirstSearch with other information products and services that the library offers. Library can:

* Enhance visibility of and access to the library collections
* Link to the library's catalog
* Activate links to full-text
* Specify a list of libraries to which the users can limit their search results
* Create 'virtual catalogs' of up to 3 databases to set up persistent cross database searching
* Customize the FirstSearch interlibrary loan request form for the users

Periodical Title Finder

One of the most popular tools available to librarians at the OCLC website, the Periodical Title Finder is now updated weekly via an automated process that runs across databases on the OCLC FirstSearch service. The Title Finder includes information such as the beginning and ending date for citations and full text articles indexed in FirstSearch databases. This information comes directly from the database producers. Users can search for a title to determine which database(s) in the FirstSearch service index it. Alternatively, they can elect to download a list of titles indexed in a particular database.

FirstSearch Documentation

OCLC provides extensive documentation for FirstSearch, such as:

* Getting Started with FirstSearch (quick reference guide)
* IP Address Recognition: Getting Started
* FirstSearch Databases Available from OCLC's Z39.50 Server

* Using OCLC FirstSearch (a quick reference guide covering the basics of using FirstSearch; also available in French and Spanish)
* Managing the FirstSearch Service (planning, setting up and administering FirstSearch in the library)
* Administrative Module Reference Guide (customizing FirstSearch for the library's users)
* FirstSearch/ILL Direct Request Link Quick Reference (setting up the link to let users generate ILL requests for materials cited in FirstSearch databases)

OCLC Services

Through FirstSearch, OCLC provides easy access to hundreds of the most valued databases in the world. In addition to WorldCat, OCLC also owns and manages a number of other databases accessed through FirstSearch. All are included in the FirstSearch Base Package.

OCLC-owned and managed databases include:

OCLC ArticleFirst : OCLC index of articles from the contents pages of journals

* More than 12,000 sources and over 12.7 million records.
* Includes items listed on the table of contents pages of journals.
* Describes one article, news story, letter or other item from a journal in each record.
* Provides a list of libraries that have the journal title for most items.

OCLC Electronic Books : An OCLC catalog of online electronic books available through libraries worldwide

* More than 210,000 e-books
* Includes all e-books cataloged by OCLC member libraries, covering all subjects

OCLC Electronic Collections Online : It is an OCLC collection of scholarly journals

* More than 3,000 sources and over 350,000 records.
* Includes all of the original content and images of articles.
* Includes bibliographic information for all journals.
* Lets library view abstracts and full-text articles from journals to which the library or institution subscribes.

OCLC PapersFirst : OCLC index of papers presented at conferences worldwide

* More than 2.3 million records.
* Covers every published congress, symposium, conference, exposition, workshop and meeting received by The British Library Document Supply Centre.

OCLC ProceedingsFirst : An OCLC index of worldwide conference proceedings

* Covers every published congress, symposium, conference, exposition, workshop and meeting received by The British Library Document Supply Centre.
* Contains in each record a list of the papers presented at each conference.

OCLC WorldCat : OCLC catalog of books, web resources, and other material worldwide

* Contains all the records cataloged by OCLC member libraries.
* Offers millions of bibliographic records.
* Includes records representing 400 languages.

OCLC WorldCat Dissertations and Theses : OCLC catalog of dissertations and theses available in OCLC member libraries

* More than 5 million records in the database
* Covers all dissertations, theses and published material based on theses and dissertations cataloged by OCLC members, covers all subjects

*   Many are available electronically, at no charge,
       directly from the publishing institution

PUBMED

PubMed, available via the NCBI Entrez retrieval
system, was developed by the National Center for
Biotechnology Information (NCBI) at the National Library
of Medicine (NLM), located at the U.S. National Institutes
of Health (NIH). Entrez is the text-based search and
retrieval system used at NCBI for services including
PubMed, Nucleotide and Protein Sequences, Protein
Structures, Complete Genomes, Taxonomy, OMIM, and
many others. PubMed provides access to citations from
biomedical literature. LinkOut provides access to full-
text articles at journal Web sites and other related Web
resources. PubMed also provides access and links to the
other Entrez molecular biology resources. Publishers
participating in PubMed electronically submit their
citations to NCBI prior to or at the time of publication. If
the publisher has a web site that offers full-text of its
journals, PubMed provides links to that site as well as
biological resources, consumer health information,
research tools, and more. There may be a charge to access
the text or information. It is necessary use the Batch
Citation Matcher to match citations to PubMed using
bibliographic information such as journal, volume, issue,
page number, and year, or the Entrez Programming
Utilities that provide access to Entrez data outside of the
regular Web query interface.

PubMed Coverage

PubMed provides access to bibliographic
information that includes MEDLINE, as well as:

*   The out-of-scope citations (e.g., articles on plate
       tectonics or astrophysics) from certain MEDLINE
       journals, primarily general science and chemistry
       journals, for which the life sciences articles are
       indexed for MEDLINE.

* Citations that proceed the date that a journal was selected for MEDLINE indexing.

* Some additional life science journals that submit full text to PubMedCentral and receive a qualitative review by NLM.

MEDLINE

MEDLINE is the NLM's premier bibliographic database that contains references to journal articles in the life sciences with a concentration on biomedicine. A distinctive feature of MEDLINE is that the records are indexed with NLM's Medical Subject Headings (MeSH). The database contains citations from 1950 to the present, with some older material. New citations that have been indexed with MeSH terms, publication types, GenBank accession numbers, and other indexing data are available daily (Tuesday through Saturday) and display with the tag [PubMed - indexed for MEDLINE].

In Process Citations

PubMed's in-process records provide basic citation information and abstracts before the citations are indexed with NLM's MeSH Terms and added to MEDLINE. New in-process records are available in PubMed daily (Tuesday through Saturday) and display with the tag [PubMed - in process].

Publisher-Supplied Citations

Citations received electronically from publishers appear in PubMed with the tag [PubMed - as supplied by publisher]. New publisher supplied citations are available in PubMed Tuesday through Saturday. Most of the progress to "in-process" status and later to "indexed for MEDLINE" status. However, not all citations will be indexed for MEDLINE and therefore will retain either the tag [PubMed - as supplied by publisher] or [PubMed]. Publishers may submit citations for articles that appear on the Web in advance of the journal issue's release. These ahead-of-print citations also display the tag [Epub ahead of print].

PubMed Journal Information

The Journals Database can be searched by subject or by using the journal title, the Title Abbreviation, the NLM ID (NLM's unique journal identifier), the International Organization for Standardization (ISO) abbreviation, and the print and electronic International Standard Serial Numbers (pISSNs and eISSNs). The database includes journals in all Entrez databases (e.g., PubMed, Nucleotide, Protein).

PubMed Citation Matchers

Use the Single Citation Matcher for finding the citation for a particular article using title words or citation information, or to find an entire volume or issue of a journal, or to generate a bibliography by a first author.

The Batch Citation Matcher allows users to match their own list of citations to PubMed citations, using bibliographic information such as journal, volume, issue, page number, and year. The Citation Matcher returns the corresponding PMID. This number can then be used to easily link to PubMed. This service is frequently used by publishers or other database providers who want to link from bibliographic references on their Web sites directly to PubMed citations.

Difference Between MEDLINE and PubMed

MEDLINE is the largest component of PubMed (http://pubmed.gov), the freely accessible online database of biomedical journal citations and abstracts created by the U.S. National Library of Medicine (NLM®). Approximately 5,000 journals published in the United States and more than 80 other countries have been selected and are currently indexed for MEDLINE. A distinctive feature of MEDLINE is that the records are indexed with NLM's controlled vocabulary, the Medical Subject Headings.

In addition to MEDLINE citations, PubMed also contains:

* In-process citations which provide a record for an article before it is indexed with MeSH and added to MEDLINE or converted to out-of-scope status.

* Citations that precede the date that a journal was selected for MEDLINE indexing (when supplied electronically by the publisher).

* Some OLDMEDLINE citations that have not yet been updated with current vocabulary and converted to MEDLINE status.

* Citations to articles that are out-of-scope (e.g., covering plate tectonics or astrophysics) from certain MEDLINE journals, primarily general science and general chemistry journals, for which the life sciences articles are indexed with MeSH for MEDLINE.

* Some life science journals that submit full text to PubMedCentral and may not yet have been recommended for inclusion in MEDLINE although they have undergone a review by NLM, and some physics journals that were part of a prototype PubMed in the early to mid-1990's.

One of the ways users can limit their retrieval to MEDLINE citations in PubMed is by selecting MEDLINE from the Subsets menu on the Limits screen.

Other PubMed services include:

* Links to many sites providing full text articles and other related resources

* Clinical queries and Special queries search filters

* Links to see citations to related articles

* Single citation matcher

* The ability to store collections of citations, and save and automatically update searches

* A spell checker

* Filters to group search results

NLM distributes all but approximately 2% of all citations in PubMed to those who formally lease MEDLINE from NLM.

Pubmed Services

1. PUBMED Journals

* Searching can take place by topic, journal title or abbreviation, ISSN, or browse by subject terms.
* Searches can be limited to PubMed journals and/ or currently indexed.
* Lists of all Entrez journals and those with links to full-text web sites are available.

The Journals Database can be searched by subject or by using the journal title, the Title Abbreviation, the NLM ID (NLM's unique journal identifier), the International Organization for Standardization (ISO) abbreviation, and the print and electronic International Standard Serial Numbers (pISSNs and eISSNs). The database includes journals in all Entrez databases (e.g., PubMed, Nucleotide, Protein).

2. MeSH Database

MeSH is the U.S. National Library of Medicine's controlled vocabulary used for indexing articles for MEDLINE/PubMed. MeSH terminology provides a consistent way to retrieve information that may use different terminology for the same concepts.

* The MeSH database is used to find Medical Subject Heading Terms and build a search strategy.
  MeSH database tutorials are used for:
* Searching with the MeSH Database
* Combining MeSH Terms
* Applying Subheadings and other features of the MeSH Database

3. PubMed Single Citation Matcher

* This tool is used to find PubMed citations. Library

may omit any field.

* Journal may be the full title or the title abbreviation.
* For first and last author searching, use smith jc format.

4. Batch Citation Matcher

To retrieve PubMed or PMC UIs for fewer than 100 citations enter each citation string on a separate line using the following input format:

journal_title|year|volume|first_page|author_name|the_key| is used. To retrieve more than 100 citations the email function is used instead of the text box below:

* Enter the email address. Citations will be sent via email if an address is provided.
* Create a file using the citation input format and save it locally, then enter the filename or Browse to choose it from the system directory.
* Email requests may take a few minutes to process and be sent to the email address.

5. PubMed Clinical Queries

This provides the following specialized PubMed searches for clinicians:

* Search by Clinical Study Category
* Find Systematic Reviews
* Medical Genetics Searches

After running one of these searches, library may further refine the results using PubMed's Limits feature. Results of searches on these pages are limited to specific clinical research areas.

BIOSIS

BIOSIS information solutions for the global life sciences community are now provided by **Thomson Scientific**. The databases are the most complete resource for finding life sciences information quickly and efficiently. BIOSIS select documents from thousands of sources worldwide, index and abstract them into citations which describe their content, and maintain databases for searching citations — adding more than 600,000 new entries each year. *BIOSIS Previews®*, *Biological Abstracts®* and *Zoological Record* are available on several leading information platforms including *ISI Web of Knowledge*, the powerful web-based platform that delivers a powerful combination of content, tools and technology.

Features

Interdisciplinary : BIOSIS databases integrate important subjects from many different fields all across biology.

International : More than 90 nations are represented in BIOSIS databases.

Easy to Search : BIOSIS databases use a unique indexing system that allows flexible, efficient searching.

Informed by Diverse Sources : Library can find citations for articles, meetings, patents, book chapters, and more in BIOSIS databases.

Databases

1. BIOSIS Previews®

BIOSIS Previews serves the every need for finding life sciences references. No matter where life sciences information is published, *BIOSIS Previews* gives library the most efficient, reliable way to find it. Researchers, librarians, and students worldwide use *BIOSIS Previews* to stay current on topics from botany to genetic engineering.

BIOSIS Archive for Biological Abstracts and BIOSIS Previews : delivers all the bibliographic records from 49 *Biological Abstracts* print volumes 1926 to 1968. It consists of 1.8 million records relevant to working biologists, from journals, patents, conference reports and books, and in fully indexed and searchable form. The original scientist abstractors and editors focused on selecting the most relevant international items in life sciences, and often wrote extensive abstracts and enhanced titles that had added indexing terms as search aids. Modern indexing terms and search functions have been added to further ease search.

Comprehensive coverage

BIOSIS Previews abstracts and indexes information from more than 5,500 sources all around the world, including:

Journal articles (sample record) : Citations taken from more than 5,000 international serials

Meeting and conference reports (sample record): Search over 165,000 documents from more than 1,500 meetings

Books : Includes detailed information on contents

Patents (sample record) : Searchable by date granted, US patent number, and other details.

Current information

Numerous features make *BIOSIS Previews* unmatched in the life sciences for both currency and global coverage. *BIOSIS Previews* is continually adding to its database:

* Over 560,000 new citations each year
* Information from more than 5,000 international serial sources
* Weekly updates

It is found that more than 18 million total records dating back to 1926.

Selective searching

BIOSIS context-sensitive indexing allows *BIOSIS Previews* to preserve the authors' intended use of terms. With it, *BIOSIS Previews* returns only the most relevant records with each search.

2. Zoological Record

Zoological Record (*ZR*) is the world's oldest continuing database of animal biology. More than 140 years of experience has made *ZR* a respected resource for:

* information from every field in animal biology
* projects in academic, government, and commercial organizations
* reliable and in-depth information searches

Because *ZR*'s coverage extends back to 1864, it has long acted as the world's unofficial register of animal names. But this is only one aspect, as its scope of coverage represents every area of animal biology, from biodiversity and the environment to taxonomy and veterinary sciences.

Zoological Record Archive provides the original bibliographic and taxonomic indexing data from print volumes 1977 to 1864. With over 1.8 million indexed and searchable records, and with unified and mapped terminology, the *Archive* makes *Zoological Record* – the oldest continuing bibliographic database in life sciences – the most complete record of animal science and taxonomy literature for living and fossil species.

Features

* Covers 5,000 serials, plus many other sources of information including books, reports, and meetings
* 72,000 indexed records added every year
* 3.4 million records available in electronic formats
* Available in print, on CD, via the Internet and online
* Choose to purchase individual print sections of the database, or subscribe to an electronic format that gives library a variety of access options, including networking the database

Benefits

Ease of use : Each one of the 3.4 million records in

ZR has been indexed with *ZR*'s specialized indexing system, ensuring that searches are both comprehensive and easy to conduct.

Combine resources with other organizations : A consortium plan is available for those who subscribe electronically

3. Biological Abstracts: The Key to the World's Life Sciences Journals

Comprehensive coverage and context-sensitive indexing make the information in **Biological Abstracts** (BA) essential for all life sciences researchers. BA directs users to information on life science topics from botany to microbiology to pharmacology, serving to connect researchers with critical journal coverage. Whether library study botany, pharmacology, biochemistry, or evolutionary ecology, BA has the journal articles that the research depends on.

Total Journal Coverage : BA indexes articles from over 3,700 serials each year. This publication also offers:

* Over 350,000 new citations each year
* 90% of new citations include an abstract by the author (sample records)
* 11.3 million archival records are available back to 1926

BIOSIS Archive for *Biological Abstracts* and *BIOSIS Previews* delivers all the bibliographic records from 49 *Biological Abstracts* print volumes 1926 to 1968. It consists of 1.8 million records relevant to working biologists, from journals, patents, conference reports and books, and in fully indexed and searchable form. The original scientist abstractors and editors focused on selecting the most relevant international items in life sciences, and often wrote extensive abstracts and enhanced titles that had added indexing terms as search aids. Modern indexing terms and search functions have been added to further ease search.

Global Information : BA articles originate from journals all around the world, and cover topics in every life sciences discipline. If the information library need lies in the life sciences, BA should be part of the information solution.

Plus, BIOSIS indexing, MESH disease terminology, and CAS Registry Numbers all help electronic BA users find the most relevant records efficiently.

The Choice of Formats : Subscribers can access BA on CD, through the Web, or in print. Electronic versions of BA are updated quarterly. Print versions are issued twice each month.

4. Biological Abstracts / RRM: Supplemental sources, essential research

Good journal coverage is just part of the picture. Some of the most exciting and cutting-edge information is released at meetings, months before any journal publications. Biological Abstracts/RRM (Reports, Reviews, Meetings) makes certain library don't miss this information, and gives library the edge of having the latest data.

Each year, BA/RRM adds 215,000 references to non-journal documents. This information comes from:

Meetings and Conferences : More than 165,000 citations per year taken from more than 1,500 meetings

Literature Reviews : Over 24,000 references to review articles

US Patents : 29,000 patents added annually

Books, software, and other media : 9,000 reviews and references for books, CD-ROMs and other life sciences media

Updated quarterly, the non-journal information in BA/RRM can both precede and complement the journal data - offering a total assessment of any life sciences field. Plus, like all BIOSIS publications, context-sensitive indexing keeps the terms in same context as the original publication, so that user sees the words used just as the author intended.

5. Abstracts of Entomology: Easy-to-Browse Current Awareness Sources of Entomological Literature

Abstracts of Entomology contain over 20,000 new references each year. Abstracts of Entomology is a monthly current awareness publication providing the most extensive references to entomological studies reported in worldwide life science literature. All references in this publication are derived from the BIOSIS Previews database.

Coverage : Nearly 5,500 international serial publications, as well as meeting literature, books, and other sources are reviewed for inclusion.

Subjects covered in Abstracts of Entomology include:

*   agronomy
*   integrated pest management
*   biochemistry
*   parasitology
*   economic entomology
*   suburban entomology
*   genetics
*   systematics

Format : References are displayed using a standard scientific bibliographic format, and organized by subject area for easy browsing and current awareness.

The indexes in each issue provide three modes of access to the literature:

*   **Author Index :** Listed in alphabetical order, the Author Index includes full author names when provided.

* **Organism Index :** The Organism Index allows for hierarchical access to kingdom, family, and genus species names. This enables the user to easily find references to related organisms.

* **Subject Index :** The Subject Index has an easy-to-scan back-of-book format. Arranged alphabetically, the Subject Index lists all significant words from the title as well as descriptive words added by BIOSIS indexers. All significant words used to describe the original document appear in the Subject Index, including genus species, common names, geographical regions, and scientific and commercial drug names.

Annual Cumulative Indexes : Cumulative Indexes allow users to locate references faster and more efficiently by cumulating an entire year's worth of information.

Mail Dates : Abstracts of Entomology is mailed monthly. The Cumulative Indexes are mailed annually in January

6. Abstracts of Mycology:Easy-to-Browse Current Awareness Sources of Mycological Literature

Abstracts of Mycology contains 17,000 new references each year. Abstracts of Mycology is a monthly current awareness publication providing the most extensive references to mycological studies reported in worldwide life science literature. All references in this publication are derived from the BIOSIS Previews database.

Coverage : Nearly 5,000 international serial publications, as well as meeting literature, books, and other sources are reviewed for inclusion.

Subjects covered in Abstracts of Mycology include:
* antifungal agents
* plant biochemistry

* biological control
* public health
* genetics
* soil microbiology
* pharmaceutical botany
* systematics

Format : References are displayed using a standard scientific bibliographic format, and organized by subject area for easy browsing and current awareness. The indexes in each issue provide three modes of access to the literature:

* **Author Index** - Listed in alphabetical order, the Author Index includes full author names when provided.

* **Organism Index** - The Organism Index allows for hierarchical access to kingdom, family, and genus species names. This enables the user to easily find references to related organisms.

* **Subject Index** - The Subject Index has an easy-to-scan back-of-book format. Arranged alphabetically, the Subject Index lists all significant words from the title as well as descriptive words added by BIOSIS indexers. All significant words used to describe the original document appear in the Subject Index, including genus species, common names, geographical regions, and scientific and commercial drug names.

Annual Cumulative Indexes : Cumulative Indexes allow users to locate references faster and more efficiently by cumulating an entire year's worth of information.

Mail Dates : Abstracts of Mycology is mailed monthly. The Cumulative Indexes are mailed annually in January.

7. BasicBIOSIS: The student's guide to life sciences research

BasicBIOSIS provides just the right coverage for a start in the life sciences - keeping tabs on enough publications to stay current and informed without overwhelming users.

With BasicBIOSIS, users benefit from:

* Citations from over 300 crucial life sciences and news publications
* Thorough coverage in topics throughout the life sciences
* More than 400,000 total records updated monthly

Thorough Coverage : BasicBIOSIS journals are carefully selected to touch on all the major life sciences disciplines. Search takes place over 300 publications, including these life sciences journals:

* Audubon
* Journal of the American Medical Association (JAMA)
* Nature
* Popular Science
* Science

It covers these important science and technology news sources, and many more:

* The New York Times
* Newsweek
* The Wall Street Journal
* U.S. News and World Report

Topical and Current Data - Perfect for Users : BasicBIOSIS is a rolling file, so it always holds the most recent four years' worth of records. By searching with BasicBIOSIS, the students can be assured of seeing only relevant, current information. BasicBIOSIS is available in electronic format, and can be purchased by individual institutions or by consortia.

8. BIOSIS Search Guide: An Essential Tool for All Users of the BIOSIS Databases

The 2001- 2002 BIOSIS Search Guide contains valuable information to assist both novice and expert searchers in retrieving the most precise search results from BIOSIS Previews, and electronic versions of Biological Abstracts and Biological Abstracts/RRM. The Search Guide provides information about each indexed term that makes searching quicker and more intuitive:

* Expanded Vocabulary Guide contains an updated list of more than 20,000 terms indexed by BIOSIS

* Addition of Biosystematic Codes to the Vocabulary Guide enables library to immediately focus the search in one area.

* Authority File's scope and history notes help users broaden or narrow a search.

* Controlled keywords, taxonomic Families, chemical synonyms, and CAS Registry Numbers give additional information for optimal search retrieval.

* Sample searches show how to structure a search on all of BIOSIS's vendor platforms.

Highlights

1. BiologyBrowser - links to science news stories, evaluated web sites, and more
2. Product updates
3. Product update archive
4. Case studies
5. Back Years
6. Relational Indexing
7. Search strategies: the following examples reflect the search strategies:

Example:

HOW DO AGRICOLA, EMBASE, AND MEDLINE MEASURE UP TO BIOSIS?

BIOSIS and Agricola

Sample Search Topics:

* Agriculture/Horticulture
* Bioprocess Engineering/Bioengineering
* Veterinary Medicine
* Public Health

BIOSIS and EMBASE

Sample Search Topics:

* Genetics / Molecular Genetics
* Pharmacognosy / Botanicals
* Pharmaceuticals
* Bioprocess Engineering/Pharmacology

BIOSIS and MEDLINE*Sample Search Topics:*

* Medical Genetics / Genetics / Proteomics
* Neuroscience
* Medical Sciences and Human Medicine
* Pharmacology and Pharmocognosy

BIOSIS vs MEDLINE vs EMBASE

Three-way search comparisons:

* Breast Cancer and Stem Cells
* Proteomics
* Medical Genetics
* Pharmacokinetics
* Multivalent Drugs
* Drug Delivery
* Diagnosis Tools

DIALOG

Earliest Dialog system was completed in 1966 under the direction of Roger K. Summit and was the world's first online information retrieval system to be used globally with materially significant databases. Today, Dialog is the worldwide leader in providing online-based information services to organizations seeking competitive advantages in such fields as business, science, engineering, finance and law. The products and services, including Dialog and Dialog DataStar, offer organizations the ability to precisely retrieve data from more than 1.4 billion unique records of key information, accessible via the Internet or through delivery to enterprise intranets. With direct operations in 27 countries, Dialog's products and services are a combination of highly accurate online research tools offering access to unique and relevant databases — designed to meet the specific needs of the wide range of users. Information professionals and end-users at business, professional and government organizations in more than 100 countries prize Dialog services to meet their searching needs.

As part of the Deep Web, which is estimated to be 500 times larger than the content accessible via Web search engines, Dialog products offer unparalleled depth and breadth of content coupled with the ability to search with precision and speed. The collection of over 900 databases handles more than 700,000 searches and delivers over 17 million document page views per month. Searchable content on Dialog services includes articles and reports from thousands of real-time news feeds, newspapers, broadcast transcripts and trade publications, plus market research reports and analyst notes providing support for financial decision-making, as well as in-depth repositories of scientific and technical data, patents, trademarks and other intellectual property data. Additional content areas include government regulations, social sciences, food and agriculture, reference, energy and environment, chemicals, pharmaceuticals and medicine.

Dialog, headquartered in Cary, North Carolina, USA,

is a business of The Thomson Corporation. Thomson provides value-added information, software tools and applications to more than 20 million users in the fields of law, tax, accounting, financial services, higher education, reference information, corporate e-learning and assessment, scientific research and healthcare. With operational headquarters in Stamford, Conn., Thomson has approximately 40,000 employees and provides services in approximately 130 countries.

PRODUCTS

Web-Based Solutions

Dialog1 : Dialog1 offers a suite of easy-to-use "one-click" interfaces. Its question-driven format allows fast access to high quality information and does not require knowledge of command language. Applications include biotech, business intelligence, chemistry, energy, engineering, intellectual property, marketing, pharmaceuticals and world news. Special features include useful search tips, file descriptions, sample records and a map interface for searching regional news.

DialogClassic Web : For experienced Dialog command language searchers who prefer access via the Internet, DialogClassic Web offers sophisticated search capabilities with the added versatility of a Web-based enviroinment to more than 500,000 sources of scientific, technical, medical, business, news and intellectual property information. Special features include secure Web server access, a buffer that captures and displays search results, a search log to enable easy reuse of search statements, chemical structure searching and expanded output options. DialogClassic Web features are browser-based, eliminating the need to install software.

DialogPRO : DialogPRO provides the information needed to make the right decisions in today's business environment. Created exclusively for small businesses, DialogPRO is divided into different tiers of content that are made available on a flat subscription rate. With DialogPRO library can monitor industry trends, prepare for a meeting with a client and make more informed decisions. All the top sources are in DialogPRO including the leading business, intellectual property, news, and science information. With this information at the disposal, library can identify data about potential partners, review press releases on clients or prospects, short-cut a product development process and track new business trends.

DialogSelect : DialogSelect combines easy-to-use, point-and-click search forms with built-in search intelligence. DialogSelect is organized vertically by major content areas with access to over 300 key Dialog databases. Just a few of the content areas are business, chemical, energy, food, government, intellectual property, medical, news, pharmaceuticals, reference and technology. Special features include a powerful search engine, multiple search options and automatic alerts.

DialogWeb : DialogWeb allows both advanced and novice searchers access to the full content of Dialog via the Internet. It offers both a robust Command Search mode that uses the powerful Dialog command language, and a flexible and easy-to-use Guided Search mode that does not require knowledge of commands. Fill-in-the-blank forms allow users to create and modify custom alerts. Search results are provided in either HTML or text and the records can be delivered online or offline via e-mail, fax, ftp or postal delivery.

Dialog@Site : Dialog@Site is an easy-to-use interface that allows searching of Dialog OnDisc databases through a Web browser. Special features include Boolean logic searching and browsable indexes.

DataStar : DataStar offers a comprehensive content collection with a special focus on pharmaceutical, biomedical, biosciences, chemical, computing, engineering and healthcare-related industries. DataStar also includes broad coverage of companies, and industry and business news. Hundreds of databases are available with options for both advanced searches, which take advantage of enhanced subject indexing, and easy searches for less-complex queries. Modify the interface— or even create the own database with PrivateStar. DataStarWeb is customizable to suit the needs of the organization. DataStar information can help library stay abreast of issues, trends and research affecting the industry. Track drugs from concept to market launch, reduce time-to-market for new developments, identify areas in which to focus research & development and track competition on a global and regional basis.

Dialog Open Access : An alternative to subscription service, Open Access has no passwords, monthly fees or minimum charges. All that is needed is a credit card to receive instant access to the power of Dialog through DialogSelect. Categories available through Open Access include business and news, chemistry, engineering, environment, government, intellectual property, medicine and pharmaceuticals.

Dialog TradStat : Dialog TradStat compiles official government trade statistics from reporting countries and presents them electronically, detailing over 90% of world trade at the touch of a button. Dialog TradStat allows library to assess market share and track competition, monitor trends in trade flows, identify potential trading partners, monitor price fluctuations and track the movement of products around the globe. With Dialog TradStat Lite, library can select a predefined report for imports or exports at a low predictable price.

Dialog SourceOne : Dialog SourceOne lets customers order copies of full-text materials that are not available on Dialog. With Dialog SourceOne, library have access to over 40 million patent documents – all in PDF format and available in minutes. Dialog SourceOne also provides access to journal articles, dissertations, and annual reports. SourceOne orders appear conveniently on the Dialog invoice making Dialog the one-stop solution for all the information needs.

Intranet Solutions

Dialog@Site : Dialog@Site is an easy-to-use interface that allows searching of Dialog OnDisc databases through a Web browser. Special features include Boolean logic searching and browsable indexes.

Dialog Intranet Toolkit : Dialog Intranet Toolkit allows library to create Dialog search and delivery sites that are seamlessly integrated into the organization's intranet. These sites can be tailored to the needs of the company, from the company-wide level down to the specific needs of departments and individuals. The flexible tools in Dialog Intranet Toolkit combine seamlessly with Dialog's expansive content collection to create unparalleled information solutions for the organization.

Desktop Applications

DialogLink : DialogLink will vastly improve the ability to access and distribute relevant information, and is the only way to conduct a chemical structure search on Dialog. Superior functionality allows users to export search results into Microsoft Word and Excel templates, integrate fulltext articles with Open URL compliant link resolvers, access related materials and maximize search efficiency, conduct powerful chemical queries using structure searching capabilities and more.

DataStar : DataStar, available in a Windows interface, provides access to more than 350 databases with worldwide coverage in business information, chemicals, energy, finance, food, industry analysis, market research, media, news and pharmaceuticals.

Dialog OnDisc : Dialog OnDisc products deliver a variety of databases to the desktop via network, intranet or CD-ROM. More than 30 databases are available on CD-ROM, some originating from Dialog's online files while others are exclusive to Dialog OnDisc.

Classic Products available via Telnet

Dialog : Dialog is available via a text-only inferface designed for professional researchers. It enables precise online research through the use of Dialog command language, Boolean logic, indexing systems and terminology-at the fastest possible speed. Dialog includes many powerful features for data manipulation, extraction and analysis; comparison and duplicaton detection of retrieval results; cross-file searching; relevancy ranking; customized output formatting; and much more.

DataStar : DataStar is available in a text-only interface designed for professional researchers offering a comprehensive collection of business information including news, industry analysis and market research with wide-ranging coverage of finance, media, pharmaceuticals, chemicals, energy, food and business. DataStar includes many powerful features for data manipulation, extraction and analysis; comparison and duplication of retrieval results; cross-file searching; customized output formatting; and much more.

Dialog SourceOne : Dialog SourceOne lets customers order copies of full-text materials that are not available on Dialog. With Dialog SourceOne, library have access to over 40 million patent documents – all in PDF format and available in minutes. Dialog SourceOne also provides access to journal articles, dissertations, and annual reports. SourceOne orders appear conveniently on the Dialog invoice making Dialog the one-stop solution for all the information needs.

DataStar : If library wants the company to be the first to register the next wonder drug, DataStar can help. The strength of its pharmaceutical content is unmatched, but DataStar also offers a balanced line of subject matter, from business information, to scientific data, to government statistics. As the first online service in Europe, DataStar revolutionized information delivery on a global scale. With an easy-to-use Web interface and incredibly precise search results, DataStar leads the way with Intranet integration and eLinking.

Web-based Solutions

DataStar : DataStar offers a comprehensive content collection with a special focus on pharmaceutical, biomedical, biosciences, chemical, computing, engineering and healthcare-related industries. DataStar also includes broad coverage of companies, and industry and business news. Hundreds of databases are available with options for both advanced searches, which take advantage of enhanced subject indexing, and easy searches for less-complex queries. Modify the interface— or even create the own database with PrivateStar. DataStarWeb is customizable to suit the needs of the organization. DataStar information can help library stay abreast of issues, trends and research affecting the industry. Track drugs from concept to market launch, reduce time-to-market for new developments, identify areas in which to focus research & development and track competition on a global and regional basis.

DataStarClassic on the Web : DataStarClassic users of DataStar can now take advantage of many hi-tech features formally only accessible via DataStarWeb. Because this is Web-based, there is no need to install any communications programs or use telnet sessions to access DataStar. The Web-based interface allows library to use the *Classic* search command language via the browser. Library can have access to eJournal Links, view images offered in particular databases and save documents in PDF, HTML and ASCII formats. Moreover, searchers can click the "save tracked session" button to save an entire search session once they have completed their searches. Other features include an editor to modify completed searches to re-execute them again, and an Options screen to set up personal classic commands that are frequently used.

Dialog TradStat : Dialog TradStat compiles official government trade statistics from reporting countries and presents them electronically, detailing over 90% of world trade at the touch of a button. Dialog TradStat allows library to assess market share and track competition, monitor trends in trade flows, identify potential trading partners, monitor price fluctuations and track the movement of products around the globe. With Dialog TradStat Lite library can select a predefined report for imports or exports at a low predictable price.

Desktop Applications

DataStar : DataStar, available in a Windows interface, provides access to more than 350 databases with worldwide coverage in business information, chemicals, energy, finance, food, industry analysis, market research, media, news and pharmaceuticals.

Classic Products available via Telnet

DataStar : DataStar is available in a text-only interface designed for professional researchers offering a comprehensive collection of business information including news, industry analysis and market research with wide-ranging coverage of finance, media, pharmaceuticals, chemicals, energy, food and business. DataStar includes many powerful features for data manipulation, extraction and analysis; comparison and duplication of retrieval results; cross-file searching; customized output formatting.

References

1.   http://serviceunavailable.oclc.org/digitalarchive/
2.   http://digitalarchive.oclc.org/da/ViewObjectMain.jsp?fileid=
      0000060174:000003647057&reqid=73.
3.   http://www.ncbi.nlm.nih.gov/sites/gquery
4.   http://www.ncbi.nlm.nih.gov/
5.   http://www.nlm.nih.gov/
6.   http://www.nih.gov/

7. http://www.ncbi.nlm.nih.gov/projects/linkout/
8. http://www.nlm.nih.gov/databases/databases_oldmedline.html
9. http://www.nlm.nih.gov/databases/leased.html
10. http://www.ncbi.nlm.nih.gov/entrez/query/static/clinical.shtml#studycat#studycat
11. http://scientific.thomson.com/biosis/indexing/
12. http://www.isiwebofknowledge.com/
13. http://scientific.thomson.com/products/bp/
14. http://scientific.thomson.com/products/barrm/
15. http://www.biologybrowser.org/
16. http://www.dialog.com/products/dialog1/
17. http://www.dialog.com/products/dialogclassicweb/

Index

Application 14, 221

Architecture 25
    Flat 26
    Hierarchical 27
    Network 29
    Relational 30
    Dimensional 33
Attitude
    Professional 195
    User 197
Audio-video database 88
Bibliographic database 75
    Inconsistence 81
    Planning 80
Boolean searching 106
    AND 107
    NOT 107
    OR 107
CD ROM database 88
Component, search
    Indexing 139
    Query 139
Copyright 17
Data
    Bibliographic 79
    Validity 173
    Updating 174
Database 1, 152
    Correction 53
    Definition 3
    Design and development 219
    Growth and development 144, 154
    Information service 15
    Maintenance 95
    Organization 7
    Problems 137
    Production 18
    Records and fields 7, 77
    Role and importance 162
    Scheme 13
    Structure 7
    Types 11
Database Management Systems 10, 229, 233
Database model 25, 26
    Flat 26
    Hierarchical 27
    Network 29

    Relational 30
    Dimensional 33
    Object Oriented 34
Database, types 10
    Analytic 10
    Operational 11
    Client-server 11
Derivative database 97
Fields 7, 8
    Categories 9
    Display 9
    Qualities 9
    Search 9
    Standard 8
    Full-text 8
Fields, categories 9
    Character 9
    Date 10
    Logic 9
    Memo 10
    Numeric 9
Files 36, 78
    Flat 36
    Hierarchical 36
    Relational 36
Format 77
    Mixed 97
FTS 176
Full text database 83
HTTP 222, 226
Image database 86
Indexes 139
    SQL 139
    Full-text 139
Indexing 108, 140, 172
Indigenous databases 39
    Correction 53
    Design and
development 53
    Essentials 51
    Genesis 39
    Impact 50
    Networked 57
    Properties 50
    Searching 57
    Types 54
Information
    Planning 58, 144

Updating 174
Information retrieval 104
AND 106
Boolean 106
Indexing 108
Literal 118
Natural language 108
NOT 106
Operators 120
OR 106
Query 109
Query language 111
Search term 115
Truncation 115
Wildcard 115
Information services 15
CAS 65
JSP 216
Architecture 217
Keyword 105
Labels 8
Long 8, 9
Short 8, 9
Language
Natural 108
Query 111
Linguistics 172, 176
Literal 118
MARC 76, 79
Importance 76
Fields 77
Formats 77
Marketing of databases 188
Costing 192
Manpower 157
Pricing 192
Production 18
Professional attitude 195
User attitude and behavior 197
Feed back 200
User education 201
Metadatabase 83
MS Access 214
MS SQL Server 215,
MySQL Library 228
MySQL Server 234
MYSQULY 228
Natural language 108
Numeric database 88
Online database services 238

OCLC 238
Pubmed 268
Medline 269
MeSH 272
BiIOSIS 273
DIALOG 285
Online information 159
Database 159
Gateways 159
Online publication 83
Operator 112, 120
ADJ 120
AND 121
NEAR 121
NEARn 122
Nesting 113
NOT 123
NOT ADJ 124
NOT NEAR 125
NOT NEARn 126
NOT SAME 126
NOT WITH 127
OR 128
SAME 129
WITH 130
XOR 130
Precedence 112
Proximity 133
ORACLE 215
RDBMS 215
Overview 1
Population 140
Full 140
Change-tracking 140
Incremental 141

Query 109
Nested 235
Catching 235
Query language 111
Non-procedural 111
Procedural 111
Searching 175
Basic 105
Boolean 107
Data types 111
Full text searching 139,
141, 176, 235

          Keyword 105
          Natural language 108
          Operators 120
          Plurals 114
          Problems 134
          Query language 111
          Refining 138
          Retrospective 65
          Truncation 115
          Wildcard 115
Server 231, 233
          MySQL 234
SQL 230
Subject headings 135
          Controlled vocabulary 135
Suggestion 200
Tier 224, 225
          Database 228
Training 159
          Strategies 206
Updating 174
US MARC 79
Users
          Attitude 197
          Education 201
          Feed back 200
Web application 211
Web technologies 214
          JSP 216
          MySQL server 215
          Oracle 215
          PHP 226
          Servelets 218
          SQL 230

Web scripting 226
          Open source 226
          PHP 226
Web servers 225
Wildcard 115
          Characters 116
          Literal 118
          Maximum numbers 117
          Specifying 116
XML 228